Modern Buddhist Conjunctures in Myanmar

Modern Buddhist Conjunctures in Myanmar

CULTURAL NARRATIVES, COLONIAL LEGACIES, AND CIVIL SOCIETY

Juliane Schober

UNIVERSITY *of* HAWAI'I PRESS
Honolulu

PRINTED IN THE UNITED STATES OF AMERICA

16 15 14 13 12 11 6 5 4 3 2 1

FRONTIS PHOTO: Kuthodaw Pagoda in Mandalay.
PHOTO BY ERIK WOODWARD.

Library of Congress Cataloging-in-Publication Data

Schober, Juliane.
Modern Buddhist conjunctures in Myanmar : cultural narratives, colonial legacies, and civil society / Juliane Schober.
p. cm.
Includes bibliographical references and index.
ISBN 978-0-8248-3382-4 (hardcover : alk. paper)
1. Buddhism and state—Burma—History. 2. Theravada Buddhism—Political aspects—Burma. I. Title.
BQ420.S36 2011
294.309591—dc22
2010030294

University of Hawaiʻi Press books are printed on acid-free paper and meet the guidelines for permanence and durability of the council on library resources.

Designed by Julie Matsuo-Chun

Printed by IBT Global

For Stefanie and Erik

CONTENTS

ix PREFACE

1 Introduction

15 1 Theravada Cultural Hegemony in Precolonial Burma

34 2 The Emergence of the Secular in Modern Burma

46 3 Educating the Other: Buddhism and Colonial Knowledge

62 4 Civil Buddhism in a Colonial Context

76 5 The Politics of the Modern State as Buddhist Practice

99 6 Buddhist Resistance against the State

119 7 The Limits of Buddhist Moral Authority in the Secular State

146 8 Potential Futures

155 CHRONOLOGY

159 NOTES

189 GLOSSARY

191 BIBLIOGRAPHY

203 INDEX

PREFACE

This book examines modern conjunctures of Buddhism and politics in Myanmar from a vantage point at the intersection of anthropology and Buddhist studies. I hope this study contributes to our understanding of the discourse about religion in colonial and postcolonial contexts. My inquiry into modern Burmese Buddhist practices and communities has revealed recurrent themes, such as colonialism, nationalism, education, and resistance to the political center. After tracing the Burmese discourse about these themes and their iterations in local, regional, national, and global contexts, I conclude that postcoloniality in Myanmar remains an aspiration yet to be achieved. Such a vision for the future requires civil institutions that allow a public discourse about power that can transcend the current tensions between Buddhism and the modern state.

These themes emerge and are submerged at significant conjunctures in the modern history of this nation. My narrative begins with a focus on the negotiation of precolonial Buddhist hegemonies and underscores the role of Buddhist institutions in public policy. I then trace the emergence of modern Buddhist discourse in colonial communities in light of the introduction of new and secular venues to power. They include the disruption of traditional paradigms of governance; the emergence of modern concerns like nationalism, education, and the power of the secular state; Buddhist resistance in the public place; and the impact of global patterns of consumption on Buddhist communities. The modern discourse about these themes at particular conjunctures continues to draw Buddhist communities into political arenas, either to legitimate political power or to resist it on moral grounds. In Burma, the conjunctures of Buddhist resistance to the hegemonic structures of the modern state have endured well beyond the colonial period.

My study draws on ethnographic fieldwork between 1980 and 2008, mostly in Mandalay, but also in Yangon and Bagan. Over the past three decades, my anthropological projects have focused on sacred space, monastic practice, charismatic communities, Buddhist nationalism, and the religious mobilization of Burmese citizens and resources through state rituals in Myanmar. The chapters in this book therefore draw on several periods of ethnographic research I conducted in Myanmar in 1981–1982, 1994, 2006, and 2008. In 2005 and 2006, I researched the archives of the British Library on Buddhism in Burma during the colonial period.

I have benefited from many opportunities to present earlier drafts of some of these chapters to academic audiences, and I appreciate the comments I received at the University of Toronto, Cornell, Princeton, Oxford, the National University of Singapore, and at meetings of the Association for Asian Studies, the International Burma Studies Conference, and the American Academy of Religion. Earlier versions of some passages in this book have been published elsewhere. The descriptions of Buddhist modernities in the introduction appear in my essay "Buddhism and Modernity in Myanmar." An earlier version of the chapter on educating the colonial "other" was published as "Colonial Knowledge and Buddhist Education." The passage on U Nu's biography is also found in my essay on his life published in the Encyclopedia of Buddhism. Lastly, earlier versions of some sections of my discussion of Aung San Suu Kyi's Buddhist ethics were published in "Buddhist Visions of Moral Authority and Civil Society." I have returned to these case studies here in order to illustrate the broader development of Buddhist engagements with modernity. I completed what turned out to be a first draft of this book in August 2007. The events of September 2007, which came to be known as the Saffron Revolution in the western media, led me to add chapters 7 and 8.

I owe a special debt to Professor F. K. Lehman, who is also known as U Chit Hlaing, and to Professor Frank Reynolds, who were my mentors when I began my study of Burmese Buddhism. Steven Collins, Ingrid Jordt, Donald Swearer, and an anonymous reviewer read parts of or even the entire manuscript and shared their discerning critiques and comments. What follows has been improved by their generous insights, while all errors and mistakes are my own. During my research and writing on this project, my efforts have been sustained by the inspiration of kindred minds and great conversations with friends and colleagues. I appreciate the comments and encouragements I received from Maitrii Aung Thwin, Michael Aung-Thwin, Aung Zaw, Stephen Berkwitz, Anne Blackburn, Erik Braun, Anne Feldhaus, Tillman Frasch, Frances Garrett, Janet Gyatso, Lillian Handlin, Harn Lay, Nancy Hefner, Robert Hefner, Alexander Henn, Chie Ikeya, Ward Keeler, Charles Keyes, Leedom Lefferts, Boreth Ly, Jacques Leider, Donald Lopez, Patrick Pranke, Catherine Raymond, James Rush, U Saw Law Ei Soe, Jörg Schendel, U Sein Win, Paul Strahan, John Strong, Shahla Talebi, Nicola Tannenbaum, Nora Taylor, Alicia Turner, U Thaw Kaung, Dr. Thaw Kaung, and Julian Wheatley. I was inspired by the exchanges at the Arizona Colloquium on Theravada Buddhist Encounters of Modernity at Arizona State University in 2009, in which several colleagues mentioned above participated. I want to add my appreciation for contributions to that project by Kate Crosby, Christoph Emmrich, Anne Hansen, Charles Hallisey, and Justin McDaniel. There are many friends and monks who have supported my efforts during field research in Burma, and I thank them sincerely for the kind assistance and patience they extended to me. May there be a time soon when we can express our views in public without fear of reprisal. My thinking has been enriched by comments from my students in seminars, and I want to acknowledge especially the contributions by Sherry Harlacher, Jordan Johnson, and Brooke Schedneck.

I am grateful for a grant from the Social Science Research Council in 1994. Some of the findings from this period of field research are published here for the first time. Joel Gereboff, head of the Religious Studies Faculty at Arizona State University, has been supportive throughout the project and has helped me find time to write. I also want to acknowledge travel and research support I received from the Center for the Study of Religion and Conflict, directed by Linell Cady at Arizona State University.

Christine Htoon, Michelle Hubele, Jordan Johnson, Brooke Schedneck, and Stefanie Woodward lent the careful eyes of a copy editor to various drafts of the manuscript. Stefanie and Erik Woodward gave me permission to use their photographs. Pamela Kelley, Ann Ludeman, and Margaret Black at the University of Hawaiʻi Press contributed a great deal of editorial wisdom at important junctures in the process and I appreciate especially their patience.

My children, Stefanie and Erik, graciously and patiently supported my work during periods of fieldwork and at home. Norma Hubele and Jan Stanley offered me their friendship and provided welcome distractions when my energy was fading. Sid, Jax, and the rest of the hikers made sure I got out. To all, I am grateful for their friendship, inspiration, and intellectual engagement.

Juliane Schober
AUGUST 2009

Introduction

Modern Buddhist Genealogies

> Faith and power must always, however uneasily, take a stance toward one another. The polity, more than most realms of human action, deals obviously with ultimate things.

Myanmar, formerly Burma, has been embroiled in conflicts at the nation's center and at its borders almost since its independence from British colonial rule in 1948.[1] As recently as September 2007, the so-called Saffron Revolution, a populist uprising led by monks, contested the legitimacy of the state. The discussion that unfolds in this book traces the cultural narratives of Burma's Theravada Buddhist engagement with modernity at the intersections of religion and politics. In the course of this exploration, I point to conjunctures in modern Burmese history when public discourse about Buddhism and politics fueled particular cultural debates. Such pivotal moments, or conjunctures, may lead to iterations of past conflicts or debates, but they may also open up possibilities for innovation and the emergence of new trajectories that resolve or move particular cultural debates into new directions.[2] It is at such moments that modern political formations, for instance, nationalism, secular power, education, identity, colonialism, ethnicity, and otherness, are articulated and become visible in culturally and historically specific contexts. While some potential trajectories unfold, others remain foreclosed.

In the case of Burma, Buddhist practices and institutions often insert themselves into public life, encouraging the politicization of religion. The cultural narratives I have chosen to explore here reveal genealogies of hegemony and subjugation, patronage and resistance, and power and loss. Articulations of these themes emerge at certain moments in history and eventually lose their cultural relevance, but the genealogies of their recurrence extend from precolonial times to the colonial era and eventually to the contemporary period.[3] Although these genealogies predated colonial modernity in Burma, they remain important historical forces in contexts such as colonialism, nationalism, education, and the cultural other/the foreign. In this book I focus on particular constellations, both cultural and historical, that harbor possible reiterations of the past or movement toward a new and different future. Those moments comprise the modern Buddhist conjunctures in Myanmar.

One such genealogy narrates the state's patronage of Buddhist institutions in order to enhance its political power. Another genealogy links those moments when Buddhist sentiments offer ways of resisting the power of the state. A third one harkens back in time to, or projects into the future, a perhaps utopian, but surely just Buddhist society. Competing visions of moral authority and civil society become visible in the social practices and discourse of such historical conjunctures, ranging from support for military dictatorship and its patronage of Buddhism to a Buddhist advocacy of democratic rights. Each of these visions represents an enduring struggle for a future in which engagement with modern concerns can be productively formulated. The historical movement between these genealogical trajectories charts the hegemonic discourse of then Burma and now Myanmar. Today, this country's challenge continues to be the realization of a future in which civil society can prosper without coercive power to guarantee the continuity of the state.

Nearly 90 percent of Myanmar's citizens practice a form of Theravada Buddhism, with roughly 70 to 80 percent of the population identifying as Burman. The remainder of the country's Theravada Buddhist population comprises ethnic minority groups, including the Shan, Mon, Pao, Karen, Arakanese, and others. A small number of Chinese Mahayana communities are found in urban centers like Yangon. The identification of Theravada Buddhist practices with the social and cultural category of being Burmese has been a significant factor in the nationalist efforts since the late colonial period. "We Burmese are Buddhist" first became a rallying cry during the nationalist struggle of the 1910s. Since then, this slogan has been invoked by many politicians, including Burma's first democratic prime minister, U Nu, whose practice of politics relied greatly on Buddhist sources of authority. Even in the popular imagination of Burma in the west, the country is closely identified with Buddhism, nonviolence, and rational ethics. Such perceptions also kindle an imagination of Burma as a romantic and nostalgic place, where people are "materially poor and spiritually wealthy." Modern Burmese sometimes echo these sentiments. Yet what it means to be Burmese and Buddhist has been articulated differently at particular cultural and historical conjunctures. In this book I explore some of the most significant moments in which Burmese Buddhist identities have been, and continue to be, constructed in modern contexts.

Burmese polities have defined themselves in terms of Buddhist sources of legitimacy for more than a millennium. The identification of Burmese ethnicity with Theravada Buddhist authority was already central to the hegemonic discourse of precolonial polities. The authority of the court was sustained by the Buddhist teachings that were believed to be the word of the Buddha. Monks acted as intellectual agents who propagated a Burmese understanding of the Pāli tradition to areas beyond the court capital and used Buddhist teachings to educate the population in the basic skills of literacy. In his seminal work on cosmological Theravada Buddhism, *World Conqueror, World Renouncer,* Stanley J. Tambiah highlighted two separate, yet complementary social categories in the Buddhist civilizations of South and Southeast Asia, namely, world renouncers and kings or householders, who were engaged with the world. Kings and householders sought to emulate the ideal actions of a world conqueror (*cakkavatti*), while world renouncers, traditionally Buddhist monks, emulated the ideal of renouncing worldly concerns in favor of religious practice that lessened the potential for future suffering and nurtured eventual moral perfection. Although the sacred biography of the Buddha encompasses both ideals, involvement with the world and its renunciation, Tambiah shows that Buddhist institutions have encompassed reciprocity between world renouncers and world conquerors.

In a traditional polity, social status was seen as the outcome of a ritual economy of merit that was based on spiritual rewards for material donations in support of Buddhist practices and institutions. A ritual system of exchange of donations for merit facilitated the politicization of Buddhist practices and institutions, and the sangha's greatest political power continues to rest in its ability to refuse donations from lay patrons and thus deny them their claims to merit and status. Neighboring vassals emulated the court of a *dhammarāja* to strengthen their social proximity to power. Such religioethnic sentiments were central to the Theravada Buddhist hegemonic paradigm of precolonial Burmese polities in which religious and political power were in dynamic tension. For instance, during the seventeenth to the nineteenth centuries and the reign of the later Taungoo and early Konbaun dynasties, the high culture of the royal court was framed by constructions of Theravada universalism that was seen at once as orthodox and Burman. Victor Lieberman identifies four levels of cultural integration in the administration of these kingdoms to facilitate and promote a Burmese Theravada hegemony. They include the erosion of local religious authority in favor of the crown and the sangha; the rise of a socially inclusive literature; imperial loyalties that superseded local ones; and a growing distinction between Burman and non-Burman ethnic boundaries.[4] Non-Burmans who wanted to bridge the social distance between them and Burman high culture and participate in the politics of the court, adopted its values, customs, and ritual theater.

During the eighteenth and nineteenth centuries European colonial powers subjugated most of Asia, and with the growth of colonial networks, important changes occurred in what until then had been a largely cohesive, traditional Buddhist worldview. The colonization of Burma as part of British India was protracted over the course of three wars between 1824 and 1885. The British had at their disposal a modern and efficient military to help them implement their colonial agenda. By contrast, the Burmese military functioned within the court's client networks and traditional Burmese warfare was imbued with cosmological and religious significance.[5] The military forces of the Konbaun dynasty were technologically and strategically overwhelmed by the colonial army, their resources, and their administrative networks. In the aftermath of the First Anglo-Burmese War of 1824, colonial rule imposed a new form of governance on Lower Burma that dislodged the received Theravada paradigm of power. Colonial agencies promoted a modern project that disrupted a calibrated balance of Burmese temporal and religious power, undermining the social and cultural foundations of a traditional Theravada polity. Invading British forces desecrated Buddhist spaces and turned them into military garrisons, such as Shwedagon Pagoda in Rangoon and, later, the palace in Mandalay. Their actions constituted grave affronts to the cultural and religious sensibilities of the Burmese, who soon came to experience that in this new colonial reality, political power had been stripped of its religious foundations. The British occupation of the Mandalay Palace in 1885, the last capital of the Konbaun dynasty, proved to be particularly disruptive to the ancien régime. It marked the end of the Third Anglo-Burmese War and the beginning of Burma's complete colonial subjugation, which ushered in a modern scheme of things to come. The British removed the Burmese Lion Throne, the symbol of the power of a *dhammarāja,* and plundered many of the court's possessions and royal regalia. The British sacking of the palace destroyed not only the court and its political culture, it also dispersed service groups within and outside of the palace walls and, by extension, the socioeconomic patronage ties that structured Mandalay society. The economy, supported by the rationale of Theravada hegemony, collapsed, and its symbols of power, courtly appointments, and status markers became meaningless. The culture of the court, the pinnacle of society in precolonial Burma, and its traditional institutions dissolved, while the Buddhist sangha, though greatly diminished in its authority and political relevance, endured as the only traditional institution to survive the advent of colonial rule.

To a large extent the Burmese experience of modernity was shaped by the experience of colonial subjugation. An important aspect of this experience was the colonial insistence on secularizing politics and dislodging it from a Buddhist worldview that had, until then, encompassed it. The advent of modernity therefore implied a challenge to received Buddhist values, institutions, and communities and set into motion profound transformations in received cultural patterns and modes of interaction. That a colonial administration facilitated this encounter of traditional culture with trade networks and global forces prefigured further innovation in the future. This process unfolded at particular historical conjunctures where modernizing forces eventually eclipsed traditional lifeways.[6] Colonial innovations undermined much of the rationale of the traditional economy of merit and its hegemony that were characteristic of a traditional Buddhist polity, and the collapse of traditional culture, initially in Lower Burma and, after 1886, also in Upper Burma, accelerated a restructuring of Burmese society.[7] In its wake, it also gave rise to innovative cultural strategies that privileged rational utility over religious worldviews and moral authority. The modern age was ushered in by new and decidedly colonial patterns of interaction. Access to western knowledge, resources, technologies, and networks empowered indigenous elites to negotiate new venues of economic, social, and political power.

Modern Buddhist institutions and practices emerged from colonial conjunctures that opened up venues and possibilities that had been beyond the scope of the Burmese cultural imagination. In the colonial state, political power was transacted separately from a Buddhist legitimation of power. In this new scheme of things, colonial subjects had access to a new economy, transnational networks, and western knowledge. The separation of secular politics from religious authority was a cornerstone of western post-Enlightenment political theory and British colonial practice during the nineteenth century. The association of secular power with colonial rule in Burma may also explain why the contemporary Burmese state continues to identify some aspects of modernity, such as human rights, with a neocolonial threat from the west. Such claims continue to be voiced in Burmese state-owned media and contribute to a popular perception that secularism lacks moral authority and is inherently weak and suspect.

Despite the discontinuities colonial rule created, Buddhism remained the social ground upon which many Burmese conducted profound cultural debates about various formations of modernity. The Burmese public discourse centered on issues of identity, the nation-state, the authority of civil vs. religious law, education, and the role of foreign influence. British prohibitions against political assemblies in public places deflected this discourse to the religious realm, a decision that elevated Buddhism as a potential site of resistance against the colonial state and ensured that Burmese cultural debates about modern concerns unfolded mostly within Buddhist frameworks. Although the British had envisioned not to become involved in the religious affairs of the colony, it was the prohibition of political assemblies during the colonial era that turned Buddhist contexts into the primary locations where Burmese were allowed to assemble and voice their views. In time, Buddhist actors and institutions frequently intervened in public debates about the common good in modern Myanmar.

A pervasive theme of Buddhist modernity in Asia is the effort of the state to reform Buddhist institutions, practices, and texts in order to promote the rationalization and centralization of public policies. However, monastic reforms have long been used as an instrument of the Burmese court and thus predate modern history. These reforms were not merely periodic attempts to rein in renegade monks.[8] Rather, they defined a religio-ideological framework for public policies that ministries and government departments subsequently implemented. In this way, reforms set the parameters for the administration of the state beyond the center. For example, King Bodawpaya's reforms in 1786 introduced the office of the *mahadanwun*, which, much like a contemporary Ministry of Religious Affairs, oversaw the regulation, finances, and implementation of monastic policies at the local, regional, and court level. Monastic lineages were largely subject to the political alliances of their royal patrons. Relations between the court and individual monks were thus carefully calibrated to maintain a balance between political power and its Buddhist source of legitimation.

Monastic reforms generally embrace two complementary trajectories. One strategy is to affirm the authority of the Theravada texts and especially the three baskets of the Tipitaka as the enduring word of the Buddha. Hence, reforms usually produced new renditions of Buddhist canonical texts that were believed to be free from accretions, pristine and orthodox. This process offered political opportunities to reframe a mythic discourse about the polity and help address, at least indirectly, the needs of the state. An equally significant component of Buddhist reform concerned the practices of members of the sangha. By alleging transgression against monastic discipline (*vinaya*), teaching false doctrines, or simply rank-and-file lassitude, the state was able to reaffirm the ordination, and hence the status of monastic communities, entire lineages, or individual monks who embraced the goals of reform. While some monks were defrocked amidst public attention, others would choose to be reordained within the new parameters of a "pure" lineage. Monastic reforms thus became tools the state employed to restructure the sangha, its economic assets, its institutional structures, and its relationships with lay supporters. The outcome of monastic reforms was an indication of the center's ability to uphold its hegemony, and, as a result, monks often had to relinquish some local control over monastic learning and conduct. The impact of monastic reform thus reverberated throughout the political system in complex and subtle ways and informed political policies. On occasion, Buddhist attempts at reform also resulted in trials that made examples of monastic transgressions of expected codes of conduct. Some monastic factions fell out of political favor and were dealt with severely. The accomplishment of the modern state has been to extend the impact of Buddhist reforms to the nation and to enforce policy implementation through the political administration of the state. Modern reforms were implemented during the U Nu era and later, through the Sangha Mahanayaka Council, under Ne Win and subsequent military regimes.

The genealogy of Buddhist resistance against the state is equally effervescent. Attempts to implement state control over the sangha can make visible certain forms of contestation and resistance to the center. Against the background of religious reforms propagated by the modern state directly, and stemming from a colonial neglect of religious obligations, the Burmese sangha has resisted the policies of the center in overt and covert ways. What began as Buddhist ways of mobilizing resistance during the colonial era continued in different guises under subsequent governments. Cultural expressions of monastic resistance ranged from silent withdrawal to the forest, to the armed militancy of millennial movements, and to the popular agitation of monks in colonial times and, since then, in 1962, 1988, 1990, 1996, and 2007.

The events of September 2007 showed that the sangha currently constitutes the greatest public challenge to the political authority of the military. As the number of monks approximates the number of conscripted soldiers, the sangha represents the largest institution outside the military. It is also the only cultural institution to survive, in a much weakened form, the challenges of colonialism and the modern state. As such it constitutes a moral force whose sources of authority transcend the secular power of the military. Nonetheless, the sangha also experiences fragmentation over allegiances to lay patrons with competing social interests. Buddhist and secular visions of authority offer competing venues to shape the future of civil society in Myanmar.

The sangha and the military have both emerged from Burma's colonial history wielding considerable public influence. Aung San, the national martyr who was also the father of Burma's symbol of democracy, Aung San Suu Kyi, is credited with founding the military in order to drive the British and later the Japanese out of Burma. Since independence, the military has intervened at critical moments to determine the nation's history and to contain popular uprisings and ethnic rebellions. Ne Win's military coup in 1962 ended the democratic government of U Nu, who relied upon Buddhist symbols in the construction of national identity. Since then, the state has been governed by military regimes. Today, the military and its forces comprise about 500,000 soldiers. Proponents of military rule argue that the armed forces are pivotal to the stability of the state, national unity, and the safety of its citizens. Opponents of the regime define the military's authority as essentially colonial. They argue that the junta lacks moral legitimation and functions primarily to extract resources from the country in order to enrich those in power. The state provides generously for members of the armed forces. Increasingly, revenues for state ministries, including the military, are generated independently of the state through joint venture enterprises with foreign capital. Mikael Gravers suggests that the military state in Myanmar still functions according to a colonial blueprint.[9] Many of the civil institutions characteristic of postcolonial societies, such as an independent judiciary, a well-developed system of higher education, and popular access to global economic and information networks still lie beyond the reach of most people in Myanmar today. A military's hold on power may be surprising in a nation where national ideology and civil institutions are infused by Buddhist values. Yet despite military rule, a battle continues to rage within this nation over moral justice, the limits of the state's authority, and a renewed vision of civil society. Time and resources will be required to foster civil institutions capable of replacing the military's control, while ensuring the continuity of the state.

Modern Buddhism relinquished a totalizing cosmology in which all aspects of life cohered across cultural, social, economic, scientific bodies of knowledge. Instead, contemporary Buddhist communities accept the fragmented nature of modern knowledge.[10] Modernity also transformed the centralized institutional authority of the sangha and made monastic norms of conduct subject to local reinterpretations. Printed journals like *The Light of Dhamma* were widely read and popularized the new religious roles of lay people. The colonial context not only facilitated the rise of Buddhist lay authority, but it also initiated modern transformations in knowledge and education. At the same time, many Burmese distrusted secular forms of governance and felt disenchanted with modern forms of living under colonial rule. Secularism entered Burmese public consciousness as part of the colonial discourse on politics and religion. Initially, it underscored the colonizers' refusal to assume responsibilities toward the Buddhist sangha. This reinforced a general public perception of secularism as suspect politics and helped foment anticolonial sentiments. Since independence, the Burmese state has at least nominally espoused a variety of secular political ideologies, ranging from democracy to socialism, militarism, and venture capitalism. However, modern political ideologies have failed in governing the country's center, and since the inception of the independent state, governments have consistently employed Buddhist constructions of power in order to legitimate the current political order.

The fluid practices of modern Buddhist communities often resist neat categories. Greater authority is accorded to lay practice and especially to lay meditation. Some of these modern Buddhist groups emphasize rationality, others have a social mission to transform society, and still others promote new rituals and mythologies. Some seek to revive past beliefs and practices. Some communities venerate a particular individual believed to embody moral perfection (*nibbāna*). Some developed organizations have been local or regional in scope, and others have focused on a national community. Some modern movements have expanded to include social networks of Buddhist and Burmese among global and transnational communities.

Certain modern Buddhist transformations constitute a clear departure from traditional practices. For instance, becoming ordained in the Buddhist sangha was traditionally the primary way of renouncing one's attachment to lay life. In modern contexts, Theravadins and other Buddhists have experimented with new ways to renounce the world. Modern contexts frequently require a reinterpretation of rules for monastic conduct, such as the need to purchase items and to use modern communication technologies. As cultural definitions of monastic roles have undergone innovation—a development that some describe as the waning authority of the sangha—the influence of the laity has grown considerably. New forms of ascetic practice and renunciation of the world, along with new social roles for spiritual leadership, have been promoted through meditation and other religious movements, including Socially Engaged Buddhism. In addition, the modern world of Theravada Buddhism has seen a rise in the status of women renouncers as novices (*thīla shin*). At present, however, there are no fully ordained nuns in Burma. By contrast, fully ordained women in Thailand include Bhikkhuni Voramai Kabilsingh, who received her ordination in Sri Lanka, and her daughter, Bhikkhuni Dhammananda, who is working to reestablish a new lineage for women renunciants. Other modern Buddhist movements have promoted a synthesis with political ideologies such as nationalism, militarism, democracy, or socialism. Still others have developed Buddhist strategies to accommodate the political powers of the modern state within a Buddhist worldview. The popularization of meditation among lay people has lent itself especially to ready rationalization of its teachings and has opened new venues for spiritual achievement among the laity.

An important concern of our time focuses on the modern conjunctures of religion and politics and the ways in which they shape the future of civil society.[11] The conjunctures of modernity identified here articulate a mythic discourse about the polity and its ultimate concerns. For example, during the nationalist movement and later, during the U Nu era, national development was conceptualized as stages on the path to enlightenment. The transcendent discourse during this era has been characterized by a Buddhist universalism articulated in beliefs, practices, and institutions. The chapters that follow trace a narrative in which modern Buddhist communities have produced and reproduced historical formations that intertwined Buddhism with the moral claims of the state. Modern knowledge and secular power became the historical locations in which received traditions were contested and reinvented. Burmese Buddhists have repeatedly questioned the power of the secular, modern state and its military coercion. During the two decades following the 1988 uprising, Burma functioned without a national constitution to define the limitations of secular power, and the modern state has repeatedly turned to sources of Buddhist authority to legitimate its practices.

In recent years the study of religion has benefited from renewed attention to the role of religion in public life. This shift was prompted in part by the inadequacy of theories about the inevitable secularization of the modern project. As scholars have articulated new perspectives on religion in public discourse, they have taken account of local and national communities as well as the civilizational projects of religious traditions in transnational contexts. Among modern Theravada communities, the emerging discourse reflects an awareness of a colonial or western "other," while affirming the foundational reality of an economy of merit, however fragmented and circumscribed its contemporary practices may appear. Contemporary realities no longer constitute a total social fact, as Tambiah has argued to be the case for the traditional galactic polity, but the exchange of merit for power still defines the parameters of politics in Theravada contexts.

This shift in scholarly attention challenges us to examine critically received categories of knowledge we use to apprehend our subject of study. In particular, modern Buddhist conjunctures make evident that a Weberian description of Buddhism as "otherworldly" obscures our understanding of the social engagement among modern Buddhist institutions and communities. Similarly, we must recognize that understanding authentic practice as inherently nonpolitical forces a collusion with a colonial hegemonic discourse that aims to maintain the status quo. One may add to this list of obsolete categories the normative ideal of nonviolence and similar conceptions of normative practice. It is not a scholar's role to assert that the practice of protesting monks is inauthentic and undermines their religious status. Further, we must relinquish the view that modern Buddhism has undergone a form of protestantization that has relegated religious activity to the private domain of civil society.[12] Instead, Buddhist sources of power engage in a moral discourse within their social, political, and cultural contexts. Our scholarly premise must acknowledge the public role of a Theravada Buddhist discourse in such contexts. These conceptual shifts enable scholars to appraise critically their own intellectual genealogies and produce new readings of modern Buddhist conjunctures.

The sociologist Max Weber posited that Buddhism was inherently "otherworldly" and hence not capable of becoming a social force similar to Protestant ethics that propelled the rise of capitalism in modern Europe. Weber's categorization relied on the work of the nineteenth-century indologist, Max Müller and was very influential in the late twentieth century, when many theories about Theravada Buddhist cultural practices, institutions, and societies explicitly referenced his work. Indeed, Weber's work continues to be invoked at many junctures in the study of Theravada societies and his influence has been noted in a number of recent studies by, among others, Choompolpaisal, Gellner, Keyes, and Kitiarsa.[13] In light of such influential work, I offer in the chapters that follow a critique of the Weberian premise of Buddhist otherwordliness and propose an opposite point of departure, namely, that Buddhist conceptions and practices are intimately tied to conceptions of political power in social, economic, and political realm. If such critique of Weber is innovative by any measure, it is perhaps in the consistent reminders to readers of the ramifications the Weberian premise harbors for our understanding of Theravada social and cultural practices and the need to evaluate critically our received genealogies of knowledge.

This study engages thematic intersections of modernity from the disciplinary perspectives of anthropology, religious studies, and history. I do not present an exhaustive chronology but seek to illuminate instead particular conjunctures of Buddhism and civil society that highlight modern tensions.[14] The chapters draw on several periods of ethnographic fieldwork I conducted since 1981 in Mandalay, Yangon, and Bagan and profile cultural and historical locations at which some forms of knowledge open access to power, while other bodies of knowledge lose relevance in the political context of their time.

Summary of Chapters

Chapter 1 illustrates the impact of Buddhist reforms on the affairs of the state and its public policy during the seventeenth to nineteenth centuries, when new empires formed that were modeled after the classical polities of Southeast Asia. Contrary to Weber's characterization of Buddhism as otherworldly, the cultural practices of the court were, in fact, at once religious and political. The court's construction of authority through Buddhist reforms was central to its hegemony. Religious reforms centralized the power of the court and produced a discourse of the Buddhist "other." The polity affirmed its policies through ritual networks and a this-worldly economy of merit in which social status was linked to the practice of generosity. The culture at the court of the *dhammarāja*, the righteous ruler of the center, encouraged competition for power among hierarchically structured communities and mobilized various segments in the support of its agenda.

Chapter 2 explores the ways in which modernity was articulated as part of the colonial project following the three Anglo-Burmese Wars (1824–1826, 1852, and 1885). As the British established control over the territories of Lower and Upper Burma, colonialism became a herald of modernity that limited traditional cultural realities. After the annexation of Mandalay, the Burmese experience of modernity was, in many ways, consonant with a rapid eclipse of traditional cultural values and lifeways, giving way to a sense of alienation from religious and cultural practices. The conceptual shifts of colonial modernity displaced traditional venues to power rooted in Theravada Buddhist belief and karmic practice.[15] They profoundly transformed Burmese cultural institutions, religious authority, and the everyday lives of Buddhists and, during the nineteenth century, led to divergent regional developments in Lower and Upper Burma. In this way the widespread collapse of traditional institutions accelerated a restructuring of Burmese society and led to the rise of colonial forms of knowledge.[16]

Chapter 3 examines the ways in which the Burmese encounter with modernity was informed by colonial knowledge and western education. Here, I investigate attempts by British colonizers and colonized Burmese to educate the "other" as part of a public discourse about the moral legitimacy of governance. While the impact of colonialism on monastic education was profound and tensions between western knowledge and Buddhist education still reverberate in the contemporary period, the history of Buddhist education in modernity is not a continuous narrative that offers neat distinctions and categorizations. Rather, it teaches us the disparate articulations of modern themes and their fragmented trajectories through time. The chapter highlights the debate about the place of Buddhist education in a modern public curriculum. As demand for colonial knowledge increased, Buddhist education was associated with the decline of a traditional Buddhist polity and with the sangha as a cultural institution. After independence, Buddhist literacy experienced a resurgence as Burmese intellectuals stressed the rationality of the Buddha *dhamma* as the foundation of modern science. Since then, various governments have employed monasteries to deliver basic education, especially in rural areas. While Burma is often said to maintain today a high degree of Buddhist learning among its monastic population, Buddhist education no longer retains the privileged status it commanded prior to the British presence.

Chapter 4 delineates the colonial project of constructing modern Buddhist identities. Colonial society, both Burmese and western, self-consciously sought to change traditional Buddhist practices and develop modern identities. These efforts were empowered by the growing influence of lay Buddhist associations, particularly the Young Men's Buddhist Association (YMBA). Initially a social club for an elite group of western-educated young Burmese men, the YMBA intentionally modeled itself after the YMCA and began to mobilize a rapidly growing membership under the banner of a modern Burmese Buddhist identity. While the YMBA initially benefited from the support of the colonial government, it was unable to resolve internal challenges. At the height of its popularity, fragmentation set in after a large, national convention in Mandalay in 1919. The organization was soon overtaken by competing nationalist movements composed of anticolonial Buddhist traditionalists and later also secular nationalists.

Chapter 5 focuses on national politics as a form of Buddhist practice and underscores from yet another vantage point the conjunctures of Buddhism and politics. At issue are attempts by three governments after independence to control Buddhist institutions, doctrines, and practices. Their reforms included propagating Buddhism among tribal peoples living at the periphery of the state. During the U Nu government, the Sixth Buddhist Convocation or Sangāyana fostered utopian expectations of an imminent wheel-turning monarch (*cakkavatti* [P], *setkya min:* [B]) and popularized meditation for the masses. The country's economic progress was likened to the nation's spiritual achievement of stages along the Eightfold Noble Path to Perfection. By contrast, Ne Win's reforms disrobed influential monks to curtail their charismatic influence with powerful lay supporters. Unlike U Nu, whose ascetic practice was widely admired, Ne Win was seen as a superstitious, rather than religious, person. After the 1988 uprising, the State Law and Order Restoration Council (SLORC) succeeded Ne Win and implemented extensive controls on monastic institutions. It also commissioned large-scale state rituals and sponsored the restoration of sacred sites. Through these efforts the state mobilized networks of Buddhist donors throughout the nation as supporters of the state in order to enhance its own power in the absence of a national constitution between 1988 and 2008. Many members of the sangha were silenced, and lay assistants were assigned to them to manage their money, travel, and activities. The surveillance extended particularly to young monks, many of whom had participated in the 1988 uprising.

By contrast, chapter 6 chronicles a genealogy of Buddhist resistance against the state and describes how modern movements employed Buddhist practices to resist the power of the state. In precolonial times, monks defied royal authority on occasion by eluding the king's summons and taking up solitary practice in the forest. But the kind of civil disobedience and government boycott anticolonial monks organized during in the 1920s and 1930s differed from earlier forms of dissent and the popular anti-British sentiments they created. Activist monks encouraged their lay supporters in public sermons to boycott imported goods and use only local products. Their popularity grew further through the grassroots mobilization by organizations such as the YMBA, the General Council of Burmese Associations (GCBA), and the General Council of Sangha Sammeggi (GCSS).

Chapter 7 examines the events of September 2007, the most recent instance of monastic resistance against the state, and delineates fault lines in the contestation between the sangha and the military. Amidst a widening economic disparity, the sangha has challenged the state with moral and ritual sanctions against the military junta. As the only cultural institution surviving colonial rule, the sangha has used its moral authority as political leverage and promotes socially engaged Buddhism, human rights, civil society, and democratic practices in Myanmar. Globalization and its economic demands for sources of energy have ultimately upheld the regime despite a commonly held view of the junta as internal colonizers who have benefited from extracting the country's resources at the cost of national development. The chapter concludes with interrogating the Burmese and academic uses of the notion of "political monks" and shows that this designation is itself a product of a colonial hegemonic discourse.

Chapter 8 recapitulates the trajectories of Buddhist modernity in order to draw the reader's attention to potential Buddhist futures in Myanmar. In doing so, I conclude that the tensions of modernity remain unresolved and confine moral visions of the future within the limitations of a colonial past. Myanmar's elites have yet to come to terms with half a century of totalitarian rule and the role Buddhism has played in that history. Global realities have also helped determine the options for the future through patterns of energy consumption and through access to digital-knowledge economies. These factors increase the likelihood of continued Buddhist contestations and calls for renewed social engagement and relevance in the future.

1 Theravada Cultural Hegemony in Precolonial Burma

This chapter delineates Theravada Buddhist paradigms that shaped precolonial polities in the region that became modern Burma. These empires modeled themselves after classical states of Southeast Asia in which royal patronage of Buddhist institutions helped consolidate the regional power of the court. Periodic reforms of the Buddhist sangha and the ritual mobilization of ethnic communities upheld this Buddhist hegemony. The intrusion of colonial trade networks and concurrent monetarization in Lower Burma undermined this economy of merit. As the British gained control over the regions of Lower and Upper Burma, colonialism became the cultural harbinger of modernity.

In response to the European encroachment along the coastal regions along the Bay of Bengal, King Thalon relocated the royal palace of the Restored Taungoo dynasty (1597–1752) from Pegu in Lower Burma to Ava in Upper Burma in 1635. The move occurred at a moment in early colonial history when European explorers of the Southeast Asian archipelago expanded their trade networks along the coastline of Lower Burma. Some historians characterized this shift inland of the Burmese political center as "motivated by the intransigence and xenophobia which radiated from the Court of Ava" and interpreted the relocation of the capital to Upper Burma as a defeatist retreat from encroaching European maritime trade networks.[1] More recently, Victor Lieberman has challenged this assertion of a Burmese xenophobic withdrawal.[2] He argues that the move of the center of power from Pegu to Ava was a strategic choice of the Restored Taungoo dynasty in response to the famine, war, and depopulation that had destabilized its earlier rule in the lower delta region. With this move King Thalon also shifted the kingdom's political focus away from maritime trade and renewed inland trade with other Buddhist polities. Ava, the new capital in the northern Irrawaddy river basin, consolidated a geopolitical location for subsequent Burmese kingdoms and offered new economic opportunities through lucrative land trade with Yunnan. By implementing this strategy, the Restored Taungoo dynasty realized, once again, the political hegemony of a Theravada polity and brought neighboring Buddhist groups, like the Shan, under the control of the Ava court. When an intermittent Mon rebellion eclipsed the Taungoo era in 1752, King Alaungpaya (1752–1760) founded the new Konbaun dynasty (1752–1885) and reconstituted the Burmese empire by moving the capital still further upcountry to Shwebo. Subsequent Konbaun kings moved the capital back to the banks of the Irrawaddy River, initially to Ava and later to Amarapura and Mandalay.

The *dhammarāja* model of kingship was a central principal for organizing early modern kingship during the Restored Taungoo and Konbaun dynasties. In his discussion of the Burmese polity from the seventeenth to the nineteenth centuries, Lieberman underscores the role of Theravada Buddhism as the prism through which the court promoted political and cultural integration. He writes that "the rise of an overarching culture that was simultaneously more orthodox Theravadin, more self-consciously Burman, and more sympathetic to central regulation became apparent."[3] The master narrative of court culture in precolonial Burma was articulated in its construction of Theravada orthodoxy. To an unprecedented degree, the court defined Theravada orthodoxy as Burman and established the dominance of the Burmese over neighboring ethnic groups. The empire of the Konbaun dynasty incorporated diverse ethnic groups, such as the Shan, Arakanese, Mon, Lao, and Tai, who practiced local versions of Theravada Buddhism along with the veneration of ancestors. Konbaun kings nonetheless succeeded in integrating these groups into the center's Buddhist culture and ritual system. Several factors reinforced the Burmese Theravada hegemony over other Buddhist ethnicities. Ethnic vassals were mobilized through the ritual theater of the court and through the construction of religious monuments and works of royal merit. Provincial officers were obliged to participate in annual *kandaw* rituals to demonstrate their loyalty to the court, which helped reproduce court ritual, culture, speech, aesthetics, and art at the provincial courts.[4] Participants in the provinces and ethnically different groups would be encouraged to emulate the culture of the court even if they did so only in select contexts or followed other traditions on other occasions. An extensive system of intermarriage between the court and provincial nobility further reinforced selective participation in Konbaun culture and hegemonic orthodoxy. During Bodawpaya's reign (1782–1819), the court even maintained a list of royal supporters who followed the religious practices of the king.[5]

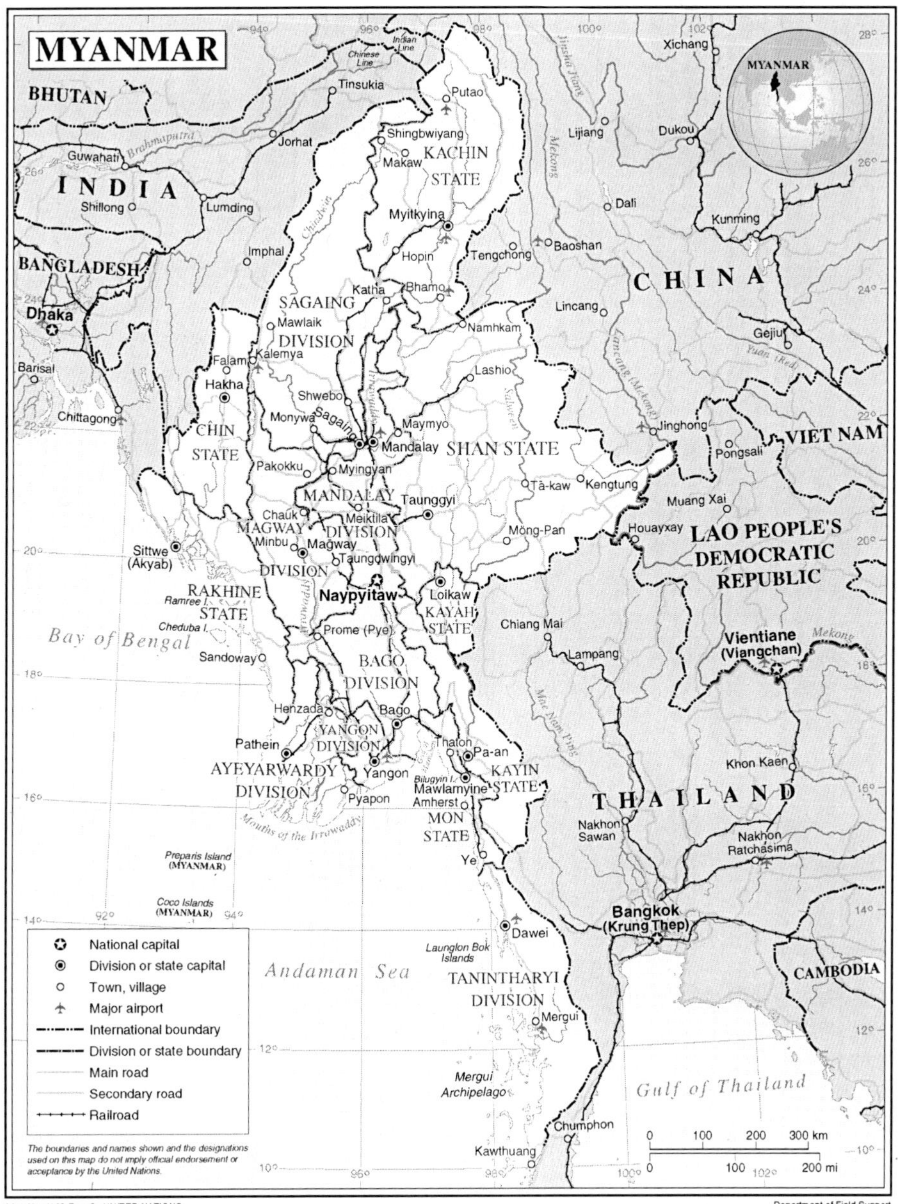

Map of Myanmar. (UN CARTOGRAPHIC SECTION, NO. 4168)

Relocating the royal capital upcountry in the seventeenth century ushered in a cultural renaissance of Burmese polities that reached its apex in the eighteenth century, when the kings of the Konbaun dynasty rebuild a Burmese empire that was based on Theravadin notions of power. In the politics of a Southeast Asian Buddhist kingdom, the court's influence typically radiated from a cosmic center to the periphery, expanding and contracting through time and cycling from periods of ascendancy to eventual decline, only to be encompassed in time in the spheres of influence of competing polities. Stanley Tambiah characterizes such Buddhist polities as galactic polities that constituted a "total social fact" and encompassed cultural, economic, and religious histories.[6] In Burma, this traditional hegemonic political system collapsed in 1885 when the British conquest of Mandalay ended the rule of Konbaun dynasty and traditional Buddhist kingship.

In the imagination of many Southeast Asian Buddhists, the Mauryan emperor Aśoka (r. 270–232 BCE) has taken on enduring mythic dimensions as an exemplary Buddhist king, who ruled in accordance with the Universal Law of the Buddha and exerted a great deal of influence over the sangha.[7] Buddhist legend attributes the emergence of the Buddhist lineage now called Theravada to Aśoka and his patronage of the Third Buddhist Council. Theravada monasteries were eventually established in Sri Lanka and, traveling along land and sea routes in Southeast Asia, the mythic dimensions of the Aśokan model had, by early in the sixth century CE, informed ideals of kingship in Southeast Asia, where kings sought to emulate his example.

The Aśokan paradigm continued to be an influential model for Burmese kings to affirm their rule over subjects and vassals, including non-Burman ethnic minorities who cultivated their distinct vernacular Buddhist traditions.[8] The contemporary state in Myanmar claims to trace its genealogy to ancient Pagan, the first Burmese empire, and credits the founding monarch, King Anawrahta (1044–1077) with establishing Theravada Buddhism there.[9] The dynasty of Pagoda Builders who ruled in the desert capital of Pagan between the eighth and thirteenth centuries built hundreds of monumental stūpas. In his history of this period, Michael Aung-Thwin shows how royal obligation toward the Buddha's dispensation (*thathana* [B], *sāsana* [P]) created spiraling economic pressures that ushered in the dynasty's eventual collapse.[10] Other factors, such as decreasing rainfall, climate changes, and the rise of coastal polities, contributed to the decline of Pagan.[11]

From a Burmese perspective, the king's religious and ritual obligations were fundamental to his political power. Ideally, the precolonial polities of Pagan and later Burmese kingdoms were ruled by a righteous Buddhist ruler (*dhammarāja*), who was expected to govern in accordance with the Buddhist

Law (*dhamma*) and fulfill the religious and political obligations of his office. The cornerstone of good governance was to create and maintain a social context in which the *sāsana* could prosper, and war and famine were kept at bay. The king's role as patron of the *thathana*,[12] his ability to ensure discipline among the sangha, and his deeds of merit were understood as the normative measures of his reign. Kings were also expected to sponsor the construction and consecration of pagodas, monasteries, and sacred icons and to mobilize resources and subjects through merit-making rituals.[13]

An elaborate annual cycle of rituals affirmed the legitimacy of the polity's hegemonic rule over its tribute-paying vassals. In the *dhammarāja*'s polity, subjects and vassals paid respect (*kandaw*) and tribute to the court in annual rituals that affirmed their position as subjects of the court. Another way to acknowledge their obligation to the court was through contributions to the king's deeds of merit. These continual affirmations of the court's legitimacy also enabled vassals to renegotiate their positions within this hierarchy. Particularly in the absence of rules for dynastic succession in Burma, the king's religious role was an important source of legitimation. The power of a *dhammarāja* was seen as manifesting itself in the contemporary expression of religious merit that the king had earned in past lives. The king's previously acquired merit provided the foundational framework for implementing the court's power over the sangha, the polity's subjects, and vassals. Royal donations to the sangha further enhanced the king's store of merit. However, the conduct of his office also made it possible for a Buddhist king to acquire negative karma, because his responsibilities required him to act in ways that caused suffering, such as enforcing criminal punishment or conducting war.[14]

Buddhist rituals generally involve ritual exchange of *dāna* for merit between lay people and monks. These networks of ritual exchange created an economy of merit that constituted the basic social fabric of traditional Theravada societies. In this economy, now as then, it is the primary religious obligation of lay people to provide for the material needs of the *sāsana*. In return for their generosity, lay people acquire merit which, in turn, determines one's rebirth and brings ethical and material rewards in future lives. A Buddhist lay community constitutes a ritual community in which an individual's status, power, and perceived store of merit are hierarchically differentiated. Giving to Buddhist causes, demonstrating generosity, and making merit are religious actions that create status differences and social hierarchies among lay people. Still today, sponsoring merit-making rituals is seen not only as a religious act, but also as an expression of power. Guests who accept invitations to participate in merit-making rituals also incur an obligation to their hosts, the "owner of merit" (*kuthou shin*), to reciprocate on another occasion. These prescribed activities can produce lavish sponsorship of religious causes and create distinct competition among ritual sponsors.

In *The Religion of India,* Max Weber characterized Buddhism as "otherworldly" and his views shaped the work of many early students of this tradition.[15] While there remains much we still do not know about early Buddhist communities, historical, textual, and ethnographic evidence shows, on the contrary, that Buddhist public acts performed by monks and laity in Buddhist societies are simultaneously—and necessarily—political and religious. This tradition early on embraced an orientation toward involvement in the social and political world through ritual practices that created an economy of merit. The courts of precolonial Burma followed a hegemonic paradigm in which Buddhist acts were at once public, political, and religious. The reforms of Buddhist institutions and practices were important instruments in the implementation of public policy. The institution of monkhood legitimated a social hierarchy in which the king's political fortune depended in many ways on his ability to make merit by mobilizing communities to undertake religious works.[16] The court promoted Buddhist networks of ritual exchange that anchored its hegemonic power.[17] Buddhist reforms reinforced centralization in traditional polities that rewarded participation in Buddhist ritual networks with access to power and social status. This mode of operation provided a political rationale for competition within and between Buddhist communities over tributary vassals. Buddhist hegemonic practice was therefore not coincidental to politics in precolonial Burma, but instead framed the parameters for the public transaction of politics.

The Bodies of the Buddha in the Economy of Merit

In Theravada practice, the legacy of the Buddha comprises two aspects, his physical remains (*rūpakāya*) and his spiritual body (*dhammakāya*). In cultural terms, *rūpakāya* encompasses the Buddha's relics, but Burmese also include in this category other sacred objects.[18] Throughout the Theravada world, the veneration of Buddhist relics and images is a popular practice as they are considered inherently powerful. Their physical presence transforms ordinary space into a cosmic center around which cultural, historical, and religious orders are constructed, and ordinary historical and cultural orders are mapped onto a transcendent reality. The presence of these Buddhist sacred objects also identifies a community of believers by means of ritual merit-making. In some ritual contexts the Buddha's physical presence, or *rūpakāya,* is represented by a set of the Tipitaka, the Theravada canon, which is believed to comprise the complete

A replica of the Tooth Relic enshrined at the Tooth Relic Pagoda in Yangon.
PHOTO BY STEFANIE WOODWARD.

teachings of the Buddha. The presence of the Buddha's *rūpakāya* constitutes a cosmic center of power, and it is common for social and ritual communities to form around them.[19] Buddhist communities at such sacred sites are defined socially and ritually through merit-making and veneration of the Buddha's *rūpakāya*. In previous essays I focused on the ritual veneration of the Buddha's remains in contexts ranging from pilgrimages to relic shrines in the solitary periphery to participation in popular state cults at the centers of Theravada polities.[20] For Burmese Buddhists, sacred places such as the famous Shwedagon Pagoda in Rangoon or the Mahamuni Buddha image in Mandalay continue to embody national significance. By the same token, local groups often identify their communities by worshiping at and offering donations to a pagoda in their vicinity.

According to popular belief and cultural discourse, the ritual veneration of Buddhist images and relics guards against the inevitable decline of the *dhamma* and *sāsana.* The presence of such sacred objects and their ritual veneration function significantly in the formative processes that define and localize Buddhist communities and cluster them around such ritual interactions. Because sacred objects like relics and Buddha images constitute potentially infinite sources of merit, the greatest religious merit and social prestige accrues to a Buddhist householder who donates an image of the Buddha. Texts and normative beliefs bestow upon the Buddhist laity the primary obligation of providing all materials required to uphold the community of monks. Indeed, material donation for Buddhist causes and patronage of the tradition's *rūpakāya* are as important to the definition of lay status as is the affirmation of the Buddhist confession of faith, namely, to take refuge in the Buddha, the *dhamma,* and the sangha.

In Burmese society monks are venerated and command authority because of their monastic status. Ideally, the sangha's role is to preserve and practice the Buddha's *dhammakāya* and to embody his spiritual message through practice, knowledge, and insight. Their disciplined observance of the teachings makes monks pure sources of merit for their lay donors. In Burma, most young boys still become novices for a short period of time to honor their parents and make merit for them. With full ordination in one of the recognized lineages, a monk gives up worldly aspirations and familial ties in order to assume a new monastic identity and life apart from lay society. Any able-bodied man can join the sangha if he meets certain conditions set forth in the *vinaya* and a lay person is willing to sponsor his ordination. In 1800, 1 to 3 percent of the male population chose that path.

The conduct of the monastic community is bound by the *vinaya,* which is interpreted with some variation among the ordination lineages (*gain:* (B), *nikāya* (P)). The sangha's internal structure is hierarchical, and monks acquire seniority with each full year they remain in the sangha. Regardless of their absolute age, junior monks are deferential to senior monks, and disciples pay homage to their teachers, resident monks show obedience to their abbot, and novices show respect to their preceptors. Traditionally, the *thathanabain* was the supreme patriarch of the Burmese sangha. He was appointed by the king, who generally looked to monastic teachers and lineages with close relations to the court. The *thathanabain* would counsel the king on matters of governance, and the king would solicit his support in political matters. While the patriarch's authority was strengthened by his proximity to the court, factionalism among *nikāya* often limited his authority over regional monastic lineages. While courts aspired to be the patrons of a centralized sangha serving the hegemonic vision of the center, monastic dissent and fragmentation were also a social reality, particularly in the peripheral regions of the court's sphere of influence.

The Burmese sangha encompassed diverse traditions of practice and study. In some monasteries, practice was dedicated exclusively to one of the many methods of meditation for which the country is well known. Other monasteries focused on the study of the Theravada textual tradition or, in Collins' expression, the Pāli Imaginaire. This literature inculcated a Buddhist worldview and structured cultural realities and social constructions. This body of texts was seen as a repository of knowledge accessible to the court and through libraries in rural monasteries. A rise in literacy also increased the production and copying of texts and promoted a shared ethic through all levels of traditional Theravada society. The cultural salience of monastic education contributed to the standardization of literary form, orthography, and content, and a broader popularization of a Burmese Theravada hegemony. By the sixteenth century, monasteries functioned as sites for instilling worldviews and teaching basic literacy throughout the Burmese empire. The British recorded a relatively high rate of literacy among Burmese men, a skill acquired during their youth spent as lay students or novices in the sangha. Instructional texts included Pāli formulae, commonly known narratives about the lives of the Buddha, and vernacular texts like the *Rājanīti,* which propounded a code of conduct for kings, and *Lokanīti* text, which extolled ethics for lay people.[21] The use of legal documents, census accounts, and commercial contracts also created a need for increased literacy in everyday life, and monastic schools (*kyaun:*), which had proliferated through the rural regions of the polity, served that purpose.[22] Lieberman notes that the increased number of professional scribes, including lay scribes, reduced the cost of producing a set of Tipitaka texts for local use.[23] Today, monastic universities in Rangoon, Mandalay, Sagain, and Pakokku still offer advanced courses of study, examinations, and monastic educational degrees.

The sangha performed a pivotal role in the cultural integration of a Theravada polity. Because of its role as an educational institution, as an intellectual elite, and as a social location for the production of cultural knowledge, the sangha profoundly shaped Burmese culture and history. Monks were regarded as repositories of knowledge about the *dhamma* and the history of the *sāsana.*

They were advisors at the court, ritual officiants in the village, and teachers of basic literacy at the court and in village monasteries. Monastic literati would spend time at the court, at monastic centers of learning, and then return to their places of origin. The majority of monasteries were located in towns where monks would minister to the lay community and perform merit-making rituals. A minority of monks resided at forest monasteries that offered solitary hermitages to practice meditation. An itinerant lifestyle was a significant part of the monastic vocation, and monks acted traditionally as cultural brokers between the center of the polity and its periphery, traveling between rural areas and urban centers. Although monks were dependent upon the validation of their practice through donations from the laity, they were generally considered to be repositories of the Buddha's knowledge and thus could claim greater authority and status than the king and his subjects as lay people were generally considered to be less accomplished in matters of Buddhist practice. The reciprocity between monks and their lay supporters was therefore always subject to public validation and allowed for a continual interpretation of interactions between the sangha and the political center. The authority of the king as a *dhammarāja* was dependent upon the sangha's validation of his rule in accordance with the Buddhist Universal Law. Monks performed this role by accepting donations from the court, acting as a source of merit, and providing counsel to the king. As such, the sangha was a source of merit for the king. Withholding opportunities for the king to make merit and refusing donations made to the sangha constituted a breach in this pattern of ritual exchange.

Buddhist Reforms as Public Policy during the Konbaun Dynasty

The attempts of the Burmese courts to control the sangha and reform monastic practice provided a cultural template for the consolidation of royal power. The kings of the Konbaun dynasty considered it their royal obligation to ensure that monastic behavior was in strict compliance with the *vinaya*, and they performed their role as patrons of the sangha and guardians of monastic discipline by means of religious reforms during the eighteenth and nineteenth centuries. The reforms not only defined normative beliefs and practices for the political and monastic elites, they also presented opportunities to refashion the authoritative standing of texts, examine monastic behavior, and account for the economic wealth acquired by the sangha. Successful reforms were promoted as purification and propagation of the *sāsana*, while affirming the political legitimacy of the kings. This also holds true of modern heads of state who have acted as patrons of the sangha. Reformers claimed to preserve the orthodoxy of

Theravada texts by producing editions of the Pāli canon that were purged of accretions and thus restored to what was considered to be the pristine word of the Buddha.

The claim to orthodoxy also provided a means to authorize the royal agenda. The purification of Buddhist texts was closely tied to the historical practices of elite monastic groups, whose actions came to be seen as authoritative and expressive of a particular cultural hegemony at a given historical moment. The court's control over reforms also surfaced in the administration of monastic property and related legal maneuvers. In these ways Buddhist reforms functioned as the imprimatur of the court and its efforts to concentrate its power at the center of the polity. Buddhist reforms were thus not just the work of great kings, they also served as tools for shaping public policy at the interface of Buddhist belief and political power. Ideally, the court sought to establish a perfect Buddhist society (*pativedha sāsana*) in which kings ensured the prosperity of subjects and the sangha, while monks strived for moral perfection.[24] Such aspirations provided an impetus for writing dynastic and religious chronicles that frequently recorded the location of a historic polity within a broader mythic discourse about the kind of Buddhist utopian society a *dhammarāja* typically sought to realize. For instance, the royal chronicles of Burmese reigns from the seventeenth to the nineteenth centuries speak from the vantage point of the Buddhist center, articulating a hegemonic discourse in which the court defined Theravada orthodoxy through the patterns of patronage it cultivated with the sangha.

Religious reforms were implemented during two reigns of the Konbaun dynasty, those of King Bodawpaya (r. 1782–1819) and King Mindon (r. 1853–1878), and they underscore the role of Buddhism as the dominant cultural idiom in the conduct of precolonial politics. King Bodawpaya represents a classic example of a Burmese *dhammarāja;* his reign ended just prior to the British conquest of the southern coastal regions in the First Anglo-Burmese War. King Mindon's reign exemplifies a weakened polity guided by a Buddhist monarch who uses traditional Buddhist means of legitimation in an attempt to unify the country despite its fragmentation through colonial rule. The portraits that emerge of these two kings and the histories of their respective reforms illustrate despotic and benevolent dimensions of royal power in precolonial Burma. Bodawpaya's demise was precipitated by his extreme claim that he was the future Buddha Metteya, which the sangha refused to validate.[25] Nonetheless, the functions he instituted in his Interior Ministry (mahadanwun), discussed below, can be seen as precedents for modern interactions between Buddhist and political institutions. King Mindon's reforms commenced half a century after the British acquired Lower Burma, when monetarization had already undermined the economic and political stability of Upper Burma. This decline was hastened by Mindon's inability to install a gifted successor. Despite the eventual failure of both reforms, they illustrate the ways in which kings regulated public policy through Buddhist means.

BODAWPAYA'S ZEAL

King Bodawpaya's (r. 1782–1819) reforms illustrate the integration of Theravada Buddhism and pragmatic politics during his reign that was marked by the king's ardent convictions and erratic reversals. The king's agenda was to remake Buddhist orthodoxy under his patronage and purge dissenters from his polity. In the course of two decades, Bodawpaya rigidly enforced his view on monastic discipline and textual orthodoxy in order to consolidate his control over the sangha and reform monastic practice. He ordered the sangha to reordain within the Sinhalese Amarapura lineage, which forced them to lose their monastic seniority. Preceptors were required to undergo five years of formal education and ten years of strict monastic practice to be permitted to officiate at ordinations.[26] Those who refused to submit to reordination and re-education were forced to disrobe and leave the sangha. Bodawpaya also introduced standardized monastic examinations for all seeking novice or higher ordination into the sangha. Starting in 1785, the government administered these examinations annually and emphasized strict conformity with the new standards and adherence to the *vinaya*.

In 1784 the court ruled on a long-standing monastic debate within the sangha over *vinaya* rules stipulating whether monks must cover only one or both shoulders while traveling outside the monastery. The unsuccessful one-shoulder faction, known as the Culagandhi, was lead by Atulayasa, the royal preceptor of the former King Alaungpaya (r. 1752–1760), and based its authority on local traditions and the rules of discipline practiced at local monasteries. The court determined to purge Atulayasa and his followers from the sangha and impose severe punishments on their lay supporters.[27] The successful two-shoulder faction, known as the Mahagandhi, which eventually constituted the Thudhamma majority, constructed its position in reference to the Pāli *vinaya* texts and its commentaries.

In 1786 Bodawpaya commissioned the Ministry of the Interior to integrate religious and secular functions in his administration. During his reign, and at several historical junctures since then, this ministry was the vehicle for religious reforms. It purged dissenters, implemented strict oversight over monastic affairs, and reported bi-annually on monastic examinations. At the same time, the ministry rewarded the relatives of monks with tax exemptions, if those relatives agreed to join the royal cavalry. The Commissioner for Censorship in the Ministry of the Interior (*mahadanwun*) functioned as a liaison between the sangha and the court.[28] He was also charged with overseeing the administration of Pāli examinations and disciplining monks whose behavior was deemed to transgress the *vinaya*. His office was assisted by two auxiliaries: the *wutmyewun*, the Commissioner of Religious Land, who was responsible for keeping financial records on monastic lands and on the maintenance of pagodas and pagoda slaves, and the *kathaunmyauntaik*, who implemented Bodawpaya's taxation of monastic land and managed royal revenue generated from it. Together, they constituted an effective administrative hierarchy that linked the center to regional and village levels. They also provided mechanisms by which local abbots could be called upon to defend their teachings and practices before the royal court. The king strictly enforced his view of orthodoxy in doctrinal debates before his cabinet (*hluttaw*) and punished dissenters with show trials.[29]

Bodawpaya convened the powerful Thudhamma Council in 1786 in order to impose his views of Theravada orthodoxy on the monastic institution. Initially it was composed of eight, and later twelve, senior monks who were charged with implementing monastic reforms and establishing new standards of orthodox practice.[30] In 1788 he appointed the scholar-monk Nānābhivamsa, the first Maundaun Sayadaw, as the new patriarch (*thathanabain*) of the Thudhamma Council. The Thudhamma lineage's rise to prominence occurred when Bodawpaya compelled all monks to be reordained in the tradition of the Sinhalese Amarapura Nikāya.[31] Thudhamma monks still constitute the majority in the Burmese sangha today, although their reformist claims to pure practice have been superseded by monastic lineages that emerged from reforms under King Mindon.

Jacques Leider comments insightfully that "the Sudhamma Reformation was not only the implementation of a formal process of moral and disciplinary restoration, but is also visibly worked out as a political process where the struggle for the definition of orthodoxy hit the shifting ground of daily human politics."[32] Although Bodawpaya loosened restrictions on the sangha in 1807 and abandoned his efforts altogether in 1812, his Buddhist reforms nonetheless comprised the utopian vision of a Buddhist polity (*pativedha sāsana*) by inscribing textual orthodoxy, reordaining the sangha, constructing of grand religious monuments, and missionizing among ethnic groups at the periphery of his polity.[33]

Bodawpaya's reforms aimed to revise Buddhist texts and histories. He commissioned new editions of the Pāli Tipitaka and hired copyists to produce duplicates for distribution to local monasteries, a process that benefited the standardization of Burmese orthographic conventions. Bodawpaya also wanted to revise the history of the transmission of the *dhamma*, for he claimed that the Buddha had introduced his teachings to Burma during his lifetime. This claim was an imaginative revision of the established genealogy of textual transmission from Sri Lanka to the Mon kingdom of Thaton; from there King Anawratha was said to have obtained a copy of the Tipitaka in the eleventh century. Bodawpaya was particularly critical of the work of the eminent fifth-century monk Buddhaghosa, who is believed to have translated canonical texts from Sinhala to Pāli. He further discredited Shin Arahan, the royal preceptor and reformer of the Pagan period, who is said to have brought these Pāli texts to Pagan after the fall of the Mon polity of Thaton. Bodawpaya then commissioned an eminent *vinaya* monk, the Mèhti Sayadaw to rewrite Buddhist history in a chronicle entitled *Vamsadīpanī*. That chronicle, completed a few years after its initial monastic author had passed away, focused on the transmission of the Buddha's dispensation to Burma and elevated the historical and religious significance of Bodawpaya.[34] The *Vamṣadīpanī* was the first in a series of four chronicles (*thathana win*) composed during Konbaun era. It was central to the construction of the court's orthodoxy and constituted, according to Patrick Pranke, an apologia for the Thudhamma Reformation.[35]

Such shifts in the construction of Theravada orthodoxy did not go unchallenged among the sangha, as can be inferred from the forceful implementation of Bodawpaya's reforms. A rhetoric of the Buddhist "other" emerges from the Royal Orders and from the chronicle Bodawpaya commissioned.[36] Prior to Bodawpaya's reform, the term Culagandhi designated those monks who covered only one shoulder when leaving the monastery. But in the context of Bodawpaya's reform, Culagandhi assumed a broader meaning and came to refer more generally to those monks who dissented from the court's authority and who were therefore seen as contravening the authority of Thudhamma lineage, their Sinhala derived heritage, and Pāli orthodoxy. Among these nonconformists were monks who wore hats or practiced medicine, astrology, or martial arts. Some lived in monasteries called *pwè kyaun:*, where monks were said to entertain lay people with drum-beating and fire-eating. The Mèhti Sayadaw described such heterodox practices and apocryphal texts as shameless (*alajji*), heretical (*adhammavadi*), and transmitted by "unorthodox" teachers (*acaryāvadin*). Perhaps the court's partisan rhetoric reveals that its authority over monastic practice remained something of an aspiration, rather than an accomplishment. Diversity within the sangha over the authority of apocryphal traditions and heterodox practices clearly endured well beyond Bodawpaya's reign. Resistance to the court's hegemony and its particular construction of the Theravada tradition was perhaps as much a site of monastic identification as were the claims to orthodoxy advanced by the Thudhamma Council and the

Amarapura Nikāya in Bodawpaya's capital.[37] If Bodawpaya looked beyond the foundations of his Buddhist polity, it was not toward the growing influence of European trade networks to the south. Instead, he collected a great many Sanskrit works as alternate sources of scientific knowledge with which to augment Buddhist learning and withstand encroaching western influences. His royal library is said to have contained a large number of Sanskrit manuscripts in addition to some western volumes, particularly on math, science, and architecture.

Bodawpaya undertook an immense scheme of constructing Buddhist monuments. The massive Mingun Pagoda by the banks of the Irrawaddy River, with its elaborate display of Jataka plaques lining the lower tiers, remains unfinished to this day. After his conquest of Arakan in 1785, Bodawpaya arranged for the transport of the Mahamuni image from southern Burma to Mandalay, where it was enshrined with great pageantry.[38] In 1802 the king invited the British envoy, Michael Symes, to view the colossal image in its newly constructed shrine, known today as the Mahamuni Pagoda in Mandalay. The cultural import of Bodawpaya's achievement was lost on the colonial imagination of his distinguished guest.[39] However, many contemporary pilgrims visiting the pagoda and its museum today are stunned by the grandeur of Bodawpaya's feat. They seem overwhelmed at the sight of the huge, painted tableaus installed by the State Law and Order Restoration Council in the early 1990s, which depict the mytho-history of the sacred icon and the royal procession that Bodawpaya arranged for its transfer from Arakan to Upper Burma.

King Bagyidaw (r. 1819–1837) succeeded Bodawpaya. During his reign, Burma lost the coastal regions to invading British forces. The Treaty of Yandabo ended the First Anglo-Burman War (1824–1826). Bagyidaw was deposed by King Tharawaddy (r. 1837–1846), the father of King Pagan (r. 1846–1853) and King Mindon (r. 1853–1878). King Pagan succeeded his father to the throne, but reigned for less than a decade. His brother Mindon became king at the time of the Second Anglo-Burmese war (1852-1853), when Lower Burma fell under British control, and the Kingdom of Ava lost access to the Bay of Bengal.

MINDON'S CONSTRAINTS

Burmese and western historians describe the reign of King Mindon (r. 1853–1878) as an era of cultural renaissance. In contrast to Bodawpaya's zeal, Mindon is depicted as a beneficent *dhammarāja*. However, he also faced internal challenges, including a rebellion in 1866, and he failed to appoint a successor at the end of his reign.[40] When Mindon ascended to power, his kingdom was fully engaged in a struggle for modernity that unfolded with increasing urgency. The British had already controlled Lower Burma for nearly fifty years, and Buddhist institutions there had suffered profound neglect because the political administration of Lower Burma was now under colonial rule and the British did not recognize the *thathanabain*'s jurisdiction over the sangha in Lower Burma. Monks who lived in the colonized regions of Lower Burma were effectively disenfranchised from the structures of authority that Mindon created for the sangha in Upper Burma. The colonial refusal to become involved in the administration of local religious matters further exacerbated the tensions, and many monks relocated to Upper Burma in order to live under Buddhist authority. Although Mindon attempted to stem this exodus of monks from Lower Burma and stop the disintegration of monastic authority there, by 1855 the migration of monks to the north left many village monasteries deserted.

When King Mindon at last convened the Fifth Buddhist Council in 1868, he sought to reaffirm a Theravada polity and the position of the Burmese *dhammarāja* within the *sāsana.* However, his efforts to bolster his polity against an expanding British colonial empire came too late, for the colonial power had already circumscribed the hegemony of a *dhammarāja* and begun a radical transformation of the Burmese Buddhist landscape. The Buddhist Council, the *sangāyana,* was to re-establish monastic purity and reaffirm the authority of the Pāli scriptures. Mindon centralized monastic administration under the office of the *thathanabain,* replacing many incumbents. To stem the decline in monastic discipline, Mindon prescribed, with the support of the Thudhamma Council, that monks take a vow before a Buddha image to observe the *vinaya.* In an effort to unify the sangha in the face of the religious fragmentation due to the loss of Lower Burma, he limited the number of official monastic lineages and required individual monks to register and certify their ordination in an approved lineage. Mindon's reform gave rise to new monastic sects that were to play a central role in formulating reformist Buddhist practices during the subsequent decades of colonial rule and the struggle for independence.

Revisions of the Pāli texts began in 1868. By 1871 Mindon's edition of the entire Pāli Tipitaka had been carved onto 729 marble slabs and enshrined at Kuthodaw Pagoda at the foot of Mandalay Hill in celebration of the Fifth Council. Mindon's Buddhist revival extended to Lower Burma as well, where commemorations of the Fifth Buddhist Council included renovation of Shwedagon Pagoda and the hoisting of its new spire (*hti*). While permitting the renovation of this national shrine, the British did not allow Mindon to travel to Lower Burma to attend the festivities, fearing that his presence might cause civil unrest or perhaps even a rebellion. The colonial intervention in rituals celebrating royal patronage of this nineteenth-century Buddhist revival indicated the limits of Mindon's Buddhist reign. Mindon's renaissance

This recreation of King Mindon seated on the Lion Throne is displayed in the reconstructed palace in Mandalay.
PHOTO BY STEFANIE WOODWARD.

of traditional Buddhist culture occurred too late in the process of colonization. He ultimately failed to reconstruct a Buddhist hegemony because the colonial disjunctures created through British rule over Lower Burma had already fragmented the polity of the *dhammarāja*. The economic boom in Lower Burma also exacerbated the colonial fragmentation of the Burmese sangha. While individual monks benefited from donations generated by this new prosperity, the sangha as an institution was largely independent of the Thudhamma Council's authority in Mandalay.

The office of the *thathanabain* endured in Mandalay, the capital of Upper Burma, even after the collapse of the Konbaun dynasty in 1886, but its influence was compromised by British refusal to recognize the authority of the *thathanabain* over monastic institutions in Lower Burma. The public standing of the sangha declined under accusations of lax monastic practice and the lack of authority to enforce discipline. Anticlerical sentiments grew especially strong in colonial Lower Burma, culminating in the assassination of one of the sangha's outspoken critics, Maung Po, which was rumored to have been instigated by Mindon's court.[41]

Some monks reacted to the fragmentation of the sangha under colonial rule by initiating reforms in their own communities. These groups were generally known as Culagandhi who, as during Bodawpaya's reign, distinguished themselves from Mahagandhi lineages that comprised mostly Thudhamma monks, through their emphasis on the *vinaya,* ascetic practice, and meditation. The Culagandhi minority's claim to orthopraxis eventually gained the support of Mindon's court. In Lower Burma, they included the Dwara lineage, which commenced under the leadership of the Okpo Sayadaw. He lived near Pago and had emerged as a modern monastic reformer and an influential voice critical of colonial Buddhism. His reform efforts gave rise to the Dwara lineage from which other monastic reformist and modernist dissenters eventually emerged. In order to dissuade monks from leaving Lower Burma, he maintained that the sangha was capable of self-regulation without the protection of a *dhammarāja* as long as monks committed themselves to strict observance of the *vinaya.* He stressed the importance of intention in the moral assessment of monastic practices and merit-making rituals and went so far as to challenge the ordination of members of the king's Thudhamma Council. His emphasis on the *vinaya* also inspired monastic reformers in Upper Burma, such as the Shwegyin, whose founding abbot had been a disciple of the Okpo Sayadaw. Other Mindon sects similarly stressed strict monastic discipline.[42]

In Upper Burma, reformist sects that developed during Mindon's reign included the Shwegyin Nikāya, the Hngettwin lineage who all identified as forest lineages. Following a confrontation with the sangha leadership, its founding Sayadaw gained Mindon's approval for Shwegyin monks to remain exempt from the authority of the *thathanabain* and his Thudhamma Council. Even today, Shwegyin monks take pride in their strict observance of *vinaya* rules in contrast to more lax interpretations associated with the Thudhamma majority. This emphasis on discipline underscored the divisions in the sangha between Upper and Lower Burma that were part of the colonial realities of religious life during Mindon's reign.

Concurrent with the decline and fragmentation of monastic institutions during the nineteenth century was the rise in the practice of meditation. This was accompanied by claims to spiritual authority among lay Buddhist associations, who became increasingly more prominent. Meditation, which traditionally had been a practice identified with the ordained lifestyle of monks, became increasingly popular among lay people. The rise of lay meditation and its implicit claims to attaining higher stages on the path to enlightenment further diminished the standing of sangha. Meditation also gained popularity among

Marble plates engraved with the texts of the Tipitaka were installed by King Mindon in1871. PHOTO BY ERIK WOODWARD.

monastic communities on Sagain Hill in Upper Burma, a stronghold of forest monasteries that rivaled the monastic strength of the neighboring city of Mandalay. The designation of forest monasteries emphasized their separation from the town-dwelling sangha, which, by implication, was less concerned with monastic discipline and often perceived to be more lax about its association with lay life.

After independence, the governments of U Nu in 1954 and of Ne Win and his successor regimes since 1980 also attempted to control the sangha and align Buddhist teachings with the state's ideologies. During each of these reforms, the state published new editions of the Tipitaka to standardize a normative orthodoxy and define ideal practice. These efforts to centralize monastic authority in the hands of the state encountered resistance within an ethnically diverse sangha and were only partially successful. It is misleading to describe the sangha as uniform or monolithic at any historical moment, and today the sangha continues to represent considerable local diversity in its practices, teachings, and multiethnic composition.[43]

2 The Emergence of the Secular in Modern Burma

European colonialism profoundly shaped Buddhist modernity in Asia.[1] One of the hallmarks of this conquest is the fragmentation of authority that results from the simultaneous affirmation of distinct, even contradictory bodies of knowledge like, for example, science and religion. The experience of modernity in Burma through British colonization brought about a cultural and religious crisis of authority that had an enduring impact on the country's history. Emerging from this collision of western and Buddhist worldviews was a radically changed social order that lacked the totalizing conceptual coherence of a traditional Theravada polity. Such changes often create the sort of contradictions that Charles Keyes described as a Buddhist crisis of authority.[2] They opened the door to alternative configurations of power that had not been a part of Burmese cultural knowledge. Colonial rule created administrative structures that rationalized and centralized state powers and furthered the economic and political goals of the colonizing empire.[3] These changes helped establish the colonial state and simultaneously paved the way for other forms of modernity.[4]

In Burma the rise of modern social formations was closely linked to the advent of British colonial rule, which abolished Buddhist kingship after the annexation of Upper Burma in 1886. Colonialism effectively dislodged secular power from the Buddhist worldview in which it had been embedded until the fall of Mandalay. The encounter initiated profound transformations and cultural disjunctures in the process. The introduction of colonial practices undermined the authority of traditional institutions, lifeways, and values characteristic of Buddhist polities.[5] While formation of the secular, colonial state did not succeed in erasing Buddhist conceptions of power, they greatly weakened traditional Buddhist institutions and created space for modern Buddhist formations to emerge. The British established an administration in which military, economic, and political power were transacted independently of traditional Buddhist worldviews. Colonial politics also introduced alternate ways of access to power that, until then, had not been a conceptual possibility in Burmese cultural knowledge. British rule promoted modern values and rationalized administrative structures in order to facilitate the economic and political goals of the British empire.[6] One of the most far-reaching developments in the colonial project concerned the acquisition in Burma of western knowledge, and through that, modern conceptions of national identity. The colonial government needed a large number of Burmese educated in the canons of modern knowledge to help administer its many projects.[7] The economic boom Lower Burma enjoyed at the start of the twentieth century reinforced the desirability of a western education. Joining the Indian Civil Service offered indisputable social and economic opportunities that could not be duplicated by a traditional monastic education or basic Buddhist literacy. As the colonial project unfolded, it reconfigured Burmese civil society; education was transformed, and newly introduced print media helped to popularize modern concerns.

Colonial Interventions in Buddhist Authority and the Demise of Traditional Culture

In 1824 the Government of India declared the First Anglo-Burmese War to protect the trade privileges of the British East India Company and to settle persistent border incursions along the Chittagong Hills. After the war, in 1826, Burma was forced to cede three provinces to the British, namely, Manipur, Arakan, and Tenasserim, as well as the port of Rangoon under the Treaty of Yandabo, and British colonial administration established control over Burma's coast along the Bay of Bengal. A further milestone of the colonial project was achieved the same year, when British surveyors completed a map of the boundaries of the Kingdom of Ava.[8] The Second Anglo-Burmese War, fought in 1852–1853 over infractions of the Treaty of Yandabo, led to the annexation of the area surrounding the city of Pegu and the lower Irrawaddy river basin, and this whole territory came to constitute the colony of British Lower Burma until the Third Anglo-Burmese war led to the annexation of Upper Burma in 1885).[9] As the cultural influence of the Buddhist kings in the court of Mandalay, Upper Burma, in the southern region of Lower Burma, and in the delta waned, the crisis of authority intensified. The decline of the Konbaun dynasty was ushered in by changes in the economic structures of the region that eroded the hegemonic rationale of Upper Burma's traditional polity. These changes included the mortgaging of private land to colonial bankers and traders and the monetization of the hinterlands, which made wealth portable. The growth of the colonial economy also entailed the loss of laborers from the increasingly impoverished rural areas in Upper Burma, who migrated to participate in the economic boom that characterized the regions of Lower Burma.[10]

The Third Anglo-Burmese War, in 1885, brought about the conquest of the Konbaun kingdom, ending its reign over Upper Burma. The complete annexation of Burma occurred on January 1, 1886, amidst complex tensions within the Konbaun court in Mandalay over competing views on the need to modernize the political administration of the Burmese polity. The modernist faction was led by Kinwun Mingyi, minister of the interior for King Thibaw (r. 1878–1886). Kinwun Mingyi had also played a prominent role during Mindon's reign, and his travels to France and England had convinced him of the need to reform the monarchy radically. Some British colonial administrators reported that the sangha in Mandalay resented Thibaw's political ineptitude to such an extent that it backed plans to collaborate with the British invasion of Mandalay. However, the British rejected this offer, and subsequent relations between the sangha and the British colonizers deteriorated. Annexation delivered a devastating blow to traditional cultural institutions and to the Burmese intellectual, social, and religious elites in Upper Burma.[11] The colonizers looted and burned Shwenandaw, the Royal Golden Palace in Mandalay, which was the polity's cosmic center and the seat of royal power in Upper Burma. They exiled King Thibaw, the last king of the Konbaun dynasty, to Ratnagiri on India's east coast and relocated the Lion Throne, the seat of the Konbaun dynasty's royal power, to the Calcutta Museum. The palace was transformed into a British military garrison, Fort Dufferin. Rangoon, the mercantile center of Lower Burma, became the new colonial capital of Burma and assumed greater political and economic importance. Upon annexation, Burma became a province of the Government of India until 1937, when it was separated from India after a very long struggle for direct representation. Between 1937 and 1948, the colony of Burma was administered by the British Crown.

The events of colonization had a profound impact on many facets of social life and eroded traditional Buddhist culture and values in Lower Burma, and after 1886 the collapse of the court in Upper Burma. Buddhist concepts include to this day the rule of a *dhammarāja,* the righteousness of the *dhamma,* and Burmese notions of power. Power, which denotes physical might (*ana*), influence (*oza*), one's store of merit (*hpoun*), and personal strength (*tagou*), had been central to defining a Buddhist identity. Although these conceptions of power continued to inform religious and political practices, colonial modernity reshaped many conjunctures of Buddhism, culture, and politics, and cultural institutions tied to Buddhist kingship became obsolete. Traditional cosmological Buddhist practices in ritual, art, and mythic narratives underwent modernizing transformations. Buddhist worldviews and knowledge were no longer undisputed but now were seen as being in competition with other bodies of knowledge and hegemonic structures.

Buddhist sources of authority gradually declined in a context of radically transformed cultural realities. While the sangha was the only traditional institution to survive Burma's colonial transformations, its organization and cultural relevance was greatly diminished. The British policy of noninvolvement in the religious affairs of the colony had many unintended consequences. In the view of many Burmese Buddhists, who expected the British to assume the obligations of a *dhammarāja,* secular politics lessened colonial authority. Some Burmese perceived the British refusal to act as patrons of Buddhist causes not merely as neutral, but as anti-Buddhist. This perception cast doubt on the moral legitimacy of colonial rule even among those who were sympathetic toward British initiatives.

When the British refused to accept the continuing authority of the *thathanabain* in Lower Burma after 1826, the sangha in Lower Burma became disenfranchised from the patriarch's office in Mandalay. The influence of the sangha in Lower Burma declined along with the support it once had among Burmese colonial elites in the delta regions. A disjuncture emerged in the administration of monastic affairs between the new colonial territories of Lower Burma and the remainder of the Konbaun empire, particularly the capital city of Mandalay, which to this day remains an important center of Burmese monasticism. In the absence of a centralized or unified sangha, internal fragmentation characterized the monastic engagement with colonization and modernity. Monastic lineages largely relied on their own internal organization that operated independently from one another. Reformist lineages, like the Shwegyin order, sought to assert their status through strict observance of the *vinaya.* But the vacuum in overall monastic leadership caused by the loss of the *thathanabain*'s authority accelerated the sangha's organizational disintegration and struggle for cultural relevance.

After the annexation of Upper Burma in 1886, the British refused to affirm the office of the supreme patriarch, then held by the Taungdaw Sayadaw, an appointee of King Thibaw. When this monk passed away in 1895, the colonial administration refused to exercise the traditional responsibilities of a *dhammarāja* and did not appoint a successor, diminishing this important office, which remained vacant until 1903. Many Burmese intellectuals criticized this prolonged vacancy during British colonial rule. The colonial refusal to act on this matter of great importance to traditional Burmese groups contributed to the fragmentations within the sangha. Because of this vacuum of monastic leadership, the sangha could not maintain a unified organization and struggled for cultural relevance, even though it was the sole institution of traditional culture to survive the demise of the Buddhist court. In Upper Burma the sangha eventually came to articulate an anticolonial discourse. It objected to the presence of a foreign power that refused the responsibility of the traditional state to protect the *thathana* and consequently was seen as anti-Buddhist. These developments became sites of resistance from which neotraditional, anti-British uprisings would emerge during the 1920s and 1930s.

The erosion of monastic authority is often accompanied by a concurrent rise in the status of the laity and this familiar feature of modern religious modernity is also found in Burmese Theravada Buddhism.[12] In contrast to traditional practices, lay Buddhists assumed positions of leadership, which opened up new, modern articulations of Buddhist identity and community. One such movement was the Young Men's Buddhist Association (YMBA), which we will discuss in greater detail in chapter 3. This organization was founded in Rangoon in 1906 by lay people who sought to promote nationalism, western education, and Buddhist modernism. Modern Buddhist organizations often conflated their religious and political agencies. Their efforts to define a new national and religious identity developed out of a need to accommodate the political and cultural challenges of modernity, including greater ethnic and religious diversity in colonial Burma. Among other initiatives, the YMBA agitated forcefully for the creation of a Ministry of Religious Affairs, a move that indicated a modern innovation in the administration of religious authority and responsibility. This exemplifies how a cultural and religious crisis of authority can engender new forms of Buddhist practice and beliefs that were at once in conflict and in collusion with the profound social changes Burma was experiencing under colonial rule.

Buddhist Modernity in Regional Contexts

As the Buddhist court's cultural influence on the southern delta region waned after 1825, the modern crisis of authority in Burmese Buddhist culture escalated.[13] Colonial rule created administrative structures that furthered the economic and political goals of the colonizing empire. To protect their mercantile interests, the British reorganized Burmese society and promoted administrative rationalization, modern values, and western education, creating new and secular venues to power and status amidst new trade networks of a burgeoning economy.[14] These social transformations paved the way for other forms of modernity and restructured avenues to economic and social capital that, until then, had not been part of Burmese cultural imagination. The most far-reaching impact was generated by the radical conceptual shifts that colonial rule initiated.

The experience of colonial rule, however, differed greatly between Lower and Upper Burma. The cultural and religious divisions created by the British administration of Burma and the ways in which the Burmese Buddhists responded to the challenges of modernity and secular power varied by geographic region and social class. The quality and extent of supraregional, national and, in a few instances, even transnational connections and organizations also differed. The colonial economy transformed the port city of Rangoon into a burgeoning cosmopolitan metropolis in the late nineteenth century.[15] Burmese colonial elites of the delta region increasingly articulated and reflected western secular values. By contrast, Upper Burma's population had remained largely rural and traditional in its educational background, political views, and religious practices.

The British policies toward Buddhist institutions and practices provided fuel for a crisis of monastic authority that was already under way. In the absence of a centralized sangha, the initial Buddhist engagement with colonization and modernity in Lower Burma was driven by internal fragmentation and rivalries. The *thathanabain*'s loss of control over monastic practices in Lower Burma commenced with the first colonial partition of Burma in 1825. The economic boom in the delta region enticed many monks and lay supporters to seek the liberality of new wealth. Concurrent with fragmentation of the sangha was the rise of reformist, *vinaya*-oriented lineages like the Shwegyin, Dwara, and Hngettwin, which sought to distinguish themselves from the Thudhamma majority. The reformist lineages that emerged in Lower Burma during Mindon's reign aimed to bring about discipline within their own communities while operating independently of the *thathanabain*'s office. Despite King Mindon's patronage of the Fifth Buddhist Council in 1871 and his restoration of Shwedagon Pagoda in Rangoon, the sangha remained embroiled in sectarian divisions, and the efforts of the Konbaun court did not succeed in reasserting traditional Buddhist authority in Lower Burma.

In Mandalay, Upper Burma, the court and the *thathanabain* retained a greater degree of ceremonial authority than they were able to exert in Lower Burma. To be Burmese and Buddhist in Upper Burma represented a retreat from the cosmopolitan modernity that colonial rule had fostered in Lower Burma.[16] Fragmentation within the sangha and the concurrent decline of monastic authority in the absence of a central office, however, opened up new venues, even in Mandalay, for lay elites to take on religious leadership. A variety of modern Buddhist practices and organizations emerged.[17] In addition, in response to the collapse of traditional institutions after 1886, a series of Buddhist revolts against the British presence occurred in Upper Burma in 1906, 1910, 1916, and 1930, as some monks fostered millennial expectations, especially among the rural population, of the imminent appearance of a universal monarch (*setkya min:*).[18] These revolts advocated a return to the previous status quo and re-establishment of a traditional Buddhist polity to recapture a past order of things. Such traditionalist responses to colonial rule culminated in the Saya San Rebellion of the 1930s.[19] Despite British intentions not to become involved in religious matters, the colonial government found itself confronted with various forms of resistance that were inspired by Buddhist beliefs and practices.

Transnational Hybridity in Colonial Rangoon

Scholars of colonial Asia have noted the features of a pan-Asian transnationalism that set the stage for new organizations and connections across the Buddhist world. Writing about the Sri Lankan Buddhist revival at the turn of the twentieth century, Mark Frost points to characteristic transformations of the public space that were initiated by wider opportunities for transnational contacts and communication.[20] Transnational linkages during the colonial period also created conjunctures and disjunctures in the emerging national discourse about modernity in Burma. Modern print culture and new means of travel accelerated the formation of transnational networks, particularly among western-educated literati and colonial elites in Lower Burma, for whom English had become a lingua franca. Public debates about a new sense of national identity also encouraged a renewed focus on religious values and national literatures. Indeed, appeals to culture, religion, and language were all instrumental in creating and mobilizing early nationalist sentiments in colonial Asian societies at the turn of the twentieth century. For many Burmese, their experience of colonial realities and new hybrid social forms led to disenchantment with prevailing ethical practices and confirmed for them a perceived decline of morality in the modern age. Alongside emerging visions of modern moral authority was a sense of nostalgia for the loss of traditional culture and values that reminded some Burmese of a better, if perhaps idealized, past.

The tendency to organize interest groups that transcend the social boundaries of the traditional society developed from a transnational awareness of developments elsewhere in Asia, such as the activities of the Congress Party in India, and from a perceived need to mobilize a shared solidarity in ways that were effective in a colonial modernity. During the late nineteenth and early twentieth centuries, several lay Buddhist societies emerged throughout Burma. Although their leaders were in occasional contact, and their respective publications reported on Buddhist missionary activities elsewhere, these groups did not share a common agenda and tended to operate independently from one another. Individual Buddhists traveling to Burma generally had greater impact than sustained international networks of Buddhist organizations, which enjoyed considerable influence elsewhere in Asia. Those Buddhist organizations that were established in Burma at that time illustrated broader historical trends, but developed for the most part independently from similar organization elsewhere in Buddhist Asia. In 1897 the Sāsana Nuggaha Athin (Mission Association) was founded in Mandalay, and another missionary society, the Kalyana Maikta Athin (Friendship Association), in Myingyan, soon merged with it.[21] In 1905 the Ledi Sayadaw established two complementary organizations, the Abhidhamma Thankait Athin, to promote lay meditation in towns throughout Burma, and the Thathana Hita Athin (Foreign Mission Society), to spread Buddhism abroad.[22] Most of these groups, including the Young Men's Buddhist Association (YMBA), were begun by Burmese, rather than by foreigners, and focused on propagating Buddhist teachings. Thus, while these new religious associations employed modern forms of organization, their purpose for mobilizing supporters retained a traditional Buddhist justification.[23]

At the turn of the twentieth century, Rangoon was a cosmopolitan city well placed within transnational networks that extended across the British empire and beyond. A frequent port of call for ocean liners traveling to destinations east and west, Rangoon enjoyed a booming economy that supported traveling merchants and immigrant laborers from India, China, Europe, and other places along colonial trade routes. In *Old Rangoon,* Noel Singer documents the city's colonial architecture with photographs and drawings of public spaces, which, by extension, offers insights into the city's cosmopolitan, transnational character.[24] The first railway station, which later expanded to become Phayre Street Station, Rangoon's main rail station, opened in 1877. Until that time, waterways had provided the primary transportation route, with the Irrawaddy Flotilla Company connecting markets upcountry with Rangoon and the ocean liners that linked Rangoon with other ports of call. Cars began to appear by 1905, and busses followed by 1908. Newspaper advertisements praised this port city as the "Pearl of the Orient" and an exotic destination for world travelers en route to ports of call from England to the Near and Far East. Companies like Thomas Cook supplied newly disembarking travelers with utilitarian items, prearranged sets that included bedrolls, chairs, and tables. They even offered the services of a translator and guide for newly arrived entrepreneurs eager to commence business. The sewing machine manufacturer Singer held exclusive import rights for the Burmese market. Commerce was booming.

Despite these transformations of public spaces and the economy's transnational connections in Rangoon, colonial society in much of Burma was divided along class and ethnic lines. Apart from superficial social interactions with the Burmese, most colonial administrators inhabited a social world vastly different from that of most Burmese. Prestigious colonial clubs, like the Pegu Club, admitted European members only. By 1886 *thakin*, meaning "master," had become the form of address commonly used for white colonials and members of the Indian Civil Service.[25] The social distance among these groups was enhanced by a linguistic separation, for English was used among the elite, and Burmese among the rural and service-providing communities. The fragmentation of colonial Burmese society was so pervasive that scholars like J. S. Furnivall refer to the "atomized" groups within Burmese society that shared few spheres of interactions.

Access to western education was an important marker of social class in Burmese society and widened the cultural distance between the Burmese elite and mainstream society. It also engendered profound social, cultural, and political transformations. Prospective students were attracted by the economic and social opportunities that a university education afforded. The first generation of Burmese nationalists was the product of a western education that had exposed them, among other things, to the secular politics of the Indian Congress Party and to the dimensions of modern civil society within the British Empire.[26] The early 1900s saw the greatest number of young urban Burmese obtaining a university education abroad, predominantly in Calcutta and England, and nearly all of the early YMBA leaders shared educational and cultural experience of studying abroad. This shared experience of the west cultivated modern cultural values and greater acceptance of secular political authority among Rangoon's social elite. In 1920 Rangoon College ceased to function as an extension of Calcutta University and became a university in its own right. The Rangoon University Act of 1920 envisioned a residential college with the strict standards of colonial education. This plan provoked a major student boycott, for many viewed the British vision of higher education as limiting access to university education to a privileged class only. It was a cultural and political victory for colonial nationalists that the curriculum at Rangoon University included the study of Burmese, Pāli, Pyu, and Mon, a provision the Government of India had initially not supported.

Colonialism had a profound impact on the ethnic composition of the colony and on politics of ethnicity. It facilitated transnational communities that brought greater cultural, ethnic, and religious diversity, particularly to

Lower Burma. In addition to the early Portuguese and Italian Catholic missions that had had some presence in Lower Burma since the seventeenth century, European Christians now included British and American missionaries. Muslim immigrants came from India and Bengal, as did members of various Hindu communities. Immigrants from China included Mahayana Buddhists, Daoists, and Muslim Chinese. By the mid-1930s, one million Indians had settled in Lower Burma to work for the Indian Civil Service as traders, laborers, or moneylenders. Indeed, Rangoon had become a predominantly Indian city. These demographic changes created not only economic competition between the immigrant and Burmese communities, but also engendered lasting ethnic and political tensions, especially with the Indian immigrants, both Hindu and Muslim.

The colonial government created separate paths of access to power for different ethnic groups. Burma's tribal minorities enjoyed direct access to the colonial administration, which increased their resources and eliminated the need for them to accept Burmese intermediaries. A significant number of tribal groups, many of whom practiced indigenous forms of ancestor veneration, converted to Protestant Christianity. Their conversation provided them with, among other things, access to western education in the Catholic and Protestant missionary schools. Many Karen, in particular, converted to the Baptist Church and learned English at an early age in missionary schools.

Secularism in a Buddhist World

Burmese who had benefited from a western education became familiar with diverse modern ideologies and intellectual trends, including western ideals of secular power and new forms of Buddhist transnationalism. Both profoundly shaped Burmese encounters with modernity and fostered new sentiments of national identity. Secularism entered Burmese public consciousness as part of the colonial discourse on politics and religion. Initially, it underscored the colonizers' refusal to assume responsibilities toward the Buddhist sangha, which reinforced a general public perception of secularism as suspect politics and helped foment anticolonial sentiments.

The nationalist struggle for independence in Burma encompasses a history of tension and collaboration between Buddhist and secular nationalists who joined forces against a common enemy in the colonial Government of India. The transnational linkages in colonial Rangoon nurtured a secular nationalism that had significant impact among students at Rangoon University. University students were lynchpins of political and educational reforms during the colonial period and thereafter. These students eventually formed the student-led Dobama (We Burmans), a nationalist movement during the 1930s, and its members continued to be a powerful political force well into the post-independence Burma. Many secular nationalists also looked to the Indian Congress Party and its strategies when they began to mobilize for independence from colonial rule.

Throughout the nineteenth and twentieth centuries, secular politics remained an elusive destination. Underscoring the precarious and suspect position of secularism in Burma is the fact that Theravada Buddhism does not contain a linguistic category equivalent to the idea of secularism. The term *lokiya,* meaning "this-worldliness," implies its antonym *lokuttara,* "otherworldliness," and derives its significance from a Buddhist discourse. No Burmese word designates the secular without an implicit reference to a religious worldview.[27] Debates about modernity in Burma often entailed a discourse about negotiating boundaries between the here-and-now, that is, the "secular," and the path to an eventual social and political destination that was identified with a utopian vision of Buddhism society, or even *nibbāna*, understood as a political destination.

In Burma, a discourse about a secular vision of the world set apart from *samsāra* cannot be sustained for long before it becomes submerged again into the Buddhist cultural mainstream and its hegemonic rationale. The public discourse about power thus never strays far from the central Buddhist paradigm. The appropriation of traditional sources and their symbolic uses in particular locations of authority is engrained at many levels in Burmese society. Military leaders in the past and now are rumored to be seeking protective powers of an alchemist stone (*dat loun:*) that some charismatic monks give to their followers. These objects are believed to be endowed with Buddhist powers and protect their bearers from harm. Even the most secular military potentates in Burma do not forgo traditional venues to power despite their relatively ready access to modern technology and the means of exchange and communication. Political and Buddhist visions about the future have been conflated at several junctures in the twentieth century.

Religion tends to assert a place in public discourse when colonial experience diminishes traditional authority and political institutions. At several historical conjunctures of the colonial period, Buddhism inserted itself into political contexts, and the Burmese affirmed their resistance to a separation of religious power from its utilitarian counterpart, which western thought labels as "secular." The colonial disjunctures between secular politics and a Buddhist worldview intensified in 1919, when the British government reaffirmed the administrative subordination of colonial Burma to the Government of India despite popular agitation among the Burmese for direct representation to the

British crown. This rendered the Young Men's Buddhist Association's advocacy of a civil, procolonial Buddhism increasingly unpopular and irrelevant to the Burmese public discourse about nationalism. After the eclipse of the YMBA, a retrospective form of Buddhism became the driving force in national and local politics. This was particularly true for Upper Burma, where Burmese Buddhist identity was a rallying point for anticolonial sentiments. During the early twentieth century, various social organizations and followers of charismatic leaders advocated *thathana pyu thi,* making the world safe for the Buddha's dispensation.[28] Similarly, U Nu identified stages in the country's economic and national development as commensurate with attaining stages in the Eightfold Noble Path leading to *nibbāna,* thereby linking ethical action to engagement in civil society and to meditation. Any action in the world, whether economic, military, or social, inevitably would engage traditional conceptions of power (*oza, ana, hpoun,* and *tagou*) in order to work toward a Buddhist vision of utopia or *pativedha sāsana.*

Only western interlocutors, not Burmese ones, require explications of cultural conceptions of power that are implicit in Burmese public discourse across religious and ethnic differences. Clearly, a concern with power looms large for those who have little access to it and for those who wield it excessively or arbitrarily. Newly emergent social groups and modern Buddhist communities are shaping the discourse about power and its "this-worldly" and "other-worldly" uses at those moments in history when new venues to power unfold at the frontiers of shifting conceptions of the world. Such conjunctures also harbor a great potential for unintended consequences as new leaders and communities move to fill a vacuum of power. In this way cultural strategies of the past also shape Burmese strategies for the future.[29]

In light of the prominent role Buddhism assumed in public politics during the colonial period and after national independence, the question arises whether secularism can provide a viable form of governance in contemporary Myanmar. Since independence, the Burmese state has at least nominally espoused secular political ideologies, ranging from democracy to socialism, militarism, and venture capitalism, but this modern paradigm of political power has proven to be insufficient for successfully governing the country's center.

3 Educating the Other

Buddhism and Colonial Knowledge

In the nineteenth century the Government of India imposed modern educational reforms on its colony in order to prepare local populations for careers as civil servants in the administration of the colony.[1] The aim of colonial education was to impart objective knowledge and rational methods of inquiry in modern science and technology. The curriculum and its language of instruction, English, would also serve to consolidate British rule in South Asia and, of course, Burma.[2]

Education, particularly religious education, plays an important role in the formation of the self and in shaping moral values. An eminent colonial scholar of Burmese history and the superintendent of the Archeological Survey in 1918–1919, Taw Sein Ko (1864–1930) went as far as to declare categorically that "education divorced from religion is of little value."[3] Individuals use strategies acquired through education to navigate many aspects of social life, such as issues concerning worldview, tradition, politics, and other temporal or ultimate visions of reality. The trajectories of colonial education, its institutions and policies, offer special insights into conceptual links between knowledge, religion, and power and reveal how colonial reforms of education worked to submerge local knowledge. Education can also function as an agent of social change because it informs cultural identity, national belonging, and religious reasoning.

This chapter describes the cultural history of education in colonial Burma and afterward to elucidate the ways in which tensions between Buddhist and British educational institutions impacted nationalist politics and cultural identity. Eventually the sangha refused to teach a modern curriculum, particularly mathematics, geography, and drawing.[4] Bernard Cohn, a historian of the British empire in India, has described subjects like these, as well as historiography, geographic surveying, ethnic practice and belief, surveillance, and so on as colonial forms of knowledge.[5] These methods of collecting and ordering information empowered the colonial state to become a theater for "experimentation, where documentation, certification, and representation were . . . modalities that transformed knowledge into power."[6] The sangha's refusal to teach such subjects was fueled by the perception that they were a colonial threat to monastic authority, autonomy, and ethics. The monastic resistance to educational reforms proved to have unforeseen consequences, for it eventually fostered millenarian resistance movements against colonial rule, such as the Saya San Rebellion.[7]

A second focus of this chapter is the development of a modern Buddhist curriculum in government schools an integral part of its nationalist agenda during the late colonial era. This was an agenda advocated most forcefully by the Young Men's Buddhist Association in the 1910s. The founding members of this organization had been educated in a secular colonial education system, and many had studied abroad in India or England. They advocated that schools in rural areas adhere to high educational standards of instruction in secular subjects, especially in mathematics. They further lobbied the colonial government to offer instruction in both religious and vernacular subjects like Buddhism, the Burmese language, and classical literature in public schools where modern, secular subjects and instruction in English formed the core of the curriculum.

The discussion then shifts to the constellation of Buddhism and science after independence. During the 1950s and 1960s prominent Burmese intellectuals argued that fundamental Buddhist tenets encompassed and foreshadowed many of the claims of modern science. They participated in an orientalist discourse and sought to missionize Buddhist truths among sympathetic western audiences. In that trajectory, a modern Buddhist discourse appropriated the sort of scientific rationalism that is often seen as the hallmark of modern western education, seemingly without contradiction. Here we find a reversal of the colonial structure of knowledge in that scientific knowledge was now subordinated to a modern Buddhist cosmology.[8]

Debates about secular and religious education continued to be central to the policies of Burmese governments after independence. Religious education played a significant role in the final collapse of U Nu's government in 1958, when Buddhist monks objected to decisions by the Ministry of Education to permit religious instruction in non-Buddhist faiths. After 1988 restrictions were imposed on access to education by the military regime. Pro-democracy forces have sought to focus the attention of the international community on the widespread need for access to education in order to shape the future of civil society. The military regime has also again used monasteries to deliver basic education in rural areas and among remote non-Buddhist tribal groups, an effort in part driven by a policy to integrate tribal minorities into the modern nation.

The Decline of Traditional Buddhist Education

Prior to Burma's gradual integration into the Government of India, Burmese and Europeans made various attempts to introduce western knowledge to the country. In 1723, during the Restored Taungoo dynasty, the king of Ava, "Master of the White Elephant" and "Lord of All Umbrella-Bearing Chiefs," requested through the office of a Barnabite missionary, Father Sangermano, that the papal court in Rome provide access to western knowledge, explaining that "many teachers and technicians were needed."[9] During the reign of Bodawpaya, another effort was made to introduce western knowledge and technical expertise. The historian Thant Myint U credits two members of the Burmese elite, the Myoza of Myawaddy and the prince of Mekkaya, with pioneering a renaissance in scholarship in the 1830s and 1840s that affected "many and diverse fields of knowledge, including geography, astronomy, history, and the natural sciences."[10] Christian schools were established as early as 1600 by Portuguese missionaries who wanted to serve their own trading communities on Burma's southern coastline. However, it was not until the first half of the nineteenth century that western education expanded significantly, when it became the project of Roman Catholic and American Baptist missionaries. In addition, the Rev. J. E. Marks of the British Society for the Propagation of the Gospel established St. James College in Rangoon in 1885, after residing in Mandalay during the 1870s.

Prior to the First Anglo-Burmese War, the Burmese became literate through the study of religious subjects, for education was firmly rooted in the monastic mission to preserve the *dhamma*. Formal education was largely shaped by a Buddhist cosmology and its cultural values.[11] Religious literacy was a product of that mentality, and the primary venue for gifted young men to realize educational goals and join the ranks of the literati was through the pursuit of a monastic career. Scholarship and teaching were natural extensions of a religious vocation, and formal education focused on general principles and timeless, ultimate knowledge. Its study was accessible through the institution of the sangha, the teaching practices of monks, and Buddhist knowledge engraved in palm-leaf manuscripts that were catalogued according to Theravada classifications and housed in monastic libraries.

Buddhist monasteries provided basic literacy for Burmese young people. British surveys taken in the mid-nineteenth century confirm that monastic education was firmly established throughout the country.[12] Most males spent some time as regular students (*kyaun: tha*) or as novices residing in a monastery where daily routines made study of the *dhamma* a central focus. Other male students attended monastic instruction, but continued to live with their families. Taw Sein Ko remarked that the education of girls was generally left to "untutored masters," for teaching young girls was considered beneath the "holy dignity" of monks and viewed as "unnecessary" by much of the population.[13] By 1869, however, slightly more than 5,000 girls, who were not permitted to attend monastic schools, were enrolled in 340 lay schools located in homes that had been designated as schools in some of the larger villages. Attendance at these home schools was intermittent, instructional periods were shorter, and educational expectations were less rigorous.

From at least the seventeenth century in Burma, monastic examinations sponsored by kings offered monks access to higher levels of education.[14] Taw Sein Ko writes that during the precolonial era, "competitive examinations in Pāli were held annually just before the beginning of Buddhist Lent. They consisted of written and oral parts. The principal textbooks prescribed were *Kaccayana's Grammar, Abhidhammattha Sangaha, Abhidhanappadipika, Chanda* and *Alankara*. The written portion was conducted by the officials, and the oral by the Council of *Thudhamma Sadaws* (*Mahātheras* of the *Sudhamma Sabha*)."[15] During the vacancy of the *thathanabain*'s office from 1895 until 1903, Pāli examinations were overseen by the British government and administered through religious organizations in Mandalay, the Society for the Promotion of Buddhism and the Pariyattisssanahita Society. The latter emphasizes especially competence in the *vinaya*.[16] Scholarly achievements were honored with monastic titles that continue to be rewarded today. An initial curriculum of four basic levels, known in Burmese as *pahtama-nge, pahtama-lat, pahtamak-gyi:,* and *pahtama-gyan,* led to high standards of Buddhist learning.[17] Education began with simple recitation and memorization of the Burmese alphabet, religious liturgies such as the Three Refuges, the Precepts, the Eightfold Noble Path, and formulas of homage and protection. At higher levels, Pāli language instruction complemented the memorization of increasingly extensive selections of canonical texts taken from each of the three baskets of the Tipitaka.[18] In addition, monks also studied texts like the *Mingala Sutta,* the *Lokanīti* with its astrological focus, the *Dhammanīti,* and the *Rajanīti.*[19] Monks embodied Buddhist learning, and the monastic libraries of local communities housed the palm-leaf manuscripts that served as repositories for textual study.

Monks were expected to lead a life removed from worldly affairs. Monastic teaching styles affirmed the cultural expectation that one must not challenge the authority of monastic teachers. Senior monks, like local abbots, tended to assume teaching roles and hence enjoyed considerable authority and respect. They instructed students using traditional methods such as reading aloud in unison and recitation from memory, and they seldom offered explanations or interpretations of the materials studied. Because questioning a monastic teacher might be perceived as a challenge to his authority, students would seek answers from parents and others in the lay world. The work of interpreting or filling in the gaps in basic religious knowledge occurred mostly outside the sangha within the larger social circle of the family.[20]

Monastic education in nineteenth-century Burma relied mostly on scarce copies of palm-leaf manuscripts, the material repositories of textual knowledge.[21] Although print culture flourished in Burma relatively late, we can point to several moments in an incipient print culture. In 1864 Bishop Bigandet, the Vicar Apostolic of Ava and Pegu, was instrumental in producing the first printed version of the Burmese Tipitaka.[22] The first English newspaper, *The Moulmein Advertiser,* began publication in 1846 to serve the commercial interests of the East India Company and its local representatives.[23] By 1852 Rangoon had emerged as a center for printing and publishing,[24] and by 1874 the *Yadana Naypyidaw* had become the first newspaper published in Burmese in Mandalay.[25] The growing cultural currency of colonial bodies of knowledge in print continually challenged the viability of monastic education, for which few printed materials were used.[26] Printed textbooks became available only after the British sought educational reforms in the 1870s. Still fewer textbooks were printed in Burmese, and L. E. Bagshawe notes in his excellent study "A Literature of School Books" the impoverished treatment of modern subjects found in them.

In Burma the British encountered an established system of Buddhist education that had produced a high rate of literacy among the general population.[27] Soon after the First Anglo-Burmese War, the British government began to develop educational policies for its Indian colonies. These envisioned a different kind of education that would produce local administrators trained to implement the colonial project. Furthermore, the knowledge they sought to instill among the Burmese was primarily secular in orientation. Colonial education presumed an ideology of cultural evolution that legitimated British rule over native peoples, which according to the British obliged them to fulfill the "White Man's Burden" by bringing progress to the colonies. In this western view of enlightenment, scientific rationalism empowered modern man to master all the components of progress. British reports on colonial education stated that the objectives of education in India were to further intellectual and moral improvement, to ensure a supply of government servants, and to safeguard the expansion of trade. The secondary purpose was to instill an appreciation for European knowledge of the arts, sciences, philosophy, and literature. Instruction in English was to begin at the elementary level, along with vernacular literacy. The Department of Public Instruction was charged with the reform of local school systems and with developing institutions of higher education. Christian missionaries played a significant role in delivering the colonial curriculum, for private schools implementing these policies received government funding. Disdain for local canons of knowledge was expressed by the chairman of the Committee on Public Instruction, Thomas Macaulay, who announced: "We have to educate a people who cannot at present be educated by means of their mother tongue. We must teach them our own language. . . . We must form . . . a class [of] interpreters between us and the millions we govern; a class of persons, Indian in blood and color, but English in taste, in opinions, in morals, and in intellect."[28]

In comparison with Macaulay's call for a colonial imprimatur, the proposal made in 1866 by the British Chief Commissioner Sir Arthur Phayre appeared liberal and progressive.[29] He envisioned collaboration between government institutions and Burmese monastic schools. He wanted to ensure that colonial knowledge be taught through the existing infrastructure of Burmese Buddhist monasteries. He tried to persuade the sangha to integrate modern subjects, including arithmetic and geography, into the existing monastic curriculum. His proposal offered financial incentives to Buddhist monasteries to compensate monastic teachers, to employ government certified lay teachers to teach modern, secular subjects at monastic schools, and to extend stipends to students.

Educational reforms during the late nineteenth century profoundly shaped the colonial and national history of Burma. British and Burmese notions of education were hardly commensurate. Colliding worldviews and political projects characterized the debates about educational policy, access, and reforms. Education has remained a contested issue throughout colonial and national history, informing national identity, politics, and religion, and it served as a flashpoint around which Burmese leaders rallied public opinion in the struggle for independence. The cultural chasm between Buddhist learning and colonial knowledge soon became apparent as British conservatives and the Burmese monastic patriarch both responded negatively to Phayre's proposal. It was unpopular among British conservatives because they saw it as contravening the Anglo-Indian government's policy not to become involved in the religious affairs of colonies. Phayre's plan also met with resistance among members of the sangha. Most monastic schools refused to integrate western, secular subjects into their curriculum, and few of them cooperated with his initiative, which slowed the implementation of educational reforms. In 1866 an education department was established by the local government and a plan for building a public education system was inaugurated. By 1871, five years after Phayre's initiative had been launched, only 46 monastic schools had been authorized under the government's policy. Two years later "the number of authorized monastery schools had risen to 801,"[30] about a fourth of the 3,438 monastic schools in Lower Burma.[31] By contrast, however, only 112 lay schools had registered with the government by 1873.[32]

The slow acceptance of British education policy in Burmese monastic schools was complemented by a rapid increase in demand for colonial education and for English as its medium of instruction. The colonial government decided to increase support to existing Christian missionary and secular government schools because it was eager to train potential recruits for the Indian Civil Service and promote colonial subject formations within the general curriculum. This trend was amplified after the annexation of Upper Burma in 1886.

Monastic resistance to colonial policy grew when British Chief Commissioner Sir Arthur Phayre proposed in 1866 to modernize education by assigning government-certified lay teachers to teach modern subjects in rural monastic schools.[33] This move further encouraged talented, young students to leave traditional Buddhist education in favor of government schools, which taught secular subjects in an English curriculum that could lead to opportunities in trade and the civil service. The space created by the disjuncture between Buddhist knowledge and colonial education also allowed for cultural innovations such as Burmese lay teachers.[34] Mendelson comments that the sangha's retreat from modern education transformed Burmese Buddhist practice and gave rise to new lay associations: "The loss of the educational role, formerly the exclusive role of the monk, has had profound effects upon the sangha's place in modern Burmese society. The movement to place education into secular hands was a legacy of colonialism that left a vacuum in Burmese life, for the specifically Buddhist nature of the traditional learning process was lost in the transfer to lay schools. Lay associations, formed in the realization of such a loss, attempted to promote Buddhism to make up the difference."[35]

The introduction of colonial knowledge through modern educational reforms challenged Buddhist cosmological worldviews.[36] Traditionally, knowledge (*batha*) was based on Buddhist principles, and the sangha facilitated its acquisition. Both basic literacy and higher education were firmly established within the domain of the sangha, which acted as its source and exercised authority over it. In a decision that proved to be pivotal in the history of education in Burma, the sangha firmly rejected British attempts to introduce new educational subjects into the monastic curriculum. The sangha held the purpose of formal education (*pyinnya*) to be intrinsically religious, and education properly belonged to the domain of Buddhist monks and monastic learning. Its premise rested on a Buddhist understanding of the world in which all phenomena, whether social, political, or cultural, are constituted by karmic action and regulated by the *dhamma.* Religious and other ultimate concerns encompassed secular and worldly matters (*lokiya*) that were ultimately meaningful only to the extent to which they were linked to notions of Buddhist morality. Humans were thought to be not in control of nature, but subject to it through the Universal Law. Practical or vocational knowledge was imparted primarily through contextual learning and mostly in informal settings. Buddhist knowledge as an indication of progress toward moral perfection is still thought to be highly individualized, as its acquisition, and the insights it generates, are believed to lead to *nibbāna.* This kind of religious knowledge is embedded in lineages of monastic teachers that can be traced, at least in principle, to the pristine time of the Buddha.

The sangha also objected to Phayre's attempt to deliver a modern secular education through existing monastery schools because his proposal was tantamount to a colonial redefinition of monastic authority.[37] The sangha did not want to be accountable to colonial authorities concerning their roles as teachers and resented British interference in matters internal to this institution that embodied Buddhist teachings.[38] Consequently, there was considerable resistance to the presence of government-certified lay teachers commissioned to teach secular subjects in monastic schools. This arrangement furthered the perception of colonial interference with monastic authority.

In 1891, the *thathanabain* prohibited monastic schools from implementing the colonial education curriculum, specifically the teaching of arithmetic and geography.[39] Lay teachers were not permitted to teach at monastic schools, and emissaries were sent out to reinforce these orders with local abbots, who had been enjoined not to employ government-certified lay teachers.[40] While the sangha took a negative view of the teaching of mathematics, geography, and drawing, it objected even more to interference by the colonial government. Concerned about compromising its authority, the sangha eventually refused to collaborate on policies that envisioned employing monks as teachers and adding lay teachers to the teaching staff at monasteries. The *thathanabain* argued that compliance would amount to a breach of the *vinaya,* which prohibits monks from working for compensation. This decision further hastened the decline of monastic education, which was already losing bright students to English-speaking schools, especially in urban areas. Monastic education became increasingly relegated to rural areas. The decline of monastic education contributed to the fragmentation of an institution that had wielded great authority during royal times.

As guardians of Buddhist knowledge, educators of the literati, and teachers of basic literacy in village schools, the sangha feared its authority and autonomy would be compromised by cooperation with a colonial power that was not committed to preserving the sangha's standing as a pure source of merit and ultimate source of knowledge. For the most part, the sangha stood its ground on matters of educational policy throughout the decade-long vacancy in the office of its patriarch, refusing to assume a monastic role in colonial education reforms. However, a few monasteries, especially in Lower Burma, showed at least nominal participation in the reforms by registering with the government and by accepting government school books and other forms of support. It was not until 1909 that a new *thathanabain* indicated in a letter to the director of public instruction his willingness to assume a neutral position on this issue, affirming his intent to work toward a resolution in matters of mutual interest by delegating the decision to participate in the colonial education project to local abbots.[41] The *thathanabain* voiced specific objections to Phayre's proposal, stating that monks accepting government funds were breaching *vinaya* rules because Theravada monks may not accept pay for their work. He further objected to certain proposed subjects as unsuitable for monastic study. Although he indicated his flexibility on some subjects proposed in the Education Code, he objected firmly to instruction in drawing, especially the drawing of maps.[42] He also objected to starting education in kindergarten and concluded: "Special rules should be framed for the guidance of monastic schools, and the indigenous curriculum should be adopted with such modifications as are necessitated by circumstances. In other words, only such subjects should be taught as are consistent with the tenets of Buddhism."[43]

The sangha's rejection of Phayre's proposal presaged a detrimental turn for the future of monastic education in colonial Burma. After the three decades of relative prosperity and stability between 1891 and 1918, John Cady documents a rapid increase in the number of secular government schools and a concurrent decline of government-recognized monastic education throughout all of Burma.[44] The British saw the lack of Buddhist collaboration as undermining the colonial project to educate a new class of civil servants. Christian missionary and government-funded schools flourished under colonial sponsorship and attracted talented, ambitious youths for whom instruction in English and western knowledge offered new opportunities and lifeways. A modern education afforded profitable opportunities under the colonial administration, but the economic boom in Lower Burma offered economic and social rewards for those Burmese who had obtained a western education. At the same time, these opportunities undermined the viability of a traditional monastic education and basic Buddhist literacy in modern contexts.

This trend was especially pronounced in towns and urban centers, which deepened the cultural divide between urban and rural areas that already characterized Burmese colonial experience. In contrast to precolonial Burma, when urban elites sought out monastic teachers and mentors, monastic education was now forced into rural areas. Monastic authority was further diminished by the rise in lay meditation and the decline of religious education after the collapse of centers of traditional culture, such as the court in Mandalay, that had lavishly supported monastic centers of learning. The trend away from monastic education created economic, cultural, and intellectual divisions between British-educated colonial elites and those who held on to a Buddhist rationality.

Although the institution of Buddhism, as embodied by the sangha, emerged as the only traditional organization to survive colonization, its influence and cultural vitality was much diminished. The *thathanabain*'s refusal to permit monastic schools to become conduits of colonial knowledge lessened the political and cultural relevance of the sangha. Monastic leaders did not anticipate the historic consequences of this decision, nor did they foresee the utility that colonial knowledge would have for an emerging class of Burmese civil servants. Living within a worldview in which Buddhist rationalities encompassed all practical knowledge, the sangha could not foresee the authority that colonial knowledge would acquire within a modern way of living. From the perspective of the traditional sangha, practical, applied, and vocational subjects had always been taught in the informal context of the worldly realm; it did not fall within the monasteries' educational mission.

The patriarchal decision indicated more than a Buddhist rejection of secular rationalism and colonial knowledge: it constituted a defense of monastic education as rooted in the *vinaya* and, more generally, as a defense of monastic status vis-à-vis a colonial regime that had shown it scant respect. By positioning itself in opposition to the colonial regime, the sangha eventually created an arena for resistance against colonialism, secular power, and modern knowledge combined. It located early Burmese anticolonial movements within a premodern Buddhist context. Increasingly, the sangha as an institution and monks as political actors became focal points of anticolonial resistance around which Burmese national identity was affirmed, and this was articulated through millennial movements and other forms for neotraditional Buddhism.

By the early twentieth century Burmese colonial elites in the cosmopolitan port city of Rangoon had been educated largely abroad in India and England. English had become the educated language among the upper class, while colloquial Burmese was used mostly in interactions with lower-class Burmese and in rural areas. Familiarity among the elite with Burmese classic literature and cultural and religious knowledge had nearly vanished. Along with the attractions of their new cosmopolitan horizons, modern innovations, and rapid social change, many Burmese also became increasingly disenchanted with the unfulfilled promises of the modern age and experienced estrangement from their own cultural traditions. Phayre's plan to involve the monasteries in delivering secular education was finally abandoned in the Education Committee report of 1924, but by then western education had been firmly established, and the fragmented sangha was experiencing considerable internal turmoil.[45]

Emerging from this collision of western and Buddhist worldviews was a radically changed social and political order; more significantly, the experience of modernity in Burma brought about a cultural and religious crisis of authority that had an enduring impact on the country's history. The authority of Buddhist worldviews, values, and knowledge was no longer undisputed, but in competition with other bodies of knowledge and structures of power that captured radically transformed cultural realities. Concepts such as the rule of a *dhammarāja* and the righteousness of the *dhamma* were now challenged by the modern realities of colonial rule. Many Burmese subjects of the British Crown now found themselves displaced to the periphery of an entirely different, affluent, and, at best, irreligious world.

Colonial Education and the Rise of Nationalism

A new challenge to colonial education emerged when the Young Men's Buddhist Association agitated for a reintroduction of Buddhist and Burmese subjects into the educational curriculum. This organization also gave voice to a popularly felt need among urban and middle-class Burmese to enhance lay authority in religious matters. Perhaps indicative of a popular disenchantment with modern lifeways, the YMBA championed a modern rationalism and an educational agenda centered on Buddhist and vernacular canons. The YMBA was an urban, colonial organization that aimed to instill nationalist sentiments based on Buddhist principles through mass education and the public schools.[46] It emerged independently from its Sri Lankan namesake in Rangoon in 1906 as a religious, cultural, and welfare-oriented organization that would serve as an umbrella structure for a variety of disparate groups.[47] Known in Burmese as Buddha Batha Kalyana Yuwa Athin (Association to Care for the Wholesomeness of Buddhism), it was explicitly modeled after the organizational and social objectives of the Young Men's Christian Association. In particular, the group imitated the organizational structure of the YMCA and its use of

A novice peers out of the window of a monastic school in Taunggyi in 2008. PHOTO BY ERIK WOODWARD.

print materials to mobilize and educate the public. Print was an important asset in "the development of a Burmese nationalist organization,"[48] one that articulated its nationalist agenda, primarily around issues of education.

In its early years the YMBA's leadership embraced many colonial values. Its national objectives were to strengthen the national spirit or race (*amyo*), to uphold a national Burmese culture and literature (*batha*), and to advance Buddhism (*thathana*) and education (*pyinnya*). Support for a national language (*batha*) was critical, since English had become the primary language among the Burmese colonial elite, and instruction in Burmese literacy and literature was primarily located within the monastic education system that had already suffered tremendous attrition. The idea of establishing a renewed and modern perspective on Buddhism (*thathana*) pervaded the YMBA's mission. The group encouraged moral self-reform among fellow Burmans[49] and advocated the prohibition of intoxicants, including liquor and tobacco. The YMBA also discouraged traditional Buddhist rituals associated with ostentatious spending, such as funerals, weddings, and novice initiations.

The YMBA undertook many initiatives on education (*pyinnya*) to promote a modern educational system that incorporated instruction in Burmese and in the fundamentals of Buddhism. Concerned about the pervasive influence of western education on Burmese national identity,[50] it promoted schools where Buddhism was part of the curriculum and sought government funding in parity with colonial support for Christian missionary schools.[51] It petitioned for the appointment of a minister of Buddhist Affairs and for instructors of Buddhism (*dhammakathika*) to teach religious fundamentals in public schools. The YMBA pushed for Burmese as the medium of instruction in national schools and worked to make basic education compulsory, which included setting standards in mathematics in rural areas.[52] Aware of the declining relevance of monastic education in shaping Burma's future, the YMBA pursued a religious and modern educational orientation, implicitly acknowledging its preference for modern schools that incorporated religious instruction by lay teachers over traditional monastic education. The history of the YMBA thus reveals significant conjunctures of colonial and Buddhist education, and from this intersection a spectrum of nationalist movements developed subsequently. Chapter 4 returns in greater detail to the role of the YMBA in the emergence of Buddhist modernity.

Educating Westerners: Scientific Discourse about the *Dhamma*

In the late nineteenth and early twentieth centuries, rational and scientific discourse was the primary mode through which orientalists and western converts gained an understanding of the Buddhist *dhamma*. In Burma, as elsewhere in the Theravada world, Buddhists engaged in educating colonizers about the Universal Law and the history of the dispensation (*sāsana*), and to do this they employed a "scientific" discourse that appealed to western audiences.[53] Their efforts appealed to two western audiences, the colonial orientalist scholars of the late nineteenth century and western converts to Buddhism in the mid-twentieth century. For the colonial scholar engaged in the discovery, classification, and enumeration of Buddhist doctrines, texts, and histories, this rationalist discourse confirmed their efforts to define the pristine origins of the tradition.[54] For western converts, a rational system of ethics, structured by causality, held a strong appeal. Both proselytizing projects displayed an intuitive affinity between Buddhist philosophy and western intellectual inquiry and seemed to imply an unqualified affirmation of modern rationalism in Buddhist terms.

A range of modern Buddhist teachings may be adduced to support this contention, and several modernist Buddhist organizations developed to bridge the divide between Buddhism and science.[55] The well-known Buddhist scholar U Shwe Zan Aung (1871–1932) explored the relationship between Buddhism and science and asserted that Buddhism, while never departing from its original canonical texts, encompassed scientific discoveries, past and future, in the way a philosophy of science foreshadowed scientific discoveries.[56] In support of his contention, Shwe Zan Aung pointed to comparative analytical methods and rules of criticism the two bodies of knowledge shared: both encouraged the study of phenomena and both relied on observation as a method, with the Buddhist cultivation of insight being the highest form of observation. He asserted that Buddhism proclaims generalizations of the highest order, such as the theory of ceaseless flux, the theory of karma, and the theory of causality. He claimed that the Buddha's teachings foreshadowed modern sciences like psychology, geography, astronomy, geology, cellular biology, chemistry, and so on, and his discussion linked key concepts of each scientific discipline to corresponding Buddhist notions. Asserting that Buddhist explication at times proceeds allegorically, he even likened Mount Meru to the axis of the earth and the North Pole to the desired abode of gods. He concluded that Buddhism was undogmatic and universal because its philosophy underlay all of science. As his exposition shows, in the Buddhist education of western converts, the Universal Truth of the *dhamma* frames the modern discourse of science, rational inquiry, and secular knowledge.

A similar point was conveyed in a lecture delivered in 1958 by the Honorable U Chan Htoon, a judge of the Supreme Court of the Union of Burma and secretary-general of U Nu's Buddha Sāsana Council. He addressed the Conference on Religion in the Age of Science in Star Island, New Hampshire, in the following way: "Scientific knowledge has shown itself not only negative towards dogmatic and 'revealed' religion, but positively hostile to it. . . . In the case of Buddhism, however, all the modern scientific concepts have been present from the beginning. There is no principle of science, from biological evolution to the general Theory of Relativity that runs counter to any teaching of Gotama Buddha."[57]

The attempt by Burmese Buddhists to justify the validity of their Buddhist worldview on grounds of western rationalism and scientific knowledge can be seen as a measure of success of British educational efforts. In delineating selected historic conjunctures of Buddhism, modernity, and politics, we can discern how intellectual and cultural strategies, like modern rationalism, can be employed to mobilize particular audiences in the process of educating the other, be they Burmese or western.

Buddhism and Education in Post-Independence Politics

Tensions between traditional Buddhist and modern colonial knowledge created a genealogy of contestation in the Burmese struggle for national identity. The rejection of colonial knowledge in monastic education in the late nineteenth century had a lasting impact and eventually contributed to a politicization of education in the Burmese public sphere, where educational policy has been pivotal since the advent of the colonial project in Burma.[58]

Buddhism and education once again emerged as a political flashpoint after independence. A major factor in the collapse of U Nu's government in 1962 was the issue of state support for religious education, and especially for Buddhist education. As prime minister, U Nu promoted the Sixth Buddhist Synod to revitalize Buddhist institutions and practices, to lend religious legitimation to his political office, and to control the public influence of the sangha. However, U Nu's government was increasingly pressured by the sangha to make Buddhism a state religion. Following a lengthy and complex negotiation, a constitutional amendment was passed in August 1961 to adopt Buddhism as the state religion. Because the state religion act defined non-Buddhists as second-class citizens, ethnic and religious minorities were alienated from the nation-building project. U Nu accommodated sangha demands for Buddhist instruction as part of state-funded, public education, but he was unable to secure the sangha's acceptance of educational rights for non-Buddhist minorities. Sangha leaders refused to accept policy provisions for non-Buddhist minorities that would have entitled them to offer religious instructions on private property with nongovernment funds.[59] Negotiations between U Nu's government and the sangha finally collapsed over state support for non-Buddhist religious education in public schools. Against the background of U Nu's failure to control the sangha's unrelenting demands and the threat of ethnic groups to secede from the Union of Burma, the military exploited the political power vacuum in 1962 in a move that weakened both Buddhist and democratic institutions. The military takeover ended more than a decade of parliamentary democracy and the Burmese Way to Buddhist Socialism, an ideology Ne Win's predecessor, U Nu, had advocated. The educational demands of the sangha had emerged again as a pivotal force in the project of nation-building, subject formation, and modernization after Burma's independence in 1948.

The collapse of U Nu's government in 1962 ushered in decades of military rule, economic deprivation, and cultural isolation. Ne Win's government and its successor regimes have continued to politicize education through the strategic closure of schools and institutions of higher education on claims of a national need to prevent or quell student unrest. The failures of educational policy and practice, and particularly the prohibition against teaching in English in public schools during the 1970s, intensified Burma's isolation during Ne Win's regime. While instruction in English has been reintroduced into the public school curriculum, the present regime continues to restrict access to higher education. Students at Rangoon University emerged as leaders in the popular uprising in 1988. In the 1990s the government again augmented the role of Buddhist monasteries in delivering basic education, especially among non-Buddhist tribal minorities and proceeded to disperse educational campuses, especially for higher education, in order to disperse the potential for student unrest. However, this dispersal of educational locations was not matched by resources, and access remains restricted to those whose families enjoy special privileges.

Since the 1990s various civil rights advocates, including the Human Rights Documentation Unit of the National Coalition Government of the Union of Burma (NCGUB) and Aung San Suu Kyi, have appealed to the international community to promote education at all levels in Burma, arguing that four decades of military rule have had a negative impact on the quality of and access to education in Burma.[60] The lack of government support for education, they argue, has had disastrous effects on basic human rights, including popular political participation in the shaping of civil society and public health care. Restricted access to education, particularly to higher education, has become a major hurdle in the development of modern civil society in Burma. Nonetheless, the numerous private schools that have opened in towns and cities in an effort to compensate for the state's restrictions on education attest to the high regard for education in Burmese culture.

The cultural history of education in colonial and independent Burma is not a continuous narrative that distinguishes consistently between modernity and tradition, secularism and religion, rationalism and Buddhist cosmology. My purpose here has been to show how the history of modern education in Burma unfolded and to highlight historical tensions in a discourse that opens up new linkages between religious values, modern knowledge, and secular rationalism. Buddhist and nationalist concerns weave through the public project of education during the colonial period and the independent nation-state in complex and often fragmented episodes that link the agendas of local actors with the cultural trajectories of institutions and concerns for the greater good of civil society. Education, it seems, is always someone's project. Our attention therefore must focus on the cultural and political contexts and audiences at specific moments. The moment discussed here has been when educational values and policies emerged as pivotal agents of social change, profoundly shaping the course of Burmese colonial and national history.

4 Civil Buddhism in a Colonial Context

The previous chapters discussed some of the ways in which British rule in Burma introduced secular structures that expanded the power of the modern state and undermined traditional Buddhist authority.[1] Colonial rule dislodged worldviews characteristic of traditional cosmological Buddhist polities and created many social disjunctures. The initial Burmese experience of modernity was therefore characterized by a cultural eclipse of received institutions and lifeways. This process had a particularly detrimental impact on the culture of Upper Burma, which still identified with the former royal capital of Mandalay.[2] But the collapse of the traditional culture hastened the restructuring of Burmese society through colonial forms of knowledge and classification, particularly in Rangoon and its surrounding area.[3] The British failure to respond to the cultural disintegration of Buddhist authority did, however, open up a social space for civil Buddhist communities to organize themselves and develop a modern agenda. This chapter focuses on these modern Buddhist communities that emerged in response to the decline of the traditional culture and linked to transnational organizations that sought to propagate Buddhist ideas in new ways. In this context of transnational modern Buddhism, a different kind of organization emerged, one emphasizing lay authority and mobilizing communities to work toward a new modern form of Buddhist nationalism. In particular, my discussion returns to the Young Men's Buddhist Association (YMBA), its accomplishments and eventual submergence within a wider nationalist struggle.[4] In delineating these developments, we encounter yet another iteration of what it means to be Burmese and Buddhist at the dawn of nationalism.

Transnational Buddhist Networks

During the late nineteenth and early twentieth centuries, transnational collaborations developed among diverse Buddhist organizations throughout Asia. The Mahabodhi Society, the Young Men's Buddhist Association in Sri Lanka and elsewhere in the Buddhist world that Burmese consider distinct from the Burmese organization discussed below, the International Buddhist League, and other established international networks. These organizations regularly published reports about their missionary activity across Asia.[5] In Burma, however, Buddhist transnational connections developed at a slower pace. Few enduring collaborations were made and attempts to integrate Burmese organizations into wider Buddhist networks received little response. There are, however, some notable exceptions to the general reluctance among Burmese to address colonial issues as part of reviving the authority for Buddhist practices and institutions. They include foreign Buddhists like the American Colonel Henry Steel Olcott (1832–1907), the British Charles Henry Allan Bennett (1872–1923) who ordained as Ananda Metteyya in 1901, and Gordon Douglas, the first Englishman to become ordained as a Buddhist monk, Ashin Asoka, in 1899.[6]

Henry Steel Olcott dedicated much of his life to revitalizing Asian religions and creating what he thought was a modern, unified Buddhist doctrine. He was involved in several missions to promote a Buddhist revival among Theravadins. At the invitation of King Thibaw, Olcott briefly visited Burma in 1885 to set up a branch of the Theosophical Society for Burmese Buddhists, but this organization did not achieve prominence there.[7] Olcott returned to Burma twice in 1891, to arrange for the translation of his *Buddhist Catechism* into Burmese and to gain approval for his Buddhist Platform. The Buddhist Platform comprised a set of foundational principles Olcott had formulated with the intention that they would serve as the basis for a universal set of doctrines that all Buddhist would share. When he presented his truths to the sangha in Mandalay, he readily gained their approval, or, perhaps more accurately, the *thathanabain* and other monastic leaders did not disagree with Olcott's list. Yet Olcott did not succeed in enlisting the sangha in his missionary efforts, and his effort to establish local branches of the International Buddhist League soon dissipated.[8]

The project of Charles Henry Allan Bennett aimed to convert British audiences to Theravada Buddhism. An ardent British convert to Buddhism himself, Bennett wanted to propagate Theravada Buddhism in Britain and bring the "Empire of Righteousness to Western Lands."[9] Having visited Sri Lanka, Bennett arrived in Burma in 1901, where he was ordained as a novice and took the name Ananda Metteyya. His first Buddhist Lent was spent in Mandalay where he studied the *vinaya* and also met the Ledi Sayadaw. Two years later, in 1903, he took full ordination as a monk under the sponsorship of Mrs. Hla Ong, the honorary secretary of the Mandalay branch of the Buddha Sāsana Samgama. Ananda Metteyya expanded the Buddha Sāsana Samgama to include a sister organization, the International Buddhist Society, which was directed toward an English-speaking audience. It was located in Rangoon where from 1903 to 1908 it published an English-language journal, *Buddhism,* through Hanthawaddy Press. His effort to missionize Buddhism in the west was remarkable because he succeeded in raising funds to do so among prominent Burmese. Many of his supporters also held important positions within the Young Men's Buddhist Association. In his writings Ananda Metteyya revealed himself as a determined, if not always persuasive, orator whose writings stressed the need to raise funds for a Buddhist mission in England. He appealed to the moral obligation of modern, wealthy Burmese to support his project. The extent to which Ananda Metteyya's project was successful was probably an indication of the desire on the part of some Burmese lay patrons to legitimate Buddhist traditions with British colonial society. In 1908 his Burmese sponsors financed his first Buddhist mission to England. He returned to Burma the same year. However, his poor health eventually forced him to disrobe and return to England permanently in 1914, and the activities of the missionary society ceased with his departure.

The attempts of the Burmese to construct a modern Buddhist tradition in their colonial context followed a different trajectory from those elsewhere in Southeast Asia as emerging lay Burmese organizations operated mostly independently from international Buddhist networks. In the early twentieth century, several Burmese organizations started up with constituencies that were motivated to renew Buddhist values and define a national identity (*wunthanu*). In 1897 the Sāsana Nuggaha Athin (Mission Association) was founded in Mandalay and Pakokku.[10] Due perhaps to the diminished, but still enduring authority of the sangha in Upper Burma, lay elites in Mandalay were less active in cultivating transnational ties. In Mawlamyine, Lower Burma, the Sāsana Dhara Athin (Service Association) was founded in 1899. The Rangoon College Buddhist Association was formed in 1904. At least initially, these and other new organizations, such as the Ledi Sayadaw's Abhidhamma Thankait Athin and the Thathana Hita Athin (Foreign Mission Society) saw themselves as taking on a traditional mission of propagating the Buddha's teachings (*thathana pyu thi*). Their project was innovative, however, in that their efforts were undertaken in the absence of royal patronage and relied on modern forms of mobilizing communities, such as print and other mass media.

The Formation of the Young Men's Buddhist Association

The anthropologist Michael Mendelson[11] has observed that Burmese nationalist sentiments emerged in reaction to British colonial presence and that a Buddhist identity provided a focal point for rather disparate groups engaged in resisting colonial power. His observations are particularly apt in light of the eventual outcome of Buddhist nationalism, especially in Upper Burma. But the kind of Buddhist nationalism the Young Men's Buddhist Association advocated initially in Lower Burma actually envisioned a role for the Burmese within the British empire, not apart from it. Its beginnings were rooted in developments in colonial Lower Burma and unfolded in response to the fragmentation of the sangha. Its history narrates conjunctures of colonial and Buddhist aspirations from which later nationalist movements developed.[12]

From the start, the emergence of the YMBA was framed by Burma's colonial realities and its development intersected with multiple transnational contexts. Some credit the initial impetus to form a social welfare organization with the establishment of a youth hostel in Arakan in 1902. Four years later the organization moved to Rangoon, where its offices were located on the corner of Dalhousie and Judah Ezekiel streets. There, the YMBA assumed a broader mission as a welfare organization that provided an umbrella structure for several Buddhist groups, including one at Rangoon College. A contemporary politician and writer, U Maung Maung, one of the founding members of this organization, tells the story that the inspiration to establish the YMBA originated with a group of students at Rangoon College who belonged to an ambitious, procolonial Burmese elite.[13] Several of them had studied law in India or England. U Ba Pe is credited with founding the group, along with Dr. Thein Maung, the lawyer U Thein Maung, and, among others, the "England-returned" barrister U May Ong, who joined the YMBA in 1908. U Maung Maung asserts that the initiative to organize the YMBA occurred independently of similar developments in Sri Lanka.[14] However, its founding members were likely aware of similar organizations elsewhere in the Buddhist world.

While several colonial conjunctures account for the "dawn of nationalism" among members of the YMBA, awareness of transnational, pan-Asian Buddhist aspirations or international Buddhist organizations appears to have influenced the rise and local dynamics of modern Buddhist nationalism in Burma only haphazardly. By contrast, the most influential transnational connections for secular nationalists seem to have come from India and the west. Many young, educated Burmese looked toward India, rather than Japan, for a model of political activism and constitutional reforms within the colony.[15]

The YMBA's membership comprised mostly of young, British-educated colonial elites. The first generation of leaders was the product of a modern education system, through attendance at government schools, at Christian missionary schools, or through higher education, often for an extended period of time, in India and England. Ambitious and talented, the careers and tasks they faced upon their return home propelled them to envision an identity for themselves that broke with the traditional past and affirmed the changing contexts of Burma and the British Empire.[16] Transnational connections informed these processes in other arenas of public life as well and led to the rapidly changing ethnic composition of Burma as it accommodated an expanding immigrant population from India, China, and Europe. In addition, the changing social matrix of the colonial empire heightened awareness of religious diversity in Burma.

During its founding years, the YMBA had been considered in colonial society to be an exemplar of a civil Buddhist organization. It was nurtured by, and simultaneously reacted to, British colonialism, the crisis of Buddhist authority, and modernity in Lower Burma in the early twentieth century. The YMBA initially imitated colonial society as a means of promoting its Buddhist national identity, and it became the most successful attempt to mobilize Burmese around modern Buddhist practices during the colonial era. Like other nationalist organizations, it promoted and mobilized patriotic grassroots activism (*wunthanu*) in small towns and villages in Lower Burma. In Bruce Lincoln's terms, it began as a minimalist organization with a procolonial agenda that sought to advance the Buddhist causes of a modern, western-educated Burmese elite.[17]

The YMBA's agenda appealed to a popular sentiment among colonial Burmese who longed for spiritual renewal at a time of disenchantment with modern society and a perceived loss of national identity and religious values. The YMBA addressed these sentiments and aimed to remedy the growing disenchantment. At the same time, the YMBA also spoke to Burmese cosmopolitan elites who felt estranged from their traditional cultural roots and sought to ease their discomfort by constructing a rationalized Buddhism stripped of cosmological mythologies. In response to the disintegration of the sangha as an institution, a western-educated Burmese lay elite felt increasingly motivated to define what it meant to be Burmese and to be Buddhist. During the early twentieth century, these definitions were fluid and took on national, regional, and even local characteristics. The presence of transnational connections in Lower Burma and their relative absence in Upper Burma exacerbated significantly regional and social differences.

The founding members of the YMBA allegedly coined the phrase "To be Burmese is to be Buddhist"[18] in order to define for themselves and others in their western-educated, cosmopolitan circles a religious and national identity. The identification of national sentiments with religion signaled a new, modern conjuncture that harnessed Buddhist fervor to mobilize popular support for an early nationalism. Its discourse involved many referents and identified membership in a national community with religious practices and rapidly changing worldviews. Since its initial use by members of the YMBA, this emblematic statement has been reinterpreted in later political contexts, such as during the post-independence era of Prime Minister U Nu.

Like other groups, which were oriented toward meditation, the YMBA claimed greater religious authority for lay people. However, unlike other Buddhist movements, the YMBA forged new Buddhist identities consonant with modern social and political realities. The YMBA gained widespread popularity in Lower Burma during the 1910s, when it began activities as a procolonial organization. It aimed to popularize a new national identity among the colonial elite and among an emerging middle class that was modern, Burmese, and Buddhist. It was the first lay organization to make nationalism a Buddhist missionary object (*thathana pyu thi)*, propagating the Buddha's dispensation and making the world safe for a Buddhist morality. The demise of monastic authority had created space for such lay activism, particularly in Lower Burma, where the demise of monastic authority was particularly evident. Transnational connections through education and commerce, as well as the growth of print technologies, helped mobilize the Burmese public.[19]

To a considerable degree the YMBA was a colonial project that responded to competing historical realities. In the view of the YMBA, the modern Burman was an educated colonial subject of the British Crown. At first, the YMBA developed with the tacit encouragement of colonial administrators and enjoyed considerable paternalistic protection from members of the Indian Civil Service, particularly J. S. Furnivall. The British favored tacit sponsorship of the YMBA as a civic organization to foster a public space in which native colonial elites would rally popular support for a modern Burmese identity within a colonial frame of reference. Implicit in their strategy was the aim to keep Buddhism and politics separate and to avoid interference of the colonial government with the religious affairs of the natives. British imperial policy was based on the premise of western political, post-Enlightenment theory that separated religion from the affairs of the state and relegated it to the private domain of civil society. In time, however, the colonial government would be confronted with the political challenges of emerging modern Buddhist identities and, hence, would not be able to avoid confrontations with anti-British resistance inspired by both modern and traditional Buddhist beliefs and practices.

In its early years YMBA's leadership was sympathetic to British values and etiquette. Simultaneously emulating and reacting to the kind of secular politics British colonialism had introduced to Burma, the YMBA initially adopted a civil and religious charter that championed Burmese Buddhist values in contradistinction to the identity of the British elite. It aimed explicitly to create a national identity equal to and characterized by the same modern values and activities as members of British colonial society did, who joined private fraternities like the Pegu Club, which only accepted European members. The colonial government initially encouraged the formation of this urban Burmese elite and "let it be known that government servants might . . . join the YMBA."[20] Membership in the YMBA became respectable and even fashionable. "Anybody, if a Burman or even an Indian, of account in Rangoon society could be found in the roster of the association. Almost all Burman officers in government service, Burman brokers and traders, retired officials, teachers, clerks, whether of business firms or government officers, avidly joined."[21]

To avoid being labeled a seditious or political organization, the YMBA demonstrated its loyalty to the Crown explicitly and even expressed its "servility."[22] According to Maung Maung, the YMBA viewed the British colonial presence in Burma as inevitable[23] and showed "deep awareness of the need to express repeatedly loyalty to the British Crown as well as appreciation and thanksgiving for the blessing of the British administration of Burma."[24] To acknowledge the prosperity and pacification the country had experienced under British rule, meetings of the YMBA regularly opened with the empire's anthem, "God Save the King," although "Buddha Save the King" soon superseded that allegiance to reflect the organization's Buddhist and nationalist goals.[25] Similarly, their negotiation strategies intentionally expressed a modern Burmese civility and knowledge of colonial practice: in their communications with the British government, the YMBA generally phrased its intentions as "respectful demands" and "petitioned" colonial authorities to remedy public affairs in accordance with their recommendations.

The discourse of YMBA members underscored a new kind of Burmese Buddhist identity that was of no lesser value or gentility than what YMBA members perceived the British to convey. Their intention was to reform traditional cultural practices, implicitly rejecting traditional cosmological Buddhism and many of its ritual practices. Implementing its charter to uplift Burmese society in religious, social, cultural, and economic ways, the YMBA formulated four major foci in its agenda, namely, to strengthen the country's sense of race (*amyo*) and national spirit, to enhance national culture and literature (*batha*), to revitalize Buddhism (*thathana*), and to promote education (*pyinnya*).

In both British and Burmese colonial discourse, race was an integral aspect of national identity. The YMBA reflected this view by identifying its membership as being "Burman" and not the ethnically more inclusive national designation of "Burmese." Even though ethnic Burmans constitute about 80 percent of the country's population, the YMBA's vision of nationalism clearly differed from an understanding of national identity that would encompass other ethnicities as belonging to its national community. The idea of "deracination," which the YMBA deplored, was seen as the fragmentation or loss of a Burman identity.[26] Hence, the YMBA's national vision did not indicate any recognition or accommodation of other ethnic and religious groups within the national community that they imagined for Burma. Among these urban elites of Rangoon, there was a strong sense that Burman culture, civilization, and race were nearly extinct and in need of revitalization. The causes for this threatened loss of identity were seen to be westernization, ethnic diversity, and the political influence of indigenous minorities, particularly those who had converted to Christianity. In the view of the YMBA and others, the loss of patriotic sentiments among the elite and the lack of a Burman national community were to be attributed to the erosion of Burman race, religion, and culture.[27]

The emphasis on and support for a national language (*batha*) was based on the fact that "knowledge of Burmese literature [had] almost died out among the educated Burmese classes and . . . Burmese speech tended to be confined to rural areas and the domestic sphere."[28] With the largest number of Burmese students studying in Europe during the early twentieth century, English had become the language of instruction and colloquial habit among the Burmese colonial elite. It was not uncommon for members of the upper classes and lower classes to belong to separate linguistic communities. The loss of a commonly shared language also implied a decline of knowledge and familiarity with classical Burmese literary traditions. At the same time, Burmese language and literature were taught in only a limited way in government schools. The colonial government viewed literacy in Burmese as necessary merely to convey imperial ideals to the Burmese population at large; it saw no need to educate Burmans in their own literary traditions. Rangoon College was founded in 1857, but only as an extension of Calcutta University. Moreover, instruction in literary subjects had traditionally been located within monastic education and the educational and cultural decline of the sangha was pervasive, and there had been no prior tradition of rigorous lay teaching in such subjects. To the leadership of the YMBA, these facts conveyed a loss of Burmese identity and cultural values that needed to be remedied. A cornerstone of the YMBA's agenda and petitions to the colonial government was therefore the teaching of Burmese language skills and literacy as an integral part of the curriculum in government schools.

A modernist, reformist stance on Buddhism (*thathana*) characterized the YMBA's mission. In an effort to ease the economic burden in already heavily taxed rural areas, the YMBA petitioned the Government of India to exempt monastic land from taxation.[29] It also discouraged villagers from ostentatious spending on ritual occasions like funerals, weddings, and novice initiations, which traditionally consumed a relatively large portion of their income. In order to intervene in what it considered to be excessive consumption of intoxicants like liquor and tobacco, the YMBA appealed to the colonial government to restrict the use of alcohol. Equally significant were their exhortations to fellow Burmese to engage in "moral self-reform."[30] The YMBA's encouragement of moral self-reform and "inner asceticism" among fellow Burmans is consonant not just with Weber's characterization of modern religion, but also with a wider transnational trend in Buddhist societies at the turn of the twentieth century, when western-educated elites especially voiced their disenchantment with practices that had developed as a result of popular exposure to modernity, secularism, and colonial culture.

Perhaps the most profound impact of the YMBA on the development of civil society can be traced to its efforts to reform education (*pyinnya*). A key element in their nationalist agenda was the demand for a modern education system in government schools that included instruction in the Burmese language, its literature, and Buddhism. The purpose of a modern education was to inspire a national and Buddhist consciousness among young Burmese. The YMBA recognized the value of mass education as "crucial to the development of a Burmese nationalist organization."[31] In the course of the 1910s, it developed into a populist movement that mobilized nationalist sentiments across Lower Burma. The YMBA sought government funding in parity with colonial support for Christian missionary schools and worked to bring monks (*dhammakathika*) into the public school system to teach Buddhism as part of the curriculum mandated through the Ministry of Buddhist Affairs.[32] In a speech about "The Modern Burman" in August 1908 at Rangoon College, U May Ong, then YMBA president, addressed these sentiments. "The New Burman has lost his pride of race, and with it nearly all feeling of community with his fellows. His nationality is not with him, as it is with other races, an ever-present reality, . . . a bond of sympathy between him and those around him." It was this lack of national feeling that kept him "aloof from the people at large and makes him even look down on his less-cultured brothers." This absence of communal sentiment "prevents him from forming commercial or even social combinations."[33]

He warned that unless the Burmese prepared themselves to overcome the "not unmixed blessing of a Western education" and "ceaseless, ebbless tide of foreign civilization and learning, . . . their national character, their institutions, their very existence as a distinct nationality will be swept away, submerged, irretrievably lost."[34] He further asserted that the fragmenting forces of modernization had disrupted the very cultural institutions that traditionally guaranteed the inculcation in future generations of core values and practices of what it meant to be Burmese. He further expressed his hope for the possibility of educating a Burmese boy who could enter English schools at a young age without becoming illiterate in his own language, religion, and culture. "If I were asked," he continued, "'What is a Burman?' the answer I should make would be, 'A Burman is a Buddhist.'"[35]

The mission of this association of young Burmese Buddhists was to compensate for the evils created by a lack of Buddhist values such as compassion and selflessness, a loss of humility, a lack of respect for traditional values, and "to make the Modern Burman a distinct species from the simple, sincere Burman of old."[36] The YMBA was to remedy these cultural realities and champion a modern Burmese Buddhist identity.

The YMBA was the first mass organization in Burma to reach beyond Rangoon's social elite to articulate a modern Buddhist agenda. It used mass mobilization and publications to raise national awareness among western-educated Burmese and others. Local chapters of the YMBA met on a monthly basis, and national conferences convened annually starting in 1910. At its first national meeting, twenty-two local chapters and associations were represented.[37] By 1917, at the fifth national conference in Pyinmana, the YMBA had grown to encompass forty-five branches. The YMBA also mobilized nationalist awareness through print. First published in English in 1908, the *Burman Buddhist Weekly* presented a decidedly procolonial perspective. *The Sun* began as a successful English-language newspaper published three times a week by prominent YMBA leaders U Hla Pe and U Ba Pe. In its Burmese-language version (*Thuriya*), which commenced daily publication in 1915, the paper cultivated an explicitly nationalist tone. The populist media outlets were complemented by another scholarly publication, *The Journal of the Burma Research Society*, which began publication in 1910 to bring the academic study of Burmese culture and history to an English-speaking audience. John S. Furnivall and Charles Duroiselle were cofounders of this society, which was constituted with the intention of encouraging modern Burmese scholarship in history, geography, culture, and literature. In time, it would become the flagship journal for colonial scholarship on Burma.

The rapid growth and national popularity of the YMBA also placed political power at the disposal of some leaders who may not have been well prepared for the offices and representation they soon acquired in this emerging mass organization. Overtaken by their success in inspiring a national spirit among the general population, several YMBA leaders were accused of abusing their fiscal responsibilities and their influence. Many who campaigned for election as a YMBA representative entered into coalitions with monks who supported their agenda in the sermons they gave and through their monastic networks of donors. As internal disorganization in YMBA developed, the influence of the sangha over individual YMBA representatives grew correspondingly. Consequently, the sangha's endorsement became a critical factor in the campaigns of delegates to the national council of the YMBA. Indeed, collaboration between members of the sangha and delegates appeared well rehearsed. Monks with excellent preaching abilities were in a position to assemble sizable crowds, who would then be called upon to vote for a particular delegate. YMBA delegates, in turn, would benefit personally from the funds raised through this process and from the political influence gained in this manner. They would also be expected to donate a portion of these funds to the monks who had supported their campaigns. This symbiotic reciprocity came to frame the electoral process to such a degree that it was not possible to campaign as a YMBA delegate without the endorsement from prominent members of the sangha. In the process, the authority of YMBA delegates was compromised, and some YMBA factions, such as the 21 Party, were suspected of money laundering and influence peddling. This accelerated the splintering within the YMBA and reasserted the influence of members of the sangha, who were becoming increasingly active in politics and radicalized in their opposition to British rule. The rapid growth of the YMBA outpaced the organization's ability to build an infrastructure that would assure the accountability of its delegates and prevent the organization's agenda from being taken over by feuding factions.

The YMBA's civil Buddhism was framed by competing and interrelated colonial realities at the "dawn of nationalism."[38] Within a decade, secularists as well as Buddhist maximalists, those with a traditional Buddhist or messianic orientation, had overwhelmed the YMBA's original agenda.[39] The 1920s saw the arrival of nationalist movements that ranged from secular, student-led nationalists who would eventually develop into the Dobama (We Burmans) Association, constituted in 1930, to Buddhist maximalists that included radical monastic groups. These included the General Council of Buddhist Associations (GCBS), the Young Women's Buddhist Association, the monastic Yahan Pyo, and the sort of neotraditional, millennial Buddhist resistance to the colonial regime that appeared in the Saya San Rebellion. For these maximalist groups, a Buddhist identity was integral to their anticolonial resistance, and they eventually submerged the YMBA's vision of a Buddhist nationalism and its mass organization beneath their own narratives of resistance to colonial rule. In contrast to the YMBA's civil Buddhism under colonial domination, these groups promoted a form of Buddhist anticolonialism, to which the discussion will return later.

Fragmentation of the YMBA

Between 1916 and 1920, the YMBA gradually relinquished its control over its initial agenda to whims and vagaries of impeding political factionalism that soon marginalized the YMBA's civil agenda and undermined its mass organization. A confluence of forces transformed the initially procolonial nationalist movement represented by the YMBA into radically anticolonial factions. Among them were monks who gained considerable influence in the nationalist movement during the 1920s.[40] The new General Council of Burmese Associations (GCBA) emerged to subsume and replace the YMBA and its infrastructure. These developments allowed other organizations to form. This included the General Council of the Sangha Sammeggi (GCSS), which was controlled by Burma's most radical political monks, who fomented and coordinated local sites of resistance. These changes in orientation and strategy empowered a younger generation of nationalist leaders, including monks, who endorsed a pronounced anticolonial agenda, while at the same time, many among the founding generation of the YMBA left that organization to assume judicial and similarly significant positions with the colonial government.

One of the foremost religious challenges to the influence of the YMBA developed from within its own ranks. In 1916 the YMBA's public standing was tested by the "No Footwear Campaign" that increasingly galvanized Burmese popular sentiment.[41] At the Shwedagon Pagoda, a sign encouraged visitors to comply with a prohibition against wearing shoes on sacred Buddhist ground. Appended to this recommendation was an exemption for Europeans who generally did not remove their shoes.[42] U Thein Maung, a lawyer from Bassein and a prominent YMBA member, provocatively removed that portion of the sign. The fact that European visitors to pagodas generally did not remove their shoes was sacrilegious behavior in the eyes of many Burmese Buddhists. Rooted in the ritual practices of traditional, cosmological Buddhism, this sort of desecration of sacred space was unacceptable, and there were not just a few isolated cases. Such behavior was offensive to traditionalists and modernists alike. In order to deflect confrontation, British administrators generally announced in advance when they planned to visit sacred Buddhist sites. In 1916 *The Sun* published an incendiary report about a British couple visiting Shwedagon who did not remove their shoes. It focused accountability for the lack of compliance on Burmese pagoda trustees, who were also prominent YMBA members. Thein Maung's populist agitation mobilized Burmese public opinion and transformed an initially religious concern into one that was political, anticolonial, and nationalist. In 1917 the venerated Ledi Sayadaw (1846–1923) published a treatise in Burmese, *On the Impropriety of Wearing*

Cartoon originally published in *The Sun* (*Thuriya*) in 1918.
THE IMAGE IS REPRODUCED FROM NOEL F. SINGER, *OLD RANGOON*, P. 194, WITH PERMISSION.

Shoes on Pagoda Platforms, that lent further religious authority to the protest.[43] The colonial government soon banned public discussion of the issue in an effort to diffuse mounting public tension. It also withdrew its public support of the YMBA and began to monitor more closely the movements of YMBA members. In order to diffuse the "foot wearing" issue, the colonial government ruled in 1918 that it was delegating to local monastic authority any final decision to implement a general prohibition against wearing shoes on pagoda grounds.

An emerging secular nationalism, the student movements that precipitated strikes in 1920, 1936, and 1938, and the prolonged struggle for home rule for Burma, which attained only partial success in 1923, all contributed to the erosion of the YMBA's mass appeal. The colonial government ordered schools to expand instruction about loyalty to the British Crown. This initiative was proposed by *The Committee Appointed to Ascertain and Advise How the Imperial Idea May be Inculcated and Fostered in Schools and Colleges in Burma* (Rangoon, 1917) and met with strong resistance from the YMBA.[44] While negotiations for home rule had been granted to India, similar privileges for local representation were refused for Burma, and this exacerbated political tensions within the YMBA leadership between the older, more conservative group and the younger, more radical one. The younger leaders eventually took control of the organization.[45] U May Ong and many of his peers resigned from the YMBA and took up positions as lawyers, judges, and administrators in the colonial government. By 1920, the YMBA was rendered obsolete and submerged, initially, by the General Council of Burmese Associations (GCBA), which aimed to include Indian and Christian minorities in the nationalist movement. Under the powerful influence of the sangha, however, the organization was soon renamed the General Council of Buddhist Associations (GCBA) and shortly thereafter, it transformed itself again into the General Council of the Sangha Sammeggi (GCSS), ceding control to another faction of Burma's politically engaged monks. As the conflict between British and Burmese national interests intensified, public debate about what constituted a national Burmese identity developed both in Buddhist and secular directions. The secular nationalist movement was led by university students, among them the famous Thirty Comrades, who became the country's heroes in the independence struggle and whose members became the country's political leadership after independence. Various anticolonial Buddhist groups, such as the GCSS, eventually eclipsed the YMBA's accommodating orientation toward the colonial government and created space for a radicalized Buddhist nationalism to usurp the agenda.

The internal fragmentation in the YMBA reached a turning point when Burmese nationalism became increasingly anti-British and anticolonial. The organizational tone and popular interpretation of being Burmese and Buddhist had been radically transformed from when it had first emerged among a procolonial elite. Shifting their focus from the urban elite, the new proponents of nationalist agendas sought out diverse secular, rural, and traditionalist contexts. Buddhist nationalism during the 1930s emphasized a revisionist traditionalism of what it meant to be Burmese and Buddhist. It shifted the focus of activity upcountry, away from transnational connections, and toward a millennial return of the past.

5 The Politics of the Modern State as Buddhist Practice

In Burmese history, traditional and modern states have relied on support from the monastic community to ensure their political continuity, and complex interdependencies developed as a result of the state's reliance on Buddhist legitimation. Secular institutions that confer power upon government, including participation in the political process through fair elections, have consequently suffered. This chapter explores recurrent attempts by the state to infuse political ideologies with Buddhist meaning. Modern Burmese governments—be they democratic, socialist, or military—have often tried to control the sangha in order to enhance their political legitimacy. Alternatively, they worked to keep the sangha from contesting the politics of the state. The state's efforts to control Buddhist institutions has created some liabilities, but at the same time, Buddhist worldviews and ethics have been forced to compete with secular visions of society and with political ideologies like democracy, socialism, and venture capitalism.

Reforming Buddhist institutions was an established practice for strong Burmese kings, who would "purify" the sangha from alleged decline. The reforms usually initiated realignments among monastic lineages and affirmed new norms of orthopraxis, orthodoxy, and popular piety.[1] Michael Aung-Thwin has pointed to the political and economic interests of kings during the Pagan dynasty, when reforming the sangha allowed the dynasty to divest monasteries of their land and recapture an otherwise shrinking royal tax base.[2] Since that time the Burmese state has repeatedly striven to reshape Buddhist practice and morality in the image of its own political ideology, attempting to redefine and reform traditional as well as modern forms of Buddhism. At the same time, the conduct of politics was often articulated as popular Buddhist practice.

The political implications of Buddhist practices were prevalent during the British period, when colonial Buddhist communities emerged in new and transformed historical contexts. Buddhist practices remained a salient idiom for mobilizing people and provided a focus for national identity well into the modern period. Since the early twentieth century, when the *wunthanu* associations and the YMBA were organized, national welfare and progress have been mapped onto the stages of the Buddhist Eightfold Noble Path. As Alicia Turner notes, Buddhist missionary societies therefore became the primary means for organizing the colonial Burmese public, creating civil institutions in colonial society, and mobilizing a broad range of civil causes (*thathana pyu thi*).[3]

In modern western European political tradition, religion is usually relegated to a private domain, and the state is envisioned as secular. In the Theravada Buddhist world, religion is necessarily at once political and religious. Buddhism in Burma has undergone periods of demythification and rationalization, but the state has never relinquished control over the sangha and has not permitted the complete privatization of Buddhist institutions and power outside the purview of the state. As we have seen in chapter 1, Theravada reforms did not particularly aim to modernize or privatize the domain of religion, although such aspects could be a part of the attempt to reform. Propagating the Buddha's dispensation is a cultural discourse that transcends historical contexts, but at the same time it harbors great political potential that is difficult to control. For example, during U Nu's government (1948–1956, 1957–1958, and 1960–1962), the state continually attempted to control the sangha, and ultimately the loss of the state's control over the monks was a major force contributing to its collapse. The popular revolts of 1988 and 2007 have similarly demonstrated the monks' ability to intervene in the functioning of the state.

This chapter explores how governments of the independent nation-state have controlled Buddhist institutions, particularly the sangha, in order to consolidate their political power. During the late 1950s and early 1960s, U Nu's democratic government encouraged charisma, meditation, and international Buddhist missionary efforts to implement the politics of the nation-state. It empowered the Ministry of Religious Affairs to become a forceful instrument of state policy.

By contrast, reforms carried out by the Sangha Mahanayaka Council of Ne Win's era in the 1980s aimed to contain charismatic monks, their sources of revenue, and their popular influence.[4] Ne Win's reforms imposed measures to control monastic institutions and individuals, including registration for and access to monastic examinations. The role of the Ministry of Religious Affairs was expanded to manage the public activities of religious minorities, including Christians, Muslims, Hindus, and Jews. After the popular uprising of 1988, the political guarantees of the modern state under a national constitution were suspended. The ruling elite under Ne Win's successor regimes, the State Law and Order Restoration Council (SLORC) and later the State Peace and Development Council (SPDC), have turned increasingly to Buddhist sources of legitimation and to state patronage of patterns of ritual exchange.

In doing so, the governments of the independent nation-state have reinterpreted a traditional paradigm of power, namely, the role of the *dhammarāja,* to meet the pragmatic requirements of the modern state. The military regimes in power have propagated a neotraditionalist and scripturalist understanding of the Buddha's teachings and again mobilized the nation through ritual networks and the construction of sacred sites. They have presented their political legitimacy as the contemporary culmination of an ancient Burmese dynastic lineage. They have restored Buddhist monuments built by past Burmese kings, and they have also constructed new ones at ancient sites and in the new capital, Naypyidaw, to bear testimony to their merit and power. Neotraditional and modernist Buddhist voices have in this way challenged the foundations of secular government and undermined the relevance of modern political ideologies. Yet at several junctures the state has failed to control the moral voices of monks who have challenged its policies, and chapter 6 will examine the genealogies of resistance to the state.[5]

U Nu's Millennial Path to Buddhist Socialism

The political era of U Nu followed the end of British colonialism and ushered in a parliamentary democracy in post-independence Burma. This also occurred amidst widespread millennial expectations of an imminent, powerful Buddhist ruler (*cakkavatti*) in the Theravada world, where many believed that the second half of the Buddha's dispensation had begun. U Nu's revitalization thus coincided with worldwide celebrations of the 2,500-year anniversary of the *sāsana.*

U Nu (1905–1995) was a gifted politician and a deeply religious man who served as prime minister of democratic Burma between 1948–1956, 1957–1958, and 1960–1962. He was also a remarkable orator and writer,[6] and these talents fostered his rise in politics. During his lifetime he experienced profound political and social change, and his political values reflected the early nationalist era in which he had grown up. He spent his youth in Wakema, a town in the delta region of Lower Burma, where his father was an active member of the local chapter of the YMBA. U Nu's education began at a local Anglo-vernacular government school. In an era when many of his peers studied in India or Britain, U Nu graduated from Rangoon University in 1929. For several years, he taught history, English, and Burmese in the national school system. He joined the colonial civil service in 1934 and eventually enrolled in law at Rangoon University. At the age of thirty-one, U Nu emerged as a leader in the student strike of 1936, together with Aung San and others among an elite, anticolonial group of students, many of whom would eventually assume positions of prominence after independence. Like his peers, Nu adopted the anticolonial title *Thakin* (Master). He became a leader in the prewar nationalist Dobama movement and the postwar Anti-Fascist People's Freedom League (AFPFL). He was a member of the Thirty Comrades during the struggle for independence and played a historic role in the country's transformation from a British colony to an independent nation-state. A political pragmatist and skilled negotiator, U Nu advocated democracy or the "Burmese Buddhist Way to Socialism" as exigencies dictated.

His politics were closely tied to his Buddhist beliefs, and he became increasingly religious in his adult life. Already in his twenties, he took vows to affirm a disciplined lifestyle and abstain from liquor, to be faithful to his spouse, and to observe celibacy. He meditated daily, observed a vegetarian diet, and removed himself from his family's affairs because he felt that the practice of asceticism would strengthen his political acumen. U Nu's charisma was a significant facet of his public persona. On several occasions he withdrew from public life strategically to meditate for extended periods of time because he believed that ascetic practice would affect a favorable resolution of his political challenges. He was convinced that Buddhist practice was a moral prerequisite for public office, and he used his popularity to promote a Buddhist welfare state and Buddhist national culture in Burma. His strong religious convictions encompassed both modernist meditation and cosmological beliefs, and in his 1987 inaugural speech for the Center for Burma Studies at Northern Illinois University, he affirmed the power that local spirit lords (*nat*) exert over worldly matters.

When U Nu became the first prime minister of independent Burma in 1948, following the murder of Aung San, he was aware of the fact that a secular state would offer only a weak paradigm for governing the country. On the advice of Nehru, he promoted a programmatic Buddhist revival (1947–1958) to further nationalism. The revival was intended to secure world peace and progress, ensure the expansion of the state into tribal areas, bring stability, and institute Buddhism as Burma's state religion. He opted to synthesize the popular national fervor with revitalization efforts across the Buddhist world in order to usher in a new millennial age. U Nu commenced a Buddhist revival for which he appointed a committee of prominent lay people, the Buddha Sāsana Council (BSC). The work of the BSC began as early as 1950 and culminated in the Sixth Buddhist Synod, Buddha Sāsana Sangāyana (1954–1956). It was modeled after earlier Buddhist councils, especially King Mindon's Fifth Buddhist Council (1871), and its mission was apparently to continue in perpetuity. He commissioned the construction of a religious complex, Kaba Aye Pagoda, to house the Buddhist texts, and Kaba Aye became the site of important state rituals, including the veneration of the Buddha's Tooth Relic, which had temporarily been conveyed from Sri Lanka to Burma. Such diplomatic exchanges celebrated both the midpoint of the Buddha's dispensation and a modern Buddhist identity among new Asian nations.

As early as the late nineteenth century, meditation had become an increasingly popular practice among lay people.[7] During U Nu's era, however, lay meditation became an exceedingly popular movement, comparable to the *wunthanu* associations that had inspired earlier generations during the nationalist struggle. U Nu persuaded the Mahasi Sayadaw, U Sobhana Mahāthera (1904–1982), to work with the powerful Buddha Sāsana Council to establish a nationwide network of meditation centers. The Mahasi Sayadaw had already earned a reputation as a respected Pāli scholar for his introduction to Buddhaghosa's influential treatise, the *Path of Purification* (*Visuddhimagga atthakatha*).[8] As Ingrid Jordt explains, the new network of meditation centers used the same meditation techniques developed by the Mahasi Sayadaw.[9] Meditation teachers were certified as instructors in the Mahasi method, a form of *vipassanā* (insight) meditation, while meditators themselves received diplomas that attested to their achievement of certain stages of insight in their mastery of the Eightfold Noble Path. As Jordt argues, lay meditation in the Mahasi tradition effectively became a popular mass movement in which many entertained messianic expectations.[10]

The ethos of U Nu's reforms, the *sangāyana,* emphasized mass rituals and cosmology, inspiring popular piety and magnifying the prime minister's charisma. They coincided with an era of prosperity for the new nation that was commonly seen as a karmic consequence of Burma's religious practice.[11] U Nu's charismatic leadership inculcated the new nation with a popular ideology, the "Burmese Buddhist Way to Socialism," which presented the country's modernization and development as gradual steps in the Eightfold Path toward enlightenment. It posited that material plenty should not serve individual greed and indulgence, but instead support the needs of a national community engaged in the practice of the path toward enlightenment. U Nu's reforms contrasted with earlier reforms in that they actively promoted a millennial Buddhist revival, encouraged cultic practices, and promoted new groups within the sangha. A decidedly modern revitalization of Buddhism and Burmese national identity formed the historical legacy of U Nu's era.

In popular Burmese culture, U Nu embodied millennial expectations for many who saw in him a benevolent and righteous Buddhist monarch (*dhammarāja*), a Universal Monarch (*setkya min:*), or even a future buddha whose superior knowledge would help his community reach *nibbāna.* His personal political and religious charisma was so enhanced by this charged context that some expected his leadership of the modern, independent Burmese to be remade into the image of a traditional Buddhist king. U Nu established a Ministry for Religious Affairs that provided the state with a mechanism for regulating religious practice among the laity, monks, and minority religions. His government sponsored monastic reforms, organized large-scale Buddhist rituals, and eventually sought to institute Buddhism as the state religion. Known as the Third Amendment to the constitution, the bill envisioned that an image of the Buddha would be placed in every courthouse, all state schools would promote veneration of the Buddha, and recitation of *suttas* and would compel students to study Buddhist teaching. Although the bill stopped short of requiring holders of political offices to be Buddhist, it created a de facto second-class citizenship for non-Buddhist citizens of the state, which exacerbated existing religious and ethnic divisions.[12] With this proposed amendment, U Nu hoped to consolidate his power by giving in to escalating monastic demands.

However, the efforts by the U Nu government to revitalize Buddhism had taken precedence over effective leadership in modernizing the economy and building infrastructure for the nation.[13] His government deteriorated under economic pressures despite—or, as his critics assert, because of—his religious practice and the state's support for Buddhism. Eventually U Nu was unable to contain the escalating pressures from the sangha, from political factions within his government, and from separatist rebellions fought by ethnic minorities. Maximalist factions within the sangha accelerated the demise of U Nu's government, as did ethnic insurgencies and the military's interventions. Monks demanded that Buddhist instruction in public schools be required and that ethnic minorities be prohibited from offering equivalent religious instruction. The pressures to institute Buddhism as a state religion and withdraw state support for the religious education of the Hindu, Muslim, and Christian communities ultimately undermined what had been a democratic government, one that was now unable to integrate ethnic minorities into the national community. Insurgencies developed in order to preserve the sort of access to secular power that ethnic minorities had enjoyed during the colonial era. They wanted to secure a secular state or, alternatively, to create an independent state of their own. These tensions surrounding Buddhism and its relations to other religious communities among citizens of the modern state opened the door for a secular, military power under Ne Win to take over Burma's government.

A secular military scored a decisive coup in 1962, when U Nu's government disintegrated under pressure from Buddhist factions. Ne Win's coup d'état ended parliamentary democracy and limited the role of Buddhism in the state until the 1980s. As the British had done in 1942, Ne Win imprisoned U Nu from 1962 to 1966. In 1973, U Nu went into exile in Thailand and emigrated later to India. He returned to Burma in 1980, when he was pardoned and asked to oversee a new edition of the Pāli canon commissioned by the Sangha Mahanayaka Council. In the aftermath of the popular uprising and the collapse of Ne Win's regime in 1988, U Nu established an interim government in a futile effort to regain political office. The regime that succeeded Ne Win, the State Law and Order Restoration Council (SLORC) again placed U Nu under house arrest from 1989 until 1992. He passed away on February 14, 1995.

Socialist Fundamentalism under Ne Win's Government

Fundamentalism is a religious response to the presence of secularism and pluralism in the modern state that promises a return to a pristine doctrine and a utopian future.[14] Toward the end of the socialist period in Burma, the secular state initiated fundamentalist Buddhist reforms in order to contain millennial or messianic Buddhist groups that could potentially undermine the power of the state. Scripturalism was invoked to sanction the state's moral authority and foster a politically disengaged, yet pious Buddhist community and a centralized sangha. That vision of moral authority empowered the secular state to carry out these reforms as a modern interpretation of the traditional responsibilities of a *dhammarāja.*[15] The fundamentalist rhetoric of the reforms popularized a pious lay ethic and presented yet another iteration of Burma as a Buddhist nation to the international world. The state's rhetoric emphasized the need to demonstrate to foreigners, particularly those from the west, a pure Buddhist nation, comprised of disciplined monks and pious lay people.

Initially, Ne Win's military regime (1962–1988) organized social and professional groups into socialist workers' collectives. The early infrastructural reforms of the Socialist Union of Burma focused on economic, social, educational, and political arenas. Although the Ne Win government was structured like the Soviet state, religion remained a vibrant part of public practice and discourse, and the attempt to institute monastic registration in 1974 failed at first. The government began to restructure the sangha in a fashion analogous to workers' collectives in the early 1980s.[16] The reform aimed to contain the activities of several charismatic leaders and communities that cultivated ties to illicit economic enterprises at the margins of, and in opposition to, the socialist state. The Ne Win reforms extended government control over internal monastic affairs to a far greater degree than the reforms implemented during the U Nu period. The state gradually abandoned its secular ideology and began a comprehensive effort to fashion a civic religion that was to combine a scripturalist, nonpolitical sangha with the traditionalist popular piety of a socialist Burmese workforce.

The Ministry of Religious Affairs convened a council of monastic dignitaries, the Sangha Mahanayaka, glossed in English publications as the Convocation of the Sangha of All Orders for the Purification, Propagation, and Perpetuation of the Buddhist Dispensation at Kaba Aye in Rangoon.[17] Most members of this council were less distinguished than the monks assembled during U Nu's *sangāyana*. For instance, the Mingun Sayadaw, who had presided over U Nu's reforms, remained distant from the Sangha Mahanayaka Council. The state, meanwhile, determined the Council's agenda and did not tolerate dissent in formulating its policies.

The Council oversaw comprehensive reform efforts at the request of and in close collaboration with the Ministry of Home and Religious Affairs in order to bring Buddhist institutions under the control of the state.[18] Its purpose was to forge greater uniformity among monastic lineages in matters of doctrine and to restrict official recognition to nine *nikāya* only.[19] Its goals were to centralize the administration of monastic institutions in the hands of the state, renew monastic registration, control monastic property, and determine the succession of abbots in monasteries. Registration of all monks was intended to document proper ordination and membership in one of the accepted lineages. The reluctance to comply was reflected in low 1984/5 census figures of approximately 300,000 registered monks.[20] The council also revised the monastic curriculum and examinations and put in place administrative structures to oversee the training of abbots. In keeping with the importance of textual orthodoxy in the Theravada tradition, the council was also charged with producing a new English rendition of the canon.[21] To enhance popular support for the reforms, the government invited U Nu to return from exile and lead a project to publish a new edition of canonical texts. The state employed monks in development and education projects among predominantly animist or Christian tribal minorities, who increasingly reported incidents of forced conversion at the nation's periphery. The achievements of the Sangha Mahanayaka were celebrated each full moon day with lavish rituals at Kaba Aye, at which the government conferred honorary titles on the Council's dignitaries. These titular awards were augmented by large donations to the sangha from the state's workers' associations. In addition, the government provided generously for the daily needs of the monastic leadership it had assembled in the Sangha Mahanayaka Council.

The state prosecuted the preaching of alleged false doctrines (*adhamma*) and wrongful monastic conduct,[22] *vinaya* infractions, and disputes over monastic property in an ecclesiastic court system the state had established. The appointment of monks to these courts was made in collaboration with the Ministry of Religious Affairs. The *vinaya* courts cooperated with civil judiciary branches that investigated concurrent infractions of civil or criminal law by monks, who were often disrobed as a result of these proceedings. The organization of the clerical hierarchy mirrored the state's administration in the political and economic domains and linked the central executive branch at Kaba Aye in Rangoon to village tracts throughout the country.[23] Structuring monastic institutions in parallel with the political administration extended the state's reach. Local representatives and a shadow structure of lay assistants mediated the Council's involvement in local monastic affairs, enabling the state to monitor donations that individual monks received from their lay supporters. This arrangement was intended to ensure that donations by affluent lay people in the free-market sector would flow only to selected monks, who worked under the patronage of the state. In a wave of excommunications, the Council disrobed about eighty popular monks, who were charged with *vinaya* transgressions and with refusals to repent. As rumors began to circulate about the Council's harsh treatment of these monks, many Burmese speculated that the state's goal was to consolidate its control over all aspects of society. The collectivization of the sangha appeared to be a logical step in an ongoing socialist restructuring of Burmese society.

The Ne Win reforms advocated a new social ethic that was at once authoritarian, totalizing, and utopian in character. The reform publicized Buddhist social values like generosity and compassion as part of its vision for a socialist society in which the state represented workers' collectives and acted as a catalyst in traditional merit-making activities. It promoted a scripturalist reading of Buddhist teachings and encouraged Burmese Buddhists to contribute to communal merit-making ceremonies. Through its patronage of lay meditation, the state sought to capitalize on the increased status and involvement of the laity, especially civil servants and professionals. At the same time, the government derided the materialistic values of the west and promised spiritual rewards in the absence of economic development.

Millennial forms of Theravada Buddhism often employ salient symbols and harbor a latent potential for political change. During the U Nu era, millennial forms ranged from expectations about the imminent appearance of a universal emperor, or *cakkavatti,* to modernist meditation groups among the sangha and laity, but during the Ne Win era, these millennial Buddhist groups explicitly manifested an apolitical, soteriological orientation.[24] The new policies in the 1980s discouraged lay support for certain charismatic monks like the influential U Parama, then abbot of the Mt. Poppa monastery. This enterprising abbot of the monastery at Mt. Poppa accumulated generous support from politically influential donors and was consequently targeted in the purge and forced to disrobe. The state's intent was to control not only the intellectual domain of the sangha, but perhaps more importantly, the sangha's revenue. It also wanted to curb the millennial potential and networks of powerful donors who supported charismatic monks like U Parama.[25] In cities like Mandalay, the regime sought to disperse popular support for monks who might cultivate political potentials among their lay supporters. One group targeted in the reforms was the powerful, modernist Yahan Pyo organization, which had been active in the anticolonial struggle during the 1930s.[26]

Initially, many Burmese were inspired by the state's attention to renewed public morality and supported the government's efforts. Some even expressed their hope that the religious reform was the culminating, transformative achievement of Ne Win's political career. However, Ne Win's personal qualities and the lackluster reputations of members of the Sangha Mahanayaka Council did not inspire the kind of charisma that U Nu had engendered among his fellow citizens. The Council's state-sponsored merit-making rituals similarly showed a somber, mechanical quality in their performance. Popular discontent with the Council's activities was soon widely rumored. In order to appeal to traditional forms of religious practice, the state sponsored large-scale merit-making rituals in conjunction with the construction of Ne Win's *stūpa,* Mahāwizaya Pagoda in Rangoon. This monumental pagoda was intended as a testament to his religious devotion and as a source of merit for the public. Although many Burmese express considerable cynicism about Ne Win's work of merit, it is the site of many official merit-making rituals. A ritual cycle accompanied the construction that began in the 1980s and culminated in the installation of a diamond-studded spire.

It is difficult to gauge what end point had been envisioned for Ne Win's reform, because history overtook the reform agenda when the country's economy and infrastructure collapsed in 1988. Millions of Burmese citizens took to the street to protest Ne Win's government and its policies, which brought about his unexpected resignation as head of state. However, he remained influential for many years in subsequent military regimes. While the precise number of people killed, imprisoned, or displaced in the aftermath of the 1988 uprising is not known, most Burmese families were affected by these tumultuous changes in some manner. Chapter 6 will examine the ways in which the sangha facilitated a nationwide underground network of resistance during the 1988 uprising.

After 1988: State Buddhism as a Total Social Fact

After the 1988 uprising and the collapse of the Socialist Union of Burma, the military junta that followed Ne Win resumed efforts to control Buddhist institutions and legitimize an unpopular military regime. The State Law and Order Restoration Council (SLORC), which transformed into the State Peace and Development Council (SPDC) in 1997, continued to "purify, protect, and propagate" Buddhism in Burma, advocating a scripturalist understanding of the *dhamma* in a devout nation. While Burma has experienced various formulations of Buddhist nationalism since independence, SLORC began to promote a far more totalizing vision of Burmese Buddhist nationalism as a cultural and political ideology designed to legitimate the military's rule.[27] The regime's discourse combined traditional state-sangha relations with a nationalist ideology in which the military elite was the primary religious agent.[28]

This nationalist construction involved familiar Buddhist strategies that harkened back to an idealized, glorified past under powerful Burmese kings. The state sponsored the consecration of sacred places and stūpas that located the Buddha's presence within the Burmese nation and its history. In the absence of a national constitution since 1990 to define the power of the state, the military regime's patronage of Buddhism provided an alternate source of legitimation and transformed a national community into a ritual network to ensure stability and future prosperity. Buddhist practices and institutions were co-opted to enhance the moral authority of a military regime that promised future prosperity for the Burmese nation. With these efforts to reform institutions and to mobilize communities, the regime affirmed a new cosmology of the modern Buddhist state that commanded authority in ways similar to the precolonial kingdoms.[29] This totalizing ideology dismissed the relevance of any competing secular and political discourse about democracy and human rights. Burmese critics of this period of Buddhist nationalism have described it as "internal colonization"; they envision instead a "just society" where individuals are spiritually empowered through meditation and where access to wealth, power, and education is equitable.[30]

Working closely with the Sangha Mahanayaka Council, the Ministry of Religious Affairs has enforced the state's hegemony over the sangha, the laity, and non-Buddhist minorities. Through local appointments of lay councils, the Ministry of Religious Affairs has closely monitored the activities of monks and their lay supporters. The Sangha Mahanayaka Council was reconvened in Rangoon to promote a fundamentalist vision of *thathana* and places strict controls on the monastic education and training delivered in newly established monastic universities. The Council has also intensified its missionary activities among ethnic minorities living at the nation's periphery. The regime began to restore royal palaces and ancient pagodas, and various state agencies began to sponsor merit-making rituals on a massive scale. Efforts were also made to involve the Burmese transnational and international communities in the ritual networks of an economy of merit. What is important here is that the Buddhist reforms after 1988 were anchored in mutually reinforcing initiatives by the Ministry of Religious Affairs. On the one hand, they aimed to silence monastic dissent and re-educate the sangha in the service of the state; on the other hand, they popularized a national cult of relics and mobilized ritual networks among the citizenry to finance these activities.[31]

SILENCING DISSENT

The sangha had played a pivotal role in organizing the 1988 popular uprising. As chapter 6 will make clear, the sangha offered an underground sanctuary for those fleeing military intelligence forces, the police, and the army. It spontaneously transformed its institutional infrastructure to facilitate antigovernment rallies and to protect the largely unarmed protestors who resisted the government in mass demonstrations and through other forms of civil disobedience. The sangha even declared some districts in Lower Burma as "liberated" and administered by monastic courts.

After the 1988 uprising was quashed, the sangha suffered severe retribution from SLORC. The monastic purge recommenced immediately and with great force. Hundreds of monks, including elderly ones, were arrested and imprisoned for extended periods of time. An unknown number died in prison.[32] Public sermons construed to be critical of the regime in any way engendered serious retaliation. Armed guards were staged outside major monasteries in Rangoon, Mandalay, and other cities to restrict the movements of monks. The Ministry of Religious Affairs imposed tight regulations on the sangha through a hierarchy of *vinaya* courts and regional administrations that extended from the center to the local level.[33] It also implemented extensive educational reforms for monks and opened new training centers for monks entering administrative careers. Lay guardians were assigned to individual monks to monitor and intervene in their day-to-day activities, such as personal finances, travel, and relations with lay donors. State-appointed lay committees oversee donations to monks and monasteries from nongovernment donors, and the regime rewards senior monks who support its vision. The regime has used various efforts to silence and restrain junior monks who may sympathize with the pro-democracy movement, and they hold senior monks accountable for the actions of their juniors.

Missionary efforts (*thathana pyu thi*) among the national and international Buddhist community constituted an extension of SLORC's control over Buddhist institutions and practices. Most government bodies sponsored their own lay meditation and recitation societies and held temporary ordinations for their staff. Various ministries formed lay associations in collaboration with the Ministry of Religious Affairs and its Department for the Propagation and Promotion of Thathana that were dedicated to Buddhist instruction and reciting prayers and *suttas*. Teachers at all educational levels were encouraged to attend re-education courses. Civil servants and other employees of the state had to enroll in Buddhist culture courses at prominent lay meditation centers. Various lay associations of government workers were mobilized to collect donations through grassroots networks in order to finance the activities of the regime's Buddhist reforms, including the construction of Buddhist monuments, the restoration of stūpas and royal palace grounds, and other large-scale, public merit-making rituals. The amounts given by each group were announced in the media, especially the state's daily newspapers. In a manner that simultaneously evoked the precolonial social order and socialist worker collectives, professional organizations contributed donations to the sangha and shared in the merit the state's leadership had engendered on their behalf. In return, their contributions to state rituals earned them karmic rewards in the future and access to networks of political power and social indebtedness at local, regional, and national levels. This strategy increased the power of the state and limited the role of individual donors within the ritual economy of merit. It validated the military for providing the population with opportunities to make merit and undermined the moral legitimacy of those voices that were critical of the state's policies.[34]

MOBILIZING THE NATION

Veneration of the Buddha's relics and images figures prominently in cosmological Theravada Buddhism,[35] because it localizes his ritual presence within the specific community and generates religious merit, social prestige, and power for those who sponsor the occasion. The military regime's cult of relics combined Buddhist meaning with cultural nationalism and appealed to classic Buddhist notions of political power; it allowed contemporary military leaders to act as heirs to the glorious past merit of Burmese kings. The processes by which this was accomplished employed totalizing constructs of a Buddhist nationalism in the service of the modern nation-state. Like its predecessors, the SLORC and SPDC created ritual communities of an imagined modern nation-state and mobilized these networks of donors at local, regional, and national levels.[36] By creating a national cult of relics (*rūpakāya*) and sacred sites, the military has provided access to merit for the entire nation. National print and television media continually feature ministers and military leaders who, on behalf of the workers' collectives and good citizens of Myanmar, perform merit-making rituals in public contexts. Individuals contributing to and participating in such rituals affirm their place within a social and ritual hierarchy in which power relations are continually negotiated. A military general or politician who officiates in a ritual role that is carried out by a Burmese lay patron, becomes an "owner of merit" (*kuthou shin*) to whom all other contributors owe gratitude for the opportunity to make merit.[37] High-profile politicians officiate at rituals in which lavish donations are given to monks who are frequently also members of the Sangha Mahanayaka Council.[38] The merit made is seen as ensuring future prosperity and leading to transcendence of *samsāra* and the attainment of *nibbāna* in time.[39] Large segments of the population are encouraged to participate in these elaborate state merit-making rituals that evoke traditional Burmese court culture in an attempt to place contemporary celebrations into a lineage that descends from the ancient Buddhist state.[40] These mass rituals also link the periphery to the center and various social classes to the elite who epitomize the state's power. The merit derived from these state rituals accrue to the officials of the modern military state and civil elites employ these traditional patterns of patronage to consolidate pragmatic and profit-oriented class interests. The significance of these ritual patterns emerged in the context of concurrent political agendas, lending credence to the state's rhetoric of "stability, peace, and tranquility" as a prerequisite for successful modernization. The rituals projected to citizens and outside observers a Buddhist vision in which the state, sangha, and laity speak in a single voice, emphasizing righteousness and morality (*sīla*). This strategy of engaging the public in a transcendent discourse has insulated the regime from accountability to its citizens and shifted attention away from crises facing the state.

For several years during the 1990s, the state enjoined millions of its citizens to participate in a series of elaborate rituals to venerate the Chinese Tooth Relic.[41] The high points of this complex cultural diplomacy with China unfolded over six weeks in 1994, when the relic traveled in an extended procession through the nation's central regions from Rangoon to Mandalay and back to the capital. At each stop in its journey, various social groups and professional organizations prepared grand celebrations, while the national news media published donor names and amounts donated. Replicas of the relic were enshrined in pagodas built for this purpose in Yangon and Mandalay. This ritual journey was a celebrated media event and presented as part of a long-standing cultural and religious legacy that had been realized under the patronage of the state.

By 1996 replicas of the Ananda Temple in Pagan were completed in Yangon and Mandalay to enshrine the copies made of the Tooth Relic from China. Yet neither of these pagodas is frequented by many worshippers.

These ritual patterns embody a politics of giving and thereby producing obligation. They engendered massive donation drives, creating patterns of patronage in which ritual clients incurred obligations toward the center. Membership in select groups of donors also indicated access to economic and political elites. Despite a public ethos of generosity for the sake of generalized merit, the perception endured that contributions in kind and cash would bring pragmatic returns, political access, and membership in a ritual community under SLORC's auspices. While such membership entitled one to privileges, it also entailed ongoing obligations to the patronage of a political elite; there was social pressure to deliver on promised allegiance in support of prevailing power structures. The public portrayals of generosity (*dāna*) and loving kindness (*metta*) also hinted at implicit competition among donors for political recognition.

From the context of these state-sponsored rituals emerged not only nationalist visions for a modern Burmese nation-state, but also pragmatic agendas and economic objectives. The rituals mobilized mass donations for religious constructions, but also for Buddhist social welfare programs, such as hospitals, residences for the elderly, and a range of other projects in contemporary Myanmar. It was part of a broader pattern in which the state financed religious causes, social welfare, and the construction and restoration of national monuments through private contributions. Donation networks transcended the national community to include foreign dignitaries and even anonymous tourists. Buddhist-motivated fundraising was projected into transnational realms and communicated, at a symbolic level, the extent of SLORC's religious patronage over national and international communities.

However, the state's authority did not depend on symbols of Buddhist just rule alone. The regime's Buddhist ideology intersected with western ideologies by emphasizing functional rationality, stability, and economic prosperity, not merely as an outcome of Buddhist merit-making, but also as a result of the bureaucratic efficiency of a modern state. Despite this rhetoric of modernity and despite economic liberalization during the 1990s, the regime's totalizing involvement in public life in fact preempted the development of social pluralism and a modern civil society.[42] For nearly two decades after 1990, the state enacted policies that were not safeguarded by the principles of a national constitution or through a legislative process that would guarantee the rights of the nation's citizens. In the absence of such constitutional guarantees, the military regimes of SLORC and now SPDC have governed the nation by decree. In place of constitutional legitimation, they championed a rationalized vision of Buddhist nationalism to promote its popular image on cultural, political, and ideological grounds.

While at the nation's center, Buddhist missionary efforts are described as an attempt to achieve national integration and ethnic nationalism, at the periphery missionizing is perceived as an attempt to extend the central government's control and infrastructure into the territories of ethnic minorities. The state is engaged in far-reaching efforts to transform "otherness," particularly among non-Buddhist tribal minorities. In those locales representatives of the sangha have established missionary schools and built stūpas. Incidents of forced conversion have been reported by Christian tribal minorities and among Muslims in Arakan. The Ministry of Religious Affairs has also put into place parallel administrative mechanisms that create formal organizations regulating the religious activities of Christians, Muslims, and Hindus, many of whom intersect socially with the Burman ethnic majority. The regime has largely silenced, within its national boundaries, voices that speak for alternate visions of Buddhism, political power, and moral legitimation. As the state controls the social discourse about ritual and hegemonic constructs that it envisions for the nation, alternate voices must be gleaned from silence, from absence in ritual participation, and from the countertexts in the expatriate media and communities beyond Myanmar's national boundaries.

The internationalization of the regime's vision was facilitated by extensive media coverage of rituals and donation drives. To the extent that such celebrations involved diplomatic links with representatives from other Asian nations, they had become pragmatic tools in the conduct of everyday politics. Foreign dignitaries and businesspeople were explicitly asked to donate foreign currency to social and religious causes. Visits by prominent dignitaries and members of the Burmese diaspora were frequently featured in the media visiting monuments of religious and national significance.

THE STATE OF BUDDHIST CULTURE AFTER MYANMARIZATION

The decade of the 1990s was marked by a public interest in Buddhism and the glorification of Myanmar's national history. Myanmarization, the cultural agenda of the state during this period, represented a neotraditional ideology affirming a Buddhist national past. The government collected donations for extensive renovations of all major religious monuments and royal palaces (*aun myei*). The Department of Archaeology, begun as a colonial invention, was now charged with the excavation and renovation of sites declared to be

The restored Ananda Temple in Pagan. PHOTO BY STEFANIE WOODWARD.

ancient palace grounds. The Ministry of Religious Affairs worked closely with the Ministry of Culture to promote a national cult of venerating religious and historical sites. State support of national treasures focused especially on restoring the spire (*hti*) on Shwedagon Pagoda, completing Ne Win's Mahāwizaya Pagoda, and constructing the two new pagodas to house the replicas of the

Tooth Relic in Yangon and in Mandalay. A sprawling new museum was built in Pagan to highlight a cultural genealogy between the present government and the ancient Pagan empire.[43]

To accomplish these projects the government mobilized people, collected tribute payments, and imposed taxes. It also created economic networks through joint ventures that were sanctioned and celebrated by large-scale, state-sponsored merit-making rituals. A brief inventory of Buddhist and national institutions will show the range of public efforts undertaken as well as some signs of decline that have come into view since then. For instance, the compound of the Sangha Mahanayaka Council near Kaba Aye was built in the early 1980s. It continues to serve as the dwelling of the Council's forty-seven resident monks, but it is considerably less splendid in appearance. Similarly, the Mahasi Mediation Center, which enjoyed a great deal of public and government support after the U Nu era, has undergone a similar decline since the passing of its founding abbot in 1982. It is now administered by a committee of senior, uncharismatic monks.[44]

In 1998 the state inaugurated another project, the International Theravada Buddhist Missionary University (ITBMU), to provide a theological curriculum and institutional setting for training foreign Buddhists in the Theravada traditions of Burma.[45] Its annual magazine features full-page color photographs of Senior General Than Shwe, head of Myanmar's ruling military junta, and his generals. It also describes an academic institution with degree-granting programs at the graduate and undergraduate levels. Monastic dignitaries are featured to a lesser extent. In 2004–2005, more than 200 students were enrolled, about half of whom were from foreign countries. Several Chinese students were attending as part of a goodwill mission, while only a few westerners were enrolled in pursuit of a personal and spiritual quest.

Institutions of national culture, highly politicized during the nineties, convey a similarly muted image in the post-Myanmarization period. The Ministry of Culture, the National Museum in Yangon, its sister institutions in Mandalay and Pagan, and the Department of Archaeology were thoroughly politicized during the 1990s as the curators of Myanmar's national Buddhist culture. The Department of Archaeology had been established by the British in 1902, and eventually Taw Sein Ko became its director. The department ceased operations during World War II but was reestablished in 1946.[46] During the 1990s the National Museum underwent renovations, including new exhibit designs, and its cultural functions figured importantly in debates among Burmese intellectuals who questioned how the museum should represent Burmese national culture, but the complex soon receded into a hollow and deserted tomb. In the summer of 2006, it was musty and dusty and received fewer than ten visitors on most days, according to the registration book at the entrance. Only foreigners who frequented the museum were required to show their passports. Police guarded the entrance, joking with their friends and relaxing in the mid-day sun. The main exhibit focused on the history and evolution of Burmese script. A second large exhibit was dedicated to the history of Burmese royal culture. It featured replicas of royal thrones and regalia, models of courts at former capitals, the Lion Throne, paintings, and exhibits about ethnic groups and ethnomusicology. The top floor held a large exhibit on the country's national races. Around the perimeter stood several dozen mannequins of women and men dressed in locally woven cloth and styles to indicate their tribal and ethnic identities, although not much beyond ethnic dress was conveyed of their culture. A couple dressed in traditional Myanmar attire was displayed in an alcove apart from the remainder of ethnic mannequins. They were intended to stand at the center of the exhibit, but for whatever reason had been slightly removed from the long lines of "ethnic" mannequins.

In contrast to the museums in Yangon and Mandalay, the Bagan Museum attracted both foreign tourists and a considerable number of Burmese visitors, including school groups.[47] This imposing building is crowned by a spire constructed in the style of nineteenth-century palace architecture. The museum's interior ceiling repeats a royal Mandalay design in different materials, such as inlaid wood, gold paint, and *kalaga* embroidery.[48] The large, extensive exhibition halls displayed maps and models of alleged former palaces and thrones. One display contained scenes depicting the rural ways of life of past Burmese culture. Eight- or nine-foot bronze figures depicted the "original" inhabitants, seated within a recreated setting of the "ancient village" of Pagan. The atrium contained several remarkable Buddha images in stone and bronze, displays of mudras, stellae, and inscribed stone plates.

Despite these state-sponsored initiatives to promote a carefully circumscribed vision of Buddhist piety and the state support for it, many Burmese expressed cynicism about the regime's patronage of Buddhist causes. Others were reticent to become involved in Buddhist activities that they considered inherently political and stated that they focused instead on improving their standard of living in the new economy. To them this took precedence over participating in Buddhist activities and rituals that entail demonstration of overt political allegiances, such as, for instance, the 88 Generation Prayer Campaign.[49] The regime's sponsorship of mass rituals had begun to decrease at the time of my visit in 2006, which seems to signal a decline in the state's political imperative to mobilize the population through religious networks. At the same time, the state's ability to manage religious expression in any community was firmly established. New patterns of consumption, such as television and other luxuries, were now competing with the social and popular entertainment Buddhist practices have traditionally provided.

The Buddhist Hegemony of the Modern State

Burma's colonial experience created a deep-seated distrust of the secular power that it inaugurated. After independence, this generalized distrust of secular institutions undermined an emergent civil culture and simultaneously strengthened traditional domains of power, especially Buddhist institutions and military control. A weak tradition of secular politics has empowered the legacies of militarism and Buddhist institutions in Myanmar. To this day, secular modernity in Myanmar continues to be contested in various ways. The previous sections illustrated how modern political ideologies like democracy and socialism influenced modern Buddhist formations. The state's involvement in ritual communities and donation networks ensured a continuing Buddhist authority in the public domain. In the second half of the twentieth century, politicians championed these religio-political continuities as defining characteristics of the Burmese nation and thus harnessed greater influence in political parties, secular institutions, and civil society. In many contexts, therefore, cultural conceptions of power remained tied to popular notions of an individual leader's karma and charisma.

Burma's national leaders were and still are sensitive to the possibility that secularism might compromise their political potential. At certain junctures in their political careers and regardless of their ideological differences, U Nu, Ne Win, and Than Shwe have all perpetuated mythic claims of descent from Buddhist royalty. Such rumors usually originated amongst their inner circles and eventually came to be repeated in the media. Such claims are relevant to our present concerns only insofar as they give voice to a cultural plausibility within the public discourse. Each of these politicians claimed a legacy of state support for Buddhist causes in order to lend credence to their allusions to royalty. The state's sponsorship of modern Buddhist practices thus inevitably implied a move toward the reification of political power in absolutist or totalizing terms.

State rituals, donation networks, the restoration of Buddhist icons and stūpas, and finally the reconstruction of palaces all served to re-enchant a religious geography of the Burmese state that was anchored firmly in traditional cosmology. During U Nu's era, the cave temple and stūpas at Kaba Aye were constructed. Ne Win is credited with the Mahāwizaya Pagoda in Yangon, and over the past two decades the state has been engaged in massive renovations and construction of religionational sites. In Yangon, a new golden spire encrusted with rubies, sapphires, and diamonds has been enshrined atop of Shwedagon

A photo, taken in 2006, of a photograph displayed at the Shwedagon Museum, showing the renovated spire of Shwedagon Pagoda against the background of Yangon's modern skyline. PHOTO BY STEFANIE WOODWARD.

Pagoda. The renovation was commemorated with rituals, publications, and a new museum for visitors on the platform.

All significant monuments at Pagan have undergone a standardized reconstruction in an artistic style less concerned with historical authenticity and preservation than with the cultural imagination of SLORC/SPDC functionaries. The archaeological museum at Pagan built during the 1990s reflects a baroque grandeur of an imagined past. In Mandalay, a new museum complex was constructed on the grounds of the important pilgrimage site of the Mahamuni Pagoda. The two-story atrium exhibits illustrations of the life of the Buddha that merge into displays of art styles characteristic of specific Burmese historic periods. A visit to the museum culminates with a huge, three-dimensional display of the Buddha's descent upon the bejeweled staircase from Tāvatimsa Heaven, where he had preached the abhidhamma pitaka to his mother. Resplendent in his glory and accompanied by gods and enlightened disciples, the Buddha descends upon Mandalay, located at the center of an enormous geographical relief map of Asia. Also indicated on this map with gilded model stūpas are other significant sites in the history of the tradition, like those the Buddha visited during his lifetime and popular pilgrimage places throughout the Theravada world of Southeast Asia.

A recent example of the cosmology of the modern state is also found in the 2005 move of the nation's capital from Yangon to Naypyidaw, a name that translates as the Abode of Royal or Divine Beings. In a move reminiscent of King Thalon's retreat from the southern coast in 1635 to relocate his polity inland and away from contact with western foreigners, the new capital is isolated and primarily serves the regime's interest in perpetuating its control and power. Many speculations surround the relative isolation of the new administrative center that restricts access to visitors. It concentrates power in one location and protects access to government facilities in the event of another popular uprising. At the same time, its central location within the nation's territory facilitates easy access to various border regions, should the war with ethnic minorities escalate. Three huge statues of Burmese kings tower over the plaza where military parades are performed to celebrate national unity.

The Buddhist state in modern Myanmar has been progressively transformed from U Nu's populist revitalization, through purges of charismatic monks under Ne Win, until it has finally arrived at the SPDC's control over Buddhist nationalism. The state's sponsorship of Buddhist practices, institutions, and communities has engendered a totalizing vision of Burmese Buddhist nationalism that is embodied by a modern nation whose righteous actions have constructed a prosperous present arising from a seamless past.[50] While overpowering and overwhelming to many, the regime's moralizing vision of authority encounters support, scorn, and contestation among its citizens. These Buddhist modernities are at once polarized and co-opted by salient mechanisms of political legitimation in Burma. Buddhist actors and institutions have played both deliberate and unwitting roles in collusion with the prevailing political interests. The religious domain is a public arena in which political contestation, however veiled, can be articulated, and social pluralism, education, and citizenship continue to be informed by Buddhist values in Burmese culture. In chapter 6 the discussion explores the ways in which modern Buddhist conjunctures empowered political protest and resistance, giving voice to divergent interpretations of Buddhist modernity in contemporary Burma and to competing visions of modern Buddhism and its discourse about civil society.

6 Buddhist Resistance against the State

In *The Nation and Its Fragments,* Partha Chatterjee observes that the discourse of nationalism encompasses material and spiritual concerns that map onto a dichotomy of outer and inner spaces, respectively.[1] Similar conceptions have been expressed in Burmese resistance movements. Nationalists as well as later protest movements have rallied around Buddhist ideals to express their opposition to the state. This chapter looks at the ways in which Buddhist identities have helped mobilize resistance against the colonial government and against military regimes throughout the twentieth century. A common theme among those who resist the power of the state is the moral judgment they make concerning social and political contexts. They have mobilized communities to change political contexts both through nonviolent activism and by force. Others have believed their moral authority derived from spiritual achievements in meditation, which would help address the needs of the developing nation.

During the early twentieth century, themes in the nationalist discourse included the presence of foreigners in Burma, colonial rule, education, and a popular desire for spiritual renewal among Buddhist communities. The convergence of these popular concerns galvanized Buddhists in their resistance to political governments and caused them to voice their public opposition. The turbulent history of the nationalist struggle during the 1920s and 1930s was marked by the rise and subsequent fragmentation of Buddhist nationalist organizations like the YMBA, which entertained modern, reformed visions of Buddhist practice, and grassroots (*wunthanu*) groups in cities and towns. Alicia Turner describes this social process as *thathana pyu thi,* a populist movement in search of spiritual and social renewal within a Buddhist framework.[2] In the

1920s, Buddhist resistance to colonial rule took a drastic turn when the monastic General Council of the Sangha Sammeggi (GCSS) came to dominate the nationalist movement. The GCSS harbored strong antiforeign sentiments and appealed especially to rural supporters and others who competed with Indian laborers for economic survival. The GCSS represented sentiments that Bruce Lincoln calls "maximalist," which sought to reconfigure the state in religious terms.[3]

Half a century later, in the aftermath of the 1988 uprising, similar issues of national identity, economic deprivation, state coercion, access to education, and foreign influence again emerged as significant themes in the public discourse of the nation. Modern Buddhist communities, including monks and students in the pro-democracy movement, articulate critiques of contemporary politics from ethical perspectives. For many Burmese, Buddhist nationalism and a sangha supported by the SLORC, the regime that was then in power, did not constitute a valid field of merit. As the state forced the pro-democratic movement increasingly out of the public sphere, meditation centers became a refuge for opponents of the regime. Such private spaces fostered spiritual renewal and the articulation of a social and political ethic that offered a moral alternative to the regime's Buddhist nationalism. Organizations like the All Burma Young Monks or the 88 Generation saw themselves as continuing the historical legacy of earlier anticolonial resistance movements. Their comparisons of the post-1988 military regimes with colonial exploitation showed widespread distrust of the state's authority. It underscored a common perception that the Burmese national spirit continued its defiance of social injustice and exploitation.

The Radicalization of Anticolonial Buddhists

Familiar concerns provided the impetus behind anticolonial Buddhist movements of the 1920s and early 1930s: national identity, government coercion, the cultural location of foreigners, and education. The foundations for popular resistance had already been laid during the previous decade when patriotic grassroots organizations like the YMBA, the nationalist-revivalist *wunthanu athin*, professional trade associations like *sipwaye athin*, and the women's *konmayi athin* sprang up in townships and villages throughout the country.[4] According to U Maung Maung, they rallied around slogans like "Home Rule or Boycott" to voice their opposition to the Craddock Scheme, which envisioned granting less self-determination to the Burmese colony than to the colonial government envsioned for India.[5] Many of these protest organizations were inspired by U Ottama, a modern monk and nationalist who preached to his audiences to follow Gandhian methods of nonviolence and civil resistance (*satyagraha*). Like Gandhi, he advocated civil disobedience against colonial rule and using only local products, such as homespun cotton.[6]

Much of the popular discourse on these modern themes was articulated in Buddhist terms. Several reasons account for this. Colonial rule prohibited Burmese to meet in groups and permitted only religious gatherings in public. This policy, along with the British neglect of the responsibilities of Buddhist kingship, made the religious domain an obvious refuge for nationalist voices. In addition, a Buddhist worldview continued to be integral to the Burmese cultural and political imagination. The advocacy of Buddhist practices as embodying the nationalist spirit, expressed in statements such as "We Burmese are Buddhists," and as forms of resistance to secular colonial rule provided a salient motivation for mobilizing popular support.

In chapter 4, we focused on the ways the YMBA capitalized on its popularity during the 1910s, when this organization underwent rapid growth and shaped the national discourse. Its membership increased from 220 to 400 local chapters and included more than thirty national schools, ten newspapers, and three journals.[7] The rapid growth but fragmented leadership precipitated reorganization at the eighth national conference, which was held in Prome on October 29–31, 1920. At this conference the YMBA officially merged with the General Council of Burmese Associations (GCBA), an umbrella organization that also included village-level nationalist organizations (*wunthanu athin*) and the National Schools Movement.

Initially, the GCBA was composed of modern Buddhists and secularists who had a shared interest in promoting Burma's nationalist struggle. Some factions within the GCBA encouraged its local chapters that promoted nationalist sentiments (*wunthanu athin*) in villages to boycott colonial taxation. Its demands included a boycott of foreign consumer items, tax exemption for religious land, and extending the authority of the *thathanabain*'s office in Mandalay to include all of Lower Burma. The educated urban lay elites tended to support those members of the GCBA who identified with the sort of secular, nationalist struggle advocated by the Indian Congress Party. From 1921 to 1923, the GCBA worked with the Council on National Education to establish a national university at a Shwegyin monastery in Rangoon. Others, with rural constituencies that were less educated in the canons of colonial knowledge envisioned that a postcolonial Burma would return to Buddhist kingship.

The Ninth Conference, held in Mandalay in 1921, was attended by a record number, 10,000 delegates and more than 100,000 visitors from all regions of the country. U Chit Hlaing made significant concessions at this conference to GCSS monks in order to preserve the GCBA and his position as president, offering them influential positions on the central committee of the GCBA. This move eroded the power of the GCBA and deferred control over its affairs to the monastic General Council of Sangha Sammeggi (GCSS), which had usurped the leadership of the GCBA by 1924.[8]

The GCSS also gained control over the electoral strategies of political candidates in the GCBA. Many GCBA candidates seeking election collaborated with local monks, who would preach their message in public sermons. At critical junctures the election of these politicians to GCBA offices depended in national and local polls on the support of their monastic allies, many of whom were members of the GCSS. This conjuncture proved to be pivotal as much of the electoral process depended on Buddhist sources of legitimacy. The limits of the electoral process as a modern form of government were already circumscribed by Buddhist authority among organizations that led the anticolonial struggle. The influence of the sangha in the organization expanded to become its dominant voice and took over the GCBA altogether. As a result, the political strategies and religious motivations of the anticolonial movement changed as the influence of moderate Buddhists and secularists lost out to maximalists in the monastic GCSS.

Within a few years, splits occurred in the volatile GCBA, including the Hlaing Pu Kyaw faction (1924), the 21 Party (1922), the Nationalist Party (1923), the Home Rule Party (1926), the Su GCBA, and Soe Thein GCBA (1925), which eventually came to support the Saya San Rebellion.[9] These new leaders found themselves empowered by popular support and by considerable funds collected among the ranks of a national movement that was more responsive to nationalist concerns than it was concerned with observing organizational by-laws.

At the same time, the position of monks in the anticolonial struggle had been politicized. Monastic participation in the GCBA's agenda began when monks assumed teaching positions as *dhammakathikas* in the National School Movement. Lay politicians and the *dhammakathikas* shared a common interest in including Buddhist education in public schools. Other conjunctures of lay and monastic collaboration developed in the anticolonial struggle, and thus their agendas began to extend beyond a Buddhist curriculum in national schools. As young and energetic teachers, *dhammakathikas* were trained in the modern methods of Indian political activism and in English-language instruction. They effectively became the political tutors of the lay members of local *wunthanu athin* chapters. The *dhammakathikas* took an oath of loyalty to these nationalist organizations and carried identity cards. Their numbers reached 12,000. Trained rigorously to agitate the population according to Gandhi's model, they were ready to face the colonial police, military, and prison.[10]

As their political agitation become more prominent, the colonial government moved to imprison many of them. The colonial government's arrest and imprisonment of monks in robes deeply offended many Burmese, who saw this as civil disrespect for monastic law and status. In prison, these monks continued to fight for their right to wear robes instead of prison clothes, to follow Buddhist observances, and to convene as a monastic community within the consecrated space of a *sīmā*. This struggle between the authority of colonial, secular law and the authority of monastic law was iterated in several contexts. Maitrii Aung Thwin has observed that the legal tensions that emerged during this period increasingly implied a criminalization of traditional cultural practices in a colonial discourse in which monks and GCBA members were described as "undesirable" people who were defiant of the government.[11]

The nationalist struggle of the 1920s agitated many segments of Burmese society. The range of voices among anticolonial Buddhists included educated modernist lay people, who resided predominantly in urban areas, but also traditional laity and monks who had been swept up in the *wunthanu* movement in smaller towns and villages. The history of this period makes it evident, however, that although many nationalist organizations sprang up during this time, none was sufficiently institutionalized to withstand scandals, intrigues, and abuses of power within their own ranks and this fact would eventually diminish the foundations of civil institutions like the YMBA, local *wunthanu athin* chapters, and others.

Trajectories of Resistance among Buddhist Maximalists

Interwoven in the history of nationalist organizations are the biographies of monks who came to assume significant political roles in the struggle for independence. Intersecting with the decline of the YMBA and its colonial charter was the rise of U Ottama (1879–1930), a peripatetic monk who traveled widely in Asia, Europe, and the Middle East. His charismatic sermons during the 1920s stressed the decline of Buddhism under colonial rule and inspired monks and lay people to join the nationalist struggle. His anticolonial agitation and civil disobedience protesting colonial rule triggered his imprisonment several times between 1921 and the end of his life. He made sophisticated use of the print news media and collaborated within the networks of the YMBA and later the GCBA to accomplish his objectives.

His biography conveys that monastic robes were significant to him throughout his life, first to obtain an education in Burma and India, and later to make possible his itineraries to mobilize various political groups, which ranged from Bengali anticolonialists to East Asian coreligionists. Academically gifted, but unable to realize his goal of studying in England in his youth, he determined to join the sangha at the age of fifteen. He studied in Calcutta for three years.[12] After a brief visit to Burma in 1904, he returned to Bengal, where he became involved in anti-British agitations. Later, he accepted a position to teach Buddhism and Pāli at the National College in Calcutta.[13] By 1907 he accepted another teaching post in Tokyo, but left in 1910 to travel to Korea, Manchuria, China, Cambodia, Annam, Siam, Ceylon, and India; he returned to Burma in 1911.[14]

Less evident in his life story are his continuing relations with the monastic leadership in Burma. Having left Burma as a young man and returning only intermittently, his connections with the Burmese monastic establishment appear transitory and removed from the local fabric of monastic settings. Although he did not succeed in mobilizing a popular following during his early trips back to Burma, he nonetheless became an important figure in the nationalist movement. After several attempts to rally and popularize Burmese anticolonial

U Ottama.

WITH PERMISSION FROM THE IRRAWADDY.

sentiments, he eventually succeeded with the backing of the more radical young leaders in the YMBA. In 1919 U Ottama resided at the publication offices of the vernacular newspaper, *The Sun,* in Rangoon as a protégé of the YMBA. His reliance on the YMBA's reputation, audience, and organization of mass media allowed him eventually to mobilize nationalist opinions. As the economic crisis worsened in Lower Burma, political monks like U Ottama, who had ties with the YMBA and the GCBA and who had been instrumental in the founding of the GCSS in 1921, advocated popular resistance modeled after Gandhi's principles of economic self-reliance and boycott of the colonial government.[15]

Charismatic and influential as he had become, he played a significant role in the Burmese nationalist struggle in the 1920s. He came onto the political stage as a well-rehearsed agitator and was imprisoned in 1921, 1924, and 1927 for organizing civil resistance and hunger strikes. His actions inspired a younger generation of politically active monks, especially among the GCBA, whose agenda effectively had replaced the procolonial orientation of the early YMBA. Yet U Ottama passed away after an extended stay at Rangoon General Hospital, a modern public institution, and not, as one might expect of a popular monastic leader, within the sheltering walls of a monastery.[16] Despite intersecting sympathies with the Burmese General Council and the political and Buddhist transnationalism that shaped his life, U Ottama's ties to the institution of the Burmese sangha appear to have fragmented. His biographical narrative, however, illustrates how members of the sangha were engaged in an increasingly radicalized struggle in fashioning Burma's future.

More so than his mentor, U Ottama, U Wisara (1888–1929) looms large in the collective memory of Burmese nationalists to this day. He gave many political speeches on behalf of the anticolonial struggle, including an address on the occasion of Mahatma Gandhi's visit in March 1929. In the course of his nationalist struggle, U Wisara endured imprisonment and torture, and was committed to an insane asylum. He was disrobed and reentered the sangha when given the opportunity to do so. He passed away after 166 days of fasting to protest the right of monks to wear robes while incarcerated. His commemorative statue, located prominently near Shwedagon Pagoda, on U Wisara Road in Yangon, is dedicated to the anticolonial cause, and the anniversary of his death, September 29, continues to be commemorated.

In contrast to modernist monks like U Ottama and U Wisara, the majority of the GCSS were less forward-looking and modern in their orientation than retrospective and local.[17] Initially, the GCSS comprised two separate councils, in Upper Burma and Lower Burma, respectively, but they soon merged into a single organization. Following the trial of U Ottama in Mandalay, the organization developed its own momentum and took up an agenda of self-reform and self-governance, which included observance of monastic discipline and the Five Precepts, the training of monastic teachers (*dhammakathika*), and sponsorship of monastic examinations.[18] The GCSS was firmly opposed to colonial diarchy and interpreted the call for "Home Rule" as an opportunity to revitalize a Buddhist kingdom.[19]

By the end of that decade Buddhist maximalists had succeeded in capturing the anticolonialist momentum. The movement that came to be known as the Saya San Rebellion commenced on December 22, 1930, as a rebellion that cascaded through the Tharrawaddi District, Lower Burma, and eventually ended in Amarapura, Upper Burma, in August 1931. It had been sparked by a colonial refusal to grant tax relief, fueled by a lack of moderate leadership and fanned by the imagination of traditionalist revivalist sentiments. Its hero, Saya San, was a former monk who had studied alchemy and Ayurvedic practices and who eventually crowned himself king. During his service as an elected representative of the GCBA, he documented 170 cases of government mistreatment of villagers.[20] His reputation among traditionalist villagers helped him mobilize quickly and secretly an army of rebels who identified with a mythic bird symbol, the Burmese *galon*. In response, the colonial government launched "peace missions" with 11,000 British forces and Indian reinforcements to defeat the rebellion of Buddhist maximalists.[21] Saya San was executed on November 28, 1931. The attempt to return to a traditional polity had precipitated the coercive assertion of colonial power.

The potential for monastic participation in communal riots was realized during the colonial period at two conjunctures. In 1932 and 1938, anticolonial Buddhists, including monks, participated in violent riots aimed at foreigners. Mendelson, Cady, and Ikeya speak of the assault, arson, and murder monks committed in anti-Muslim riots.[22] Well-known monks published inflammatory articles in nationalist newspapers like *The New Light of Burma* and *The Sun*, which called for "urgent action against the enemies of Buddhism."[23] Foreign influence, the presence of Muslims and Indians, and the economic power they had acquired through banking, mortgaging, and even competing for low-wage porter jobs became flashpoints at which violent confrontations occurred. The Yahan Pyo Apwe (the Young Monks Association or YBA) was among the most militant voices in the sangha speaking out against the cultural, economic, and political influence of foreigners in late colonial Burma.[24] In the late 1930s this organization began to agitate the public against Indian Muslims.[25] On the streets of Rangoon, YBA monks would confront women and men wearing western-style clothing. Some of these monks came to be seen as martyrs when they were shot by the colonial government during the riots. Through their collaboration with the charismatic hermit U Khanti, for whom they administered profitable pilgrimage sites, including Mandalay Hill, the YBA had acquired considerable financial wealth and political power. The organization managed to retain its strong influence through most of the post-independence era and sided with Ne Win's military faction when the U Nu government collapsed in 1962. It was reconstituted as an infrastructural conduit during the 1988 uprising against the socialist government but was officially banned soon thereafter.

Monastic Resistance in the Aftermath of 1988

The popular uprising of 1988 was a defining moment in Burma's post-independence history. Monks and students again emerged as a political force. Amidst the chaos of the uprising, the sangha transformed itself spontaneously into an underground organization aiding the popular uprising.[26] Monks provided logistical support for widespread antigovernment mobilization, relayed information through an internal monastic network, and even stepped up to administer some judicial and civil infrastructure in those towns and areas considered "liberated" by the democratic uprising. In the aftermath of the uprising, monasteries became sanctuaries for student protesters whom the military police frequently arrested, particularly at night. As monastic robes offered anonymity to those fleeing government persecution, the monastic network became a conduit for safe travel to the border and into exile. Unofficial estimates of the state's reprisals against monks speak of hundreds killed and thousands missing or imprisoned. The state prohibited the Sangha Mahanayaka Council from carrying out its mandate to adjudicate disciplinary proceedings against monks charged with resistance activities. Even elderly monks suffered severe hardship during their arrests, and some died in prison. As many as 3,000 monks are said to have been jailed. Several hundred monks and students fled to the Thai border, where they organized resistance through newly founded organizations like the All Burma Young Monks Union (ABYMU).[27] Although a prominent organization that emerged out of the 1988 protests, the ABYMU nonetheless suffered eventual fragmentation.[28]

The military regime of the State Law and Order Restoration Council (SLORC) came to power shortly after the 1988 uprising. As previously discussed, the SLORC began a far-reaching, fundamentalist purification of Buddhist institutions and imposed restrictions on all religious groups. It took a strong stand against the sangha and identified politically engaged monks as "impostors in robes" and as subversive "communists" seeking to destroy the state. The state's violent reprisals and the fear it generated changed the atmosphere of Buddhist practice and imposed a repressive religious nationalism during the 1990s. By imposing doctrinal and economic control over the sangha and its lay supporters, the state has also worked to preempt the resurgence of millennial cults and to curb the popular influence of charismatic monks and their organizations, which have translated Buddhist social ethics into political discourse throughout the twentieth century.[29]

The state's restrictions on Buddhist institutions rekindled tensions. When 7,000 monks convened in Mandalay in August 1990 to commemorate the uprising and its martyrs, the military dispersed the crowd by force. In a rarely exercised and official act of the sangha, the monks called for a boycott of donations from members of the military and their families, thereby repudiating their ability to make merit or benefit from religious counsel. This formal boycott symbolized the excommunication of members of the military and their families from the Buddhist field of merit. After two months, and growing public sympathy for this passive resistance, the government convinced senior Shwegyin monks to prevail upon monastic leaders to avoid further confrontation and stop the boycott.

Apart from intermittent eruptions, whatever resistance networks continued to operate in Burma did so outside the public purview until the protest marches of September of 2007. On the surface, it appeared that the state controlled the Sangha Mahanayaka Council effectively and ensured compliance among its ranks despite sporadic tensions among junior monks and pervasive, generalized passive resistance. Many monks seemed to embrace the state's fundamentalism and participated in its administrative structures in a perfunctory way. While tensions persisted, some monks selectively collaborated with the state in order to elude state retribution. In addition, they seemed to accept the state's "taxation" on foreign donations.

Aung San Suu Kyi's Ascetic Engagement with Civil Society

Aung San Suu Kyi, the daughter of Burma's national martyr Aung San, entered politics in 1988. Two years later she won in a landslide election for her party, the National League for Democracy (NLD), but the military regime prevented her from assuming office. Her emergence into the national and international public spheres has proceeded under the political auspices of her electoral campaigns for the NLD. Since the electoral landslide victory in May 1990, she has served as secretary general of the NLD. As she is a strong advocate of a democratic and secular nation-state, it is unlikely that Buddhism would become a state religion under a government led by the NLD. In 1991 she was awarded the Nobel Peace Prize in recognition of her work for democratic reform in Burma, and she used the award to establish a health and education trust for Burmese. She has lived most of the past two decades under house arrest at her home on University Avenue in Rangoon, near Inya Lake, where she and her party's activities are closely monitored and frequently curtailed altogether by agents of the regime. In order to ensure that she will not be able to stand for election in 2010, her house arrest was extended again for eighteen months in 2009.[30]

She has commented on her practice of meditation, which she views as an integral part of her social engagement, and on the spiritual strengths she derives from it. Her message has been one of nonviolent resistance that emphasizes spiritual strength through meditation in preparation for political action and social change. Along with right speech and truthfulness, Suu Kyi has encouraged the practice of mindfulness (*sati*), faith (*saddhā*), energy (*viriya*), concentration (*samādhi*), and wisdom (*paññа*), all of which are considered benefits of meditation. In her *Letters from Burma,* she frames her critique of contemporary Burmese political culture from the perspective of socially engaged Buddhism, and she advocates a grassroots-level engagement with democratic reforms in order to bring about material and moral improvement in society.[31] She sees Buddhist engagement with society as premised on providing for basic human needs like adequate livelihood, public health, and education. She considers self-empowerment and social action at the local level as a contribution to the greater common good. Suu Kyi has stated that her political work has been enhanced by the practice of meditation and selflessness. She has expressed her reliance on a Buddhist ethos of nonviolence and on meditation for the spiritual strength to endure house arrest and persevere in her political work.

Ingrid Jordt notes in her study on lay mediation as a mass movement that meditation is widely practiced and has figured importantly in Burmese political discourse throughout the twentieth century. Many Burmese conceive of the silent retreat into meditation as empowering political change in society.[32] Many of Suu Kyi's supporters have taken refuge in the practice of meditation at centers that offer a temporary retreat from society and offer spiritual cultivation and freedom of thought in secluded communities. Like Gandhi's ashram, these meditation centers are separate and, perhaps at times, utopian communities engaged in common spiritual goals and social resistance against an oppressive government. At the height of the state's cult of Buddhist nationalism during the early 1990s, the meditation movement became an alternate location for Buddhist practice that was often seen as synonymous with political resistance. Its emergence was partially a response to the government's refusal to allow democracy advocates to organize public merit-making rituals or to seek ordination in the sangha. The retreat into secluded meditation centers therefore shielded supporters of the democracy movement to some extent from government scrutiny.

Insight (*vipassanā*) meditation cultivates the practice of the Eightfold

Noble Path to *nibbāna* and empowers practitioners to claim positions of superior moral accomplishment. On account of this common perception, the practice of meditation became an evocative symbol for countering the state's public sponsorship of merit-making rituals. Among the country's intellectual elites, for whom public expression of ideas is severely censored, meditation has become a venue for intellectual involvement and the articulation of a pro-democratic stance. Gustaaf Houtman has noted that many meditators believe in an intrinsic affinity between cultivating the Eightfold Noble Path through meditation and the popular desire for democracy in Burma.[33] The ideal that ascetic power can be used to renew society has historical roots in pan-Indian religious traditions. Its appeal among socially engaged Buddhists and practitioners of meditation constitutes a new interpretation of traditional Theravada doctrine according to which society benefits materially and spiritually from the presence of perfected individuals (*arahant*). Traditionally, these enlightened individuals were envisioned as world renouncers and accomplished members of the sangha. Modern interpretations, and particularly the Buddhist commitment to political activism of Aung San Suu Kyi, has allowed new perspectives to emerge on what it means to renounce the modern world and who can successfully embark upon the path to ascetic power to transform society. While socially engaged Buddhists still consider merit-making a significant part of Buddhist practice, meditation has come to assume special significance among modern lay Buddhists.

Buddhist communities in Burma are often identified with the Burman ethnic majority, and have played at times a divisive role in the construction of civil society. Ethnic minorities have often found themselves disenfranchised from the state's ritual activities, which in turn accentuates their political marginality. In contrast, Aung San Suu Kyi's vision of Buddhism has been a vehicle for conveying values like liberal democracy and the universality of human rights in a culturally salient Buddhist idiom. Suu Kyi has been outspoken about her personal beliefs and the practice of meditation. She has made extensive use of salient Buddhist narratives, idioms, and imagery to convey to Burmese audiences and to western activists her vision of civil society and moral authority in the practice of politics. Her charismatic appeal among Burmese and among Buddhists in the west has been heightened by meditation and by the discipline with which she has submitted herself to hunger strikes and prolonged periods of house arrest imposed by the state.

In exile at home, the daughter of Burma's national hero and founder of the country's army, lives the life of a world renouncer. Among the many civil rights leaders of the twentieth century, she has particularly emulated Mahatma Gandhi and his ideals of nonviolence, civil resistance against oppression, and temporary ascetic withdrawal from political engagement. In adopting Gandhi's strategies, Suu Kyi seeks to translate Gandhi's model of *satyagraha* into a modern Buddhist idiom. This translation has also entailed an innovation concerning gender, for Suu Kyi represents perhaps the first modern female ascetic to engage in civil resistance. She sees herself as a Buddhist meditator who aims to infuse the ethics of everyday politics with the spiritual and ascetic power she gains through meditation under house arrest. Reflecting on the solitude of six years' of house arrest (1989–1995), she remarked: "Like many of my Buddhist colleagues, I decided to put my time under detention to good use by practicing meditation. . . . In my political work, I have been helped and strengthened by the teachings of members of the sangha."[34]

From this ethical premise, Aung San Suu Kyi has articulated an encompassing Buddhist vision of civil society, moral authority, social justice, and political empowerment. Reminiscent of Martin Luther King's "Letter from the Birmingham Jail," her *Letters from Burma* present eloquent allegory on contemporary Burmese society.[35] This series of weekly letters was initially published in a Japanese newspaper, *Mainichi Daily News,* and later as a collection. In two of these letters, she reflects on the notion of meditation and self-sacrifice. She recounts the story of Padasari, a woman whose tragic loss of her family makes her "the epitome of the consuming fire of extreme grief" until the Buddha's teachings bring her peace of mind and "the joy of victory over the self."[36] This passage recalls Aung San Suu Kyi's own life story and separation from her family. In another letter she reminisces about her religious teachers and invokes the spiritual guidance that Buddhists derive from faith and the practice of the Eightfold Noble Path.[37] One teacher reminded her of the story of the hermit Sumedha, the Buddha-to-be, "who sacrificed the possibility of early liberation for himself and underwent many lives of striving that he might save others from suffering."[38] About another teacher, she writes: "He sketched out for me how it would be to work for democracy in Burma. 'You will be attacked and reviled for engaging in honest politics,' pronounced the teacher, 'But you must persevere. Lay down an investment in suffering and you will gain bliss.'"[39]

Her political and social ideologies are grounded in the modern ethics of socially engaged Buddhism.[40] Her statements on current events and developments in Burma have been grounded in ethical considerations about the greater common good and civic responsibility. In speeches, essays, and letters, she evokes the vision of a modern, rational Buddhist ethic in which the moral conduct of the state, social justice, and the material and spiritual welfare of individuals and families are closely linked to issues of participatory democracy, human rights, and dignity. In an essay entitled "In Quest for Democracy," she places the Burmese movement for democracy during the late 1980s into a Buddhist framework:

> Members of the Buddhist sangha in their customary role as mentors have led the way in articulating popular expectations by drawing on classical learning to illustrate timeless values. But the conscious effort to make traditional knowledge relevant to contemporary needs was not confined to any particular circle—it went right through Burmese society from urban intellectuals and small shopkeepers to doughty village grandmothers. . . . The Burmese people go to the heart of the matter by turning to the words of the Buddha on the four causes of decline and decay: failure to recover that which has been lost, omission to repair that which has been damaged, disregard for the need for reasonable economy, and the elevation to leadership of men without morality or learning. Translated into contemporary terms, when . . . democratic rights were lost to the military dicta, sufficient efforts had not been made to regain them, moral and political values had been allowed to deteriorate without concerted attempts to save the situation, the economy had been badly damaged, and the country had been ruled by men without integrity, or wisdom.[41]

Here Aung San Suu Kyi articulates a Buddhist critique of the current regime. For Burmese audiences, her words voice in culturally salient terms a political critique of bad governance and failed economic policies. In her *Letters* she criticizes other government policies, which she considers from the perspective of modern Buddhist ethics. Topics include corruption among civil servants, health-care providers, and teachers; the short-sighted, profit-oriented immorality of foreign investments fostered by the state; the arbitrary misrule of law, political repression, and threats to safety; preventing NLD members from participating in merit-making rituals and from joining the sangha; and the plight of young children. She praises the spirit of courage in the fight for democracy, deplores the immorality of the imprisonment of NLD party members, presents her party's political agenda, and expresses her hope for the future of the nation's children. Her *Letters* also contain celebrations of national, religious, and ethnic identity and tributes to the strength of national unity.

In her discussion of democracy, Aung San Suu Kyi includes the myth about the election of the first Buddhist king, Mahāsammata. Most Burmese Buddhists are familiar with this story and are likely to infer from her telling that pristine Buddhism embraces democracy just as this king restored peace and justice to a society plunged into moral and social chaos.[42] She then elaborates on Buddhist visions of good governance, using the Seven Safeguards against Decline, the Four Kinds of Assistance to the People, and the Ten Duties of Kings, which are liberality, morality, self-sacrifice, integrity, kindness, austerity, nonanger, nonviolence, forbearance, and nonopposition to the will of the people. These are the Buddhist qualities and virtues that she imagines a modern, "enlightened" civil society to possess. She sees these virtues as drawing on "time-honored values to reinforce the validity of political reforms." She writes: "It is a strong argument for democracy that governments regulated by principles of accountability, respect for public opinion and the supremacy of just laws are more likely than an all powerful ruler or ruling class, uninhibited by the need to honor the will of the people, to observe the traditional duties of Buddhist kingship. Traditional values serve both to justify and to decipher popular expectations of democratic government."[43]

Aung San Suu Kyi's writings suggest that democratic values are compatible with modern Buddhist ethics. In her *Letters* she recounts an ideal, perhaps even utopian, vision of a civil society cast in a Buddhist narrative frame, and, in doing so she employs an established allegorical pattern of social critique to comment on state policies in the public sector, especially in health and education. The opening chapter introduces the reader to her memory of a Buddhist pilgrimage she undertook shortly after her release from house arrest to a mountain monastery, Thamanya, near Pa'an. In the course of this journey, she jokingly comments on poor road conditions along the way and recalls the moral integrity of King Manuha's defiance when he was imprisioned by the founder of the first Burmese empire, King Anawrahta. Upon her arrival at the pilgrimage site, she describes the monks, female ascetics, pilgrims, and villagers who enjoy the generous benefactions of the charismatic monk U Vinaya, who facilitated construction of this ideal community, its educational facilities, and its economic security. In her conclusions she notes:

> People will contribute both hard work and money cheerfully if they are handled with kindness and care and if they are convinced that their contributions will truly benefit the public. The works of the Sayadaw are upheld by the donations of devotees who know beyond the shadow of a doubt that everything that is given to him will be used for the good of others. How fine it would be if such a spirit of service were to spread across the land. Some have questioned the appropriateness of talking about such matters as *metta* (loving kindness) and *thissa* (truth) in the political context. But politics is about people, and what we have seen in Thamanya proved that love and truth can move people more strongly than any form of coercion.[44]

Her moral vision of society, though cast in largely modern Buddhist terms, presumes an ideological framework of universal human rights and universal modern ethics. Suu Kyi's Buddhism shares with other socially engaged

Buddhists and advocates of liberation theologies the premise that religion is a positive force in social life. In her view, modern Buddhist ethical conduct has a responsibility to ameliorate social, economic, and political injustice. It empowers spiritually and morally popular resistance against oppression and coercion. Such modern religious interpretations emphasize the need for the improvement of basic social services such as health care, education, and human rights. These religious visions establish an intersection between traditional religious values and western, post-Enlightenment ideologies that emphasize human rights and a participatory political process. Aung San Suu Kyi explicitly draws on her sociological, intellectual, and ethical thinking when she writes in her address to the World Commission on Culture and Development:

> The true development of human beings involves much more than mere economic growth. At its heart there must be a sense of empowerment and inner fulfillment. This alone will ensure that human and cultural values remain paramount [in a world where] political leadership is often synonymous with tyranny and the rule of a narrow elite. People's participation in social and political transformation is the central issue of our time. This can only be achieved through the establishment of societies which place human worth above power, and liberation above control. In this paradigm, development requires democracy, the genuine empowerment of the people. When this is achieved, culture and development will naturally coalesce to create an environment in which all are valued, and every kind of human potential can be realized.[45]

Within a larger discourse, Suu Kyi remains a consistent advocate of democratic reforms grounded in a modern Buddhist ethic. Her voice is joined by others who share her vision, including some prominent Burmese monks and lay meditators and socially engaged Buddhists like the Thai activist Sulak Sivaraksa, the Vietnamese monk Thich Nhat Hanh, and the Dalai Lama, who speaks on behalf of Tibet.[46] The portrait presented to the global world of Buddhists is one in which a modern world renouncer engages in the politics of resistance against a centralized state on the basis of Buddhist interpretations of timeless values. The further removed from the context of daily life in Burma the interviewer is, the more likely is the report to emphasize religious aspects and Suu Kyi's charisma over her politics. Among western Buddhists, any familiarity with Aung San Suu Kyi is likely to focus on her religious charisma and only to a lesser degree on her political agenda or on the political realities of the contemporary Burmese state and its Buddhist citizens. Her audiences in the west include many expatriate Burmese as well as western Buddhists and secular political activists. To many who sympathize with her cause, Aung San Suu Kyi is a charismatic modern world renouncer and social activist who takes her place among defenders of righteous causes and nonviolent advocates of civil resistance, such as Mahatma Gandhi, Martin Luther King, and Nelson Mandela. To her supporters in Burma, she is a liberal Buddhist and political activist who has stepped up to assume a charismatic role that comes to her, at least in part, as the daughter of Burma's national martyr, Aung San. It is in these ways that she has become a pivotal figure and charismatic symbol for those who see the national struggle as resistance against the internal colonialism of the regime.[47]

During the 1990s the socially engaged, ethical Buddhism of Aung San Suu Kyi and her supporters lent moral authority to their resistance against the military regime. Her political and religious message articulated modern political values—such as liberalism, human rights, and the empowerment of individuals, deemed universal in the west. Conversely, the military regime represented a centralized state based on bureaucratic rationalism. In the absence of a national constitution between 1990 and 2008, the regime's power was legitimated by a Buddhist nationalism that affirmed the center's authority over differentiated levels of social and political power, thus harkening back to traditional Burmese political ideology.

The 88 Generation Students' Prayer Campaign

In contrast to early examples of Buddhist practices as expressions of political resistance, the 88 Generation movement claimed a public role in its pursuit of multireligious, national reconciliation. This group spoke out explicitly against all forms of oppression and sought to inspire a public stance against the fear that many experienced as a consequence of pressures on the population to work in collusion with a repressive government. The movement emerged in August 2006 under the leadership of individuals who had played prominent roles as students during the 1988 uprising. Having served lengthy jail sentences, Min Ko Naing, Kho Htay Kywe, and others emerged from their lengthy imprisonment with new strategies for a public engagement that emphasized a need for national reconciliation. Although critical of the regime, the 88 Generation looked to engage the generals in a political dialogue as much as it seemed to encourage the public at large to voice their experience since the 1988 uprising.[48]

This strategy of dialogical mediating inspired considerable public support and participation. Among the campaigns undertaken was the Prayer Campaign, where members gathered at Shwedagon Pagoda in Rangoon to pray for the release of all political prisoners. Their use of public prayer at this national shrine was an innovative strategy for conflict resolution, and, significantly, their leaders claimed that their prayers included Buddhist as well as Hindu, Christian, and Muslim ones to underscore the multireligious character of the nation. The members of the Prayer Campaign were subjected to harassment and assault by plainclothes individuals, often taken to be government thugs, who disrupted their public prayers. Reports on such incidents traveled quickly to media outlets run by the democratic opposition in the diaspora, where they generated international embarrassment for the military regime.

A second campaign envisioned that supporters, dressed in white shirts, would visit on Sundays the homes of relatives of political prisoners to offer moral support.[49] Aung San Suu Kyi's sixty-second birthday and ongoing house arrest was commemorated in this manner on June 19, 2007. A third initiative concerned the Open Heart Campaign, in which the 88 Generation members encouraged the general public to write letters to General Than Shwe, the current head of state and chairman of the State Peace and Development Council (SPDC), and share their personal experience of suffering and discrimination since 1988. The strategy of overcoming painful memories by writing letters to the alleged perpetrators is an established therapeutic method that the 88 Generation movement has attempted to translate into national healing. Simultaneously, this method gave a voice to the experience of political suppression in an environment where public media are tightly censored. Leaders of the movement were not immune to government retribution, and many of them were subsequently rearrested in the weeks leading up to the Saffron Revolution in September 2007. Some 88 Generation protesters were arrested repeatedly, while others were released after several weeks or months of imprisonment.

The movement's campaign appeared to have been timed to coincide with the regime's announcement in September 2007 that the process of drafting a national constitution had been completed and that a popular referendum was planned for May 2008. General elections were to follow in 2010 and initiate a transition to a multiparty system in which the military was to play a dominant role. In their 2007 manifesto, the 88 Generation stressed the responsibility of the military to ensure the right of all citizens to have access to social and economic privileges, regardless of political affiliation.[50] They pointed out that pro-democracy supporters experienced "discrimination in their pursuit of a livelihood" and that all citizens feared the loss of opportunities for economic advancement if they expressed political views.[51] Speaking to issues that affect the majority of the nation's population while affirming political rights and evoking the struggle of an entire generation that has now reached middle age, this movement drew on the sentiments of many whose personal lives had been polarized by past political events.

Conclusion

This chapter has focused on expressions of Buddhist resistance to the political power of the modern state. While Theravada kings struggled to control the moral powers and social practices of world renouncers, the modern Burmese state also faces modern Buddhist forms of resistance that have shown the power to mobilize the public and engender potentially violent confrontations. The modern state in Burma has encouraged distrust of the secular political process, a development attributable in part to the relatively brief periods of prosperity under secular governance and hence the lack of viable models that could be recalled in the collective memory of its citizens. At the same time, authoritarian military regimes have continued to project a totalizing Buddhist worldview in which the institutions of modern civil society and a secular political process have not been safeguarded. Modern conjunctures of Buddhism are often embedded in elite social communities that comprise both postcolonial hybrid practices and some traditional ones. Through its links to the Theravada diaspora, the Burmese Buddhist resistance has also been able to internationalize their local concerns to some degree and, simultaneously, localize an international Theravada Buddhist discourse about modernity. Examples of Buddhist resistance to the center therefore comprise hybrid social formations that have emerged at the intersection of two distinct global systems, namely, Buddhism, on the one hand, and western rationalism, on the other.

It is easy to imagine postcolonial hybridities that might foster a secular civilian state and a modern civil society to sustain political, economic, and social pluralism and development. But at this moment in time, it remains doubtful that any Buddhist vision of moral authority will sustain pluralist social and political formations. It will likely be the work of two or more generations to establish the postcolonial project in Burma. Present realities make it clear that the legitimation of political authority remains entrenched in the political divisions of the day and in institutional, cultural, and religious structures that are unlikely to fade quickly.

A comparison of contemporary political activism in other Buddhist countries reveals an equally diversified response to modern conjunctures. In Thailand responses include the socially engaged Buddhist voices of Buddhadasa Bhikkhu and Sulak Sivaraksa, the involvement of the Thai sangha in state-sponsored development projects, as well as the Dhammakay and Santi Asoka communities. Sri Lanka's ethnic violence has been informed by the emergence of a fundamentalist Buddhist nationalism and militancy.[52] Comparable modern social processes in the relations between the state and Buddhism are also occurring in Vietnam. The self-immolation and martyrdom of a Buddhist lay person in Hue in May 1993 engendered the largest popular demonstration against the state since 1975 and led to the imprisonment of Buddhist monks who opposed government attempts to unify and control the monastic establishment.

A common feature among these examples is the fact that Buddhist resistance movements against the hegemonic structures of modern governments often claim for themselves a moral high ground and essentialize religious truth by staking their claims on a mythic and transcendent discourse. They see themselves bound by a moral duty to missionize their vision of authority. Some even see themselves entitled to defend the *dhamma* through violent means. Given such absolutist rhetoric, many politicians submit themselves to Buddhist causes in the hope that their patronage will bring political legitimation. In other words, Buddhist modes of resistance remain powerful instruments of change precisely because modern history has shown secular power, political processes, and liberal civil society to be weak rationales for governance.[53]

7 The Limits of Buddhist Moral Authority in the Secular State

In September 2007 the world watched as tens of thousands of Buddhist monks marched in daily defiance of Myanmar's military rule.[1] The "Saffron Revolution," as it came to be called in exile media, was the most recent iteration in a genealogy of Buddhist resistance against the secular state. Despite its designation as a "revolution," the revolt did not achieve its promised transformation of the political order. Nonetheless, the events of September 2007 have figured monumentally in the minds of ordinary Burmese. The military and its supporters were widely seen as internal colonizers who extracted the country's resources at the cost of economic development. The events of September 2007 presented a clear challenge to military regime and define a conflict that is located at the core of the nation and its cultural fabric.

Since the advent of colonial rule, Buddhist resistance against the modern state has questioned the moral authority of secular government, setting the stage for competing paradigms of power. During the late colonial period of the 1920s and 1930s, the sangha actively contested British colonialism at historical conjunctures in which a traditional Buddhist worldview inspired early nationalist movements. Some of these monks came to be revered as national heroes and constitute the founding generation of Burma's so-called "political monks." During the 1988 uprising, a pivotal moment in the country's post-independence history, the Alliance of All Burma Monks was formed to organize nationwide protest marches by students and civil servants. It was an umbrella organization for several monastic groups, including the Young Monks Organization (Yahan Pyo Apwe) and the All Monks Union (Sangha Sammeggi), which traced their organization to the sangha's contestation of the British colonial state during the 1920s and 1930s.

In this genealogy, monks contested the moral authority of the state through their interpretation of the *vinaya.* The Buddhist discourse presented the conflict as one of moral authority and the Buddhist Universal Law (*dhamma*) against bad governance enacted by a secular state. In its contestation of modern secular power, the sangha justified its social involvement in public politics on the grounds of its moral authority to speak on behalf of the Buddhist laity and its economic hardship. While the Saffron Revolution represents a recent articulation of socially engaged Buddhism in contemporary Myanmar, the practices and tenets of socially engaged Buddhists are rooted in traditional monastic lifeways. Traditionally monks were a class of literati who were teachers for the population at large. They were also active in other social capacities, including as healers and purveyors of medicines. Today they run hospitals and HIV clinics, are active in environmental conservation, and they organized vital relief campaigns in the aftermath of Cyclone Nargis in May 2008, when most relief organizations were denied access to the affected regions. As a cultural institution that survived colonial rule, the sangha has used its moral authority as political leverage to promote socially engaged Buddhist ideals, human rights, civil society, and democracy in Myanmar.

These modern Buddhist conjunctures encourage us to rethink Max Weber's attribution of Buddhism as "otherworldly," a gloss that has long obscured our understanding of the inherently political implications of Buddhist practices. His notion of Buddhism validated a colonial view according to which political engagement by monks was not considered an authentic expression of Buddhist practice, but a manifestation of the tradition's inevitable decline from its pristine origins. Weber's position therefore reflects an orientalist reading of the *vinaya* that privileges some modern Buddhist interlocutors, while silencing other Buddhist voices who contest prevailing hegemonies.

What follows in this chapter is a critical appraisal of the discourse on monastic involvement in Burmese politics. This inquiry takes its departure from the premise that the social context of Buddhist practice is necessarily embedded in political realities. At the core of the social practice of Buddhist ideals lies an economy of merit in which lay people demonstrate their virtue of generosity by giving *dāna* to monks in various ritual settings. This practice of generosity helps lay people acquire spiritual rewards or merit occasioned by the monks' acceptance of their donations. Merit thus acquired becomes manifested in future spiritual and material prosperity as well as in social status and political power. The ritual exchanges that constitute a Buddhist economy of merit are performed in many contexts and affirm the legitimate status of monks and their lay supporters. Its ritual reversal, namely the refusal of donations from lay donors, requires a formal act of the sangha. Burmese monks say that this act is authorized in monastic law. The Burmese sangha invoked this *vinaya* provision in 1990, 1996, 2004, and most recently in September 2007, when this reversal of Buddhist ritual exchange precipitated a political and moral crisis on a national scale. As scholars, we must locate Buddhist hegemonic ideals within a cultural logic—namely, the economy of merit and its negotiations in everyday life—and not locate them, as Weber does, in the renunciation of the world by Buddhist monks as proposed in the orientalist work of Max Müller and his contemporaries.

We shall look at the events of September 2007 to chronicle the conjunctures of their emergence at the center of the nation and their eventual submergence within the larger context of geopolitics.[2] The discussion locates the events of September 2007 within a broader struggle for political legitimacy in which the sangha enacted once again its potential not only to mobilize its monks, but also its social networks of lay supporters. The ensuing struggle reveals the conflicting visions of moral authority held by each of the competing factions, the sangha and the military regime. The fact that many families maintain vital ties to both institutions underscores the precarious reality of ambiguous and competing loyalties. A comparison of the sangha and the military, the two pivotal institutions in contemporary Myanmar, indicates their respective strengths as well as signs of internal fragmentation. Tracing the political and academic discourse about political monks, the chapter concludes with a critical interrogation of this hegemonic rhetoric. This discourse on power is contrasted with the ethnographic constructions of a modern Buddhist ethic that centers on the social engagement of the sangha as a field of merit and as a moral authority within the Buddhist world (*samsāra*).

Chronicling the Events

In the spring of 2007 the 88 Generation movement, the All Burma Monks Association, and the international monastic organization Sāsana Moli called for a popular boycott of the regime's referendum on a proposed constitution that assured the continuing role of the military in national politics. Some of these organizations sharply criticized the United Nation's failure to prevail upon the regime to implement a reconciliatory dialogue with the NLD and to institute democratizing reforms. During the weeks and months leading up to September 2007, civil rights and labor activists organized small, sporadic protests in some Yangon suburbs. This led to the arrest of some civil rights leaders.[3] Sporadic unrest soon gave way to large protest marches led by monks who became the public voice decrying the economic suffering many Burmese experienced. Initially, the columns of marching monks in Yangon were flanked by lay people who formed a human chain on either side to protect them as they made their way through crowded areas and to signal popular support for the courageous demonstrations of these monks. By the last weeks of September 2007 the protests had escalated into massive marches led by monks in major cities like Yangon and Mandalay and in several provincial towns, such as Sittwe and Pakokku, where important monasteries are located.[4] The largest protests occurred in Yangon in the days leading up to September 26, when close to 100,000 people, mostly monks and nuns, marched through the streets in protest against the military junta and its economic policies. Across the nation, close to 300,000 Buddhist monks joined their protests and openly contested the secular power of the state over issues of social injustice. The standoff ended on September 26, when the state asserted its coercion over the moral claims of the sangha with a violent military crackdown on those protesting.

Economic pressures had furnished the immediate flashpoints for these public protests. In a surprise move, and in response to demands by the International Monetary Fund, the government abruptly stopped its subsidy for natural gas. This precipitated a sharp increase in gasoline and diesel costs as well as in the general cost of living. The sudden rise in basic expenses hit lower-income groups particularly hard, for they were already living on the margins of economic survival. This change in economic policy further exacerbated the disparity of wealth between Yangon elites and the poor in urban and provincial areas. Some monks stated that their marches were protesting the economic hardships that their lay supporters endured. One monk described the economic struggles of many lay people as follows: "Monks who receive donations from laymen and who visit households every morning to receive *hsoon* [cooked rice] witness at first hand the suffering and poverty of ordinary people. They continue to witness the deteriorating situation in the predominately Buddhist country, ruled by a military government."[5]

The failure of the state's economic policies was seen as the failure of traditional Buddhist norms of good governance. The general lack of prosperity empowered the monks' moral position against the government. Skyrocketing living expenses not only jeopardized the welfare of lay supporters, but also placed financial strain on some monasteries by increasing the number of poor already living in monastic compounds. The plight of the poor not only limited donations to monks, but also became a growing economic liability for the sangha as an institution. Monasteries had become refuges for the sick, indigent, and homeless and by default functioned as a social safety net in many local communities. This traditional function of monasteries to provide social services took on new significance in the modern context of socially engaged Buddhism.

The public protests of the Saffron Revolution evoked salient symbols at the core of traditional Buddhist practice that centered on the ritual exchanges

A protesting monk displays an overturned alms bowl to signal the sangha's refusal to accept donations in 2007. PHOTO BY SAW LAW EI SOE.

of *dāna* for merit between monks and lay people. Theravada rules for monastic conduct prohibit monks from accepting compensation for their work, which makes them entirely dependent on donations from the laity. The economy of merit affirms both the status of the monk who accepts the donations and the standing of his lay sponsor who is practicing the Buddhist virtue of generosity. This exchange is enacted in a variety of ritual interactions between monks and lay people. It constitutes the foundation of traditional Theravada social hierarchy and hegemony. Most significantly, the events of September 2007 precipitated a reversal of the traditional ritual exchange between the sangha and the laity. This formal act of the sangha is legally binding under monastic law and mandates that all monks refuse donations (*pattam nikkujjana kamma*) from unworthy donors. "Turning over one's alms bowl" (*thabeik hmauk*) is the Burmese expression designating the sangha's refusal to confer religious, social, and political legitimacy on certain lay supporters. Such a boycott is tantamount to banning from the Buddhist field of merit any lay supporter who has acted to the detriment of the *sāsana*.[6] "Monks can boycott . . . these persons through methods such as not accepting religious offerings from them, not helping them to perform any religious ceremonies, not going to and relating to them in religious ways."[7]

The ban can be revoked once the person has shown remorse and apologized to the sangha. Until the donor's actions have been remedied, however, observance of the refusal of donations is incumbent upon the entire sangha. The enactment of the *pattam nikkujjana kamma* may therefore harbor a great deal of social tension and potential communal violence. The Burmese sangha has invoked this act of refusal on several occasions in recent years. In 1990 the All Monks Union (Sangha Sammeggi) of Upper Burma declared *pattam nikkujjana kamma*, in which 7,000 monks in Mandalay refused donations from members of the military and their families in order to protest violence against ethnic minorities in the nation's tribal regions. Similar, though smaller protests were organized in 1996 and 1997. When the regime sponsored the Buddhist World Summit in Yangon in December 2004, at the apex of its propagation of Buddhist nationalism, monks also declared a boycott, refusing to accept donations from military personnel or to perform religious rites for them.

Monks clashed with local police during a protest march in early September 2007 in the provincial monastic center of Pakokku, Upper Burma. The altercation spiraled into violence when two monks were reportedly tied to a pole and beaten by local police. In retaliation, monks held local officials hostage for several hours at a monastery and burned their cars. This incident escalated the national confrontation between the sangha and the regime, for now monks were not only protesting economic injustice endured by the population in general, but also blasphemous injury to the institution and status of members of the sangha at the hands of the regime. A new organization, the All Burma Monks Alliance (ABMA), was formed in response to the mistreatment of protesting monks. In widely distributed leaflets publicizing this shameful incident, the ABMA issued an ultimatum demanding an apology from the authorities for the violent treatment inflicted upon monks in Pakokku. If the ultimatum was not honored, a nationwide *pattam nikkujjana kamma* was to commence on September 17, 2007.[8] When the deadline passed unheeded, public tension escalated daily, as more and more young monks joined protest marches, many of them carrying their alms bowls turned upside down to signal their boycott of donations from members of the military government and their families. This ostracism of the regime was in clear contrast to the support the monks accepted from pro-democracy supporters. Along the routes of the protest marches, they accepted water and food from lay supporters, including from democratic activists who shared their political goals. Among them were prominent critics of the regime, including the celebrated actor Zarganar, who, like many others, was subsequently arrested and given a harsh prison sentence.

Harn Lay's rendering of soldiers breaking up the Pakokku protests in *The Irrawaddy Online Edition,* September 6, 2007.

WITH PERMISSION FROM *THE IRRAWADDY.*

The international media stunned audiences worldwide with daily broadcasts of monks walking in single file through the monsoon-swept streets of Yangon. The images of the protesting monks conveyed disciplined determination and hinted at their physical abilities as an army of young men in robes who had taken to the streets on a pilgrimage for justice. As they marched through the streets, lay supporters flanked each side of the single-file column and joined hands in a symbolic gesture of protection, shielding the monks from potential interference with their march. The protests were organized primarily by young monks in their twenties and thirties, who found themselves thrust suddenly into leadership roles of a revolutionary movement for which they were largely unprepared. "We will march until we bring down the evil government" was the battle cry of one young leader of the All Burma Monks Alliance, U Gambira. Other dissident groups, such the All Burma Young Monks Union, which had played a significant role in the 1988 uprising, and the United Front of Monks, joined in the protests. At the height of the protests, monks encouraged their lay supporters to join them in their goal of a general strike, which they hoped would topple the regime.

In the absence of immediate government intervention, the marches gained momentum and took on the predictable routine and euphoric atmosphere of ritual performance. Protesting monks and their supporters created a national *communitas,* in Victor Turner's sense, whose moral legitimacy transcended the temporal powers of the secular state.[9] Their rallies charted the same routes that had been walked in the protest marches in 1988 and during the colonial era. Their steps retraced a sacred map of public protest that linked sacred sites, such as Shwedagon, Sule Pagoda, and other local repositories of Buddhist power with the reenacted memories of past resistance movements.[10] En route the monks chanted the *Metta sutta,* a popular incantation that extols the Buddhist virtues of loving kindness and compassion. This text, which forms part of a standard repertoire of *paritta* recitations, now became a political expression of Buddhist resistance against the regime and was seen as an invocation of Buddhist social engagement, human rights, and democracy. Indeed, democracy was viewed as a Buddhist cause in accordance with the *dhamma.* The exiled leader of the 1988 uprising, U Pandavamsa, who had been abbot of Shwe Taung Monastery and secretary general of the All Monks Union, an organization of about 80,000 monks dedicated to public education and the promotion of Buddhism, explained the political significance of this text in the following way: "The sangha . . . supports the democratization process in the country because democracy is in line with the Buddha's teaching. . . . [The] *Metta sutta* directly gives attention to the humanitarian approach to democracy. Buddhist monks have a motto in their struggle for democracy, and this is to not tackle each other and not to hurt one another. This is becoming a social ethics base of the democratic struggle of Burmese monks."[11]

Protesting monks depart from Shwedagon Pagoda to commence their march on September 24, 2007. PHOTO FROM ASSOCIATED PRESS.

Other forms of political dissent expressed in public and religious discourse also became popular. For example, charismatic monks like Ashin Nyanissara, the abbot of Sitagu Monastery in Sagain, preached sermons that contained allegorical critiques of the regime with titles such as the "Last Days of the Empire." They quickly became popular narratives of the resistance and were circulated widely on compact disks despite state censorship prohibiting their dissemination. Donald Swearer has suggested a distinction between the moral authority of the sangha that derives from ritual acts such as turning over the bowl and the kind of moral authority that derives from the dhammic moral critique that typifies socially engaged Buddhism.[12] This analytical distinction between moral critique and ritual practice illuminates concurrent dimensions of the Burmese Buddhist protests as both moral discourse and ritual acts are articulated in the multifaceted narratives about the events of September 2007.

An inspiring moment of the protest movement occurred on September 21, when a group of monks in Yangon turned unexpectedly onto University Avenue, where Myanmar's most famous advocate of democracy, Aung San Suu Kyi, was held under house arrest. Although access to this road and to her home was usually blocked, soldiers at this checkpoint allowed the monks to proceed to her compound, where they chanted the *Metta Sutta.* Emerging into public view for the first time after more than five years under house arrest, Aung San Suu Kyi came to the gate of her property where she paid respects to the monks and briefly conversed with them. The monks, in turn, blessed her and extended to her the very recognition they withheld from the regime. Initial reports of this encounter were met with disbelief until a picture taken with a cellphone camera surfaced online. It is noteworthy that the picture also showed riot police in full gear posted in front of the compound. It would seem that an arrangement must have been struck with a local commander who permitted this evocative meeting to occur, a fact that underscores the multifaceted and fragmented quality of power relations and conflicting obligations among local representatives of the regime.

The following days constituted the culmination of the events of September 2007, when monks called upon lay people to join them in their antigovernment protests, and more than a hundred thousand people marched through the cities and towns of Myanmar, seeking to end the military regime. Buddhist practices and institutions came to be viewed as salient sites of protest against the regime. The practice of religion (*thathana*) was transformed into a public political discourse that challenged the government. The same military generals who only a decade earlier had been honored as powerful patrons of the Buddhist *thathana* were now excommunicated by a younger generation of monks who were impatient with the nation's progress toward modernization.

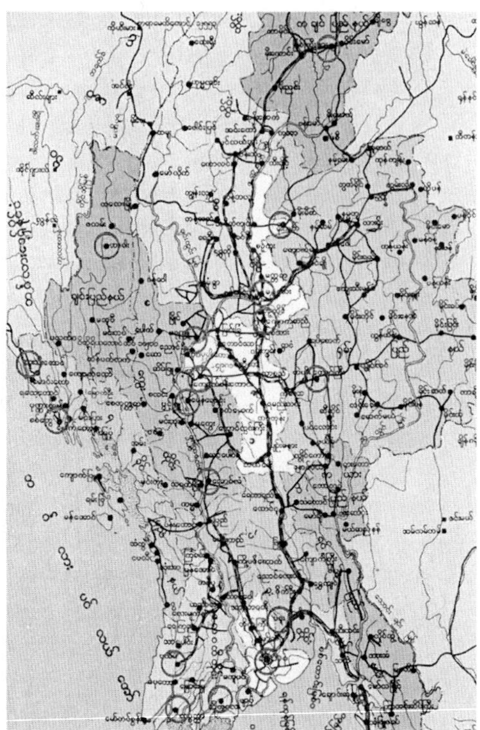

Sites of protest during September 2007. WITH PERMISSION FROM *THE IRRAWADDY*.

For several weeks the regime had permitted the protests to gain momentum throughout the nation, but it began brutal reprisals on September 26 and 27, 2007. The *New Light of Myanmar,* a government-run English-language newspaper, predicted that "national traitors will soon meet their tragic ends," as fear, terror, and doom replaced the earlier hopes attached to the events of September 2007. Police and military troops armed with automatic weapons and tear gas were put into place to quash the protests. A curfew was imposed in the major cities. In Yangon, police trucks equipped with loudspeakers announced: "We have your pictures and we will come to arrest you." The use of cell-phone cameras by its agents, tasked with surveillance during the protests, helped the regime to track down protest leaders. The news media began to report violence against monks and lay protesters. The regime's crackdown displaced a significant part of the monastic population from monasteries and other potential sites of resistance. Monastic compounds were surrounded by police, raided, and ransacked during the night. Many of the monasteries were suddenly empty, with only a handful of elderly monks left to mind the compound. Signs of violent struggle and destruction left behind revealed why these large monastic com-

Cornered, but unbeaten—the true leader. Cartoon by Harn Lay, *The Irrawaddy*, September 27, 2007. WITH PERMISSION FROM *THE IRRAWADDY*.

pounds, which had housed hundreds of monks, were suddenly abandoned. Many monks left their monastic residences and went into hiding, while others were arrested. Some returned to their places of origin or fled across the border to Thailand. Public buildings such as a racetrack and a sports arena were converted into makeshift mass prisons, where an unknown number of monks were disrobed and made to suffer harsh treatment at the hands of prison guards and interrogators. Many Burmese people feared raids on their homes at night and the arrests that would follow. Rumors circulated of secret cremations, mass graves, and a massacre at Insein Prison in Yangon. According to reports by the Human Rights Council of the United Nations and Human Rights Watch, the estimated number of deaths in the aftermath of the protests ranged from 31 to 200 people, including a Japanese journalist.[13] As many as 6,000 people may have been arrested initially, although the regime claims that the number of arrests was closer to 3,000 and that many were eventually released. Prominent participants in the protests were eventually arrested and received severe prison sentences. The armed reprisals against unarmed protesters ended outward public opposition to the regime, although isolated acts of resistance, such as the self-immolation of a monk at Shwedagon Pagoda in March 2008, and small demonstrations continue to erupt spontaneously. In the weeks that followed the eventual suppression of the monks' public dissent, the realities of state reprisal put an end to the public protests of the Saffron Revolution.

International Repercussions

Although the Saffron Revolution emerged from local conjunctures, its concerns and developments were soon reflected in a variety of international and global contexts. In his work on communal violence, Stanley Tambiah describes processes like those of the events of September 2007 in terms of focalization, which is the abstraction of local concerns, and transvaluation, which is the mapping of global concerns onto specific local issues. Both of these processes are characteristically at work in the mobilization of communal conflicts, and they are refracted in the ways in which the events of September 2007 unfolded.[14]

The immediacy of citizen reporting through digital networks played a crucial role in presenting unfolding events to international audiences. Digital technology made possible seemingly instant reporting of the protests that were distributed through exile media as well as international news organizations. Protesters were equipped with disposable cell phones to elude tracking and possible capture by the regime. On the marches, protestors carried CNN I-Report posters depicting Aung San, Aung San Suu Kyi, and other emblems of the 1988 uprising. The posters were at once symbols of defiance and a means of protection against immediate reprisals, for such interventions would immediately have been reported abroad. Under ordinary circumstances, such posters and displays of defiance would have triggered the intercession of state censors. In this context, however, protesters were able to assert their political message and signal their awareness of the public scrutiny they received in daily news reports of international media. The reflexivity of digital reporting underscores the appeal by the protesters to global audiences and set a cadence to the protest performance that was in synchrony with foreign news coverage.

The regime also employed the tools of digital reporting in its retaliation. When the crackdown commenced, the country's main public internet server was shut down, which prevented protesters from communicating with the world outside and heightening fears about the extent and methods of the regime's retribution. For some time the only communications reaching the foreign news media were transmitted through internet servers at foreign embassies in Yangon. As soon as the crackdown began, the regime successfully jammed the websites of the Burmese news media in exile, such as *The Irrawaddy News* and *Mizzima News,* whose reports on the protests had relied on sources inside Myanmar.

Burmese diaspora communities around the world organized sympathy demonstrations, and Buddhist leaders spoke out against the brutal reprisals Burmese protesters endured. The Vietnamese monk Thich Nhat Hanh, who is known for his commitment to socially engaged Buddhism, remarked that the suffering of the Burmese monks already accomplished its purpose. His statement alludes to a Mahayana ideal of a bodhisattva's compassionate sacrifice for the greater good of the Buddhist community. The Fourteenth Dalai Lama, the Tibetan leader who had just been awarded the U.S. Congressional Medal of Honor despite China's protest, commented that the beating the monks endured would cause bad karma for the perpetrators.

Yet international sympathy with the moral courage of Burmese monks to challenge the military regime did not expunge the reality of a global economy and its insatiable need for cheap energy. The regime's need to solicit legitimacy at the height of Buddhist nationalism a decade earlier was now obviated, at least temporarily, by its strategic location as a supplier of cheap energy to the global economy. While the European Union, the United States, and other countries that do not have significant imports from Myanmar imposed additional sanctions targeting individual members of the regime, their foreign assets, and their ability to obtain visas, other countries depended on Burmese natural gas.[15] The United Nations Security Council debated the events in Myanmar and dispatched a special envoy to mediate the crisis and promote a national dialog for reconciliation and democratization. International governments advocated a formal process of national reconciliation and a transition to democracy in Myanmar. But the nations in the Association of Southeast Asian Nations with important economic ties to the regime placed less pressure on Myanmar to pursue a negotiated reconciliation with its protesting opposition. Emergent economies like China, India, and Thailand continue to rely on the import of natural gas from Myanmar, which effectively shields the junta's hegemony from international pressure. For instance, 20 percent of Thailand's energy is imported from Myanmar, which generates revenue of approximately $2 billion per year for the military regime.[16] Any disruption of the energy supply would severely affect the Thai economy and that of the region. International observers were particularly attentive to the degree to which China appeared willing to prevail upon its client state, Myanmar, and its generals to implement democratic reforms. China did not welcome popular unrest on its borders at a time when the host country of the 2008 Olympic Games was carefully managing its international image. The struggle of socially engaged Buddhists ultimately lost out to the market forces of economic globalization in general and to the centrifugal needs for resources in the Chinese economy specifically.[17]

Within weeks, the *International Herald Tribune* concluded that "Burmese monks [had been] shown the limits of their moral authority."[18] Although the revolt had been put down at least on the surface, it created yet another generation of displaced and disillusioned young leaders among lay activists and monks. As a collectivity, they constitute a generation lost at great cost to the nation's future. Four monks, known by their pseudonyms as U Gambira, U Vicitta, U Obhasa, and U Padaka, were identified as key organizers. In order to force U Gambira out of hiding, authorities arrested his family members. Although he managed to elude apprehension for some weeks, he was eventually arrested, disrobed, tried on grounds of treason, and given a life sentence. This judgment by a secular court against a Buddhist monk illustrates the contestation of monastic status in the context of the Saffron Revolution and harkens back to colonial precedents of imprisoned and disrobed monks. This is a critical issue to which the discussion will return below.

The Social Engagement of the Sangha

During the events of September 2007, the sangha's public position of solidarity with the plight of their disenfranchised lay supporters constituted a form of Buddhist social engagement. The commitment of some monks to democratic reforms in Burma, however, is understood not primarily as political involvement, but as a moral obligation to advocate for the rights of those who are marginalized under the current system and to promote a process of national reconciliation.

The emergence of socially engaged Buddhism is a significant religious development in Myanmar. It advocates a modern and increasingly popular interpretation of the Buddha's teachings that emphasizes social justice, sustainable development, and peace as foundations for spiritual development. This view of seeking enlightenment by engaging society, rather than withdrawing from it, transcends traditional boundaries between Theravada and Mahayana models for practicing the path to enlightenment. Socially engaged Buddhism emphasizes the sangha's moral obligation to act in *samsāra* for the benefit of the community and thus opens a new venue for the sangha to mobilize support and influence social policy. Its ideas are rooted in traditional Buddhist notions of good governance. The Ten Duties of Kingship (*das rāja dhamma*) constitute the traditional basis for political ethics, and they specifically warn against the failure of a *dhammarāja* to provide economic prosperity. This discourse is often interpreted in light of social issues such as human rights and democracy.[19]

In his essay on the hegemonic discourse of *samsāra,* the Burmese writer and democracy activist Min Zin argues for interpreting the Buddha's teaching to address contemporary needs and points out conceptual constraints a traditional Buddhist worldview imposes on modern social realities.[20] He argues that the concept of *samsāra,* which is the cycle of rebirth, cannot do justice to the immediate needs in the modern world because its focus extends too far into the future. He challenges the received authority of the sangha as being not sufficiently effective to bring about social change. Instead, an alternate focus for Buddhist activists and interpreters of the *dhamma* should be the individual human life, rather than *nibbāna,* that transcendent stage of existence that embodies perfection and is difficult to attain, according to traditional Theravada orthodoxy. He argues for a shift in emphasis from a traditional Buddhist worldview to one that enables effective social change and in which human experience in the present is central. The interpretative move that Min Zin calls for is a characteristically modern focus on the individual and on living in a socially conditioned present. It is an interpretation that deemphasizes karmic consequences in the future in favor of transforming the present to affect social change.

While socially engaged Buddhism invokes a traditional concern for social ethics, it also charts new social responsibilities for monks and lay people. This broad range of social engagement by monks creates new forms of monastic involvement in society. Redefining the sangha's social relevance in modern contexts can be seen as an alternative to silence and confinement in meditation centers, which offered refuge to many pro-democracy activists who felt disenchanted after the 1988 uprising. The contrast between social engagement and retreat into meditation recalls Chatterjee's distinction between outward action and interiorized spirituality as complementary modes of resistance characteristic of struggles to define national identity.

The appeal of socially engaged Buddhism among Burmese people further builds on the sangha's traditional roles as teachers and healers as monks have long ministered to lay people in those capacities. More than two decades ago U Nyanissara of Sitagu Monastery in Sagain mobilized resources to develop a clean water supply and a hospital specializing in eye surgery. This project helped promote a new relevance for monks in medical contexts, creating yet another challenge to the state's inability to provide adequate health care. Monks have become increasingly active in meeting social welfare needs that the state has not addressed, such as hospice care for HIV/AIDS patients.[21]

In the aftermath of Cyclone Nargis in May 2008, monks organized many relief efforts in the affected areas. In Yangon, they formed labor columns to clear trees and other debris from public places. The sangha also mobilized its supporters to deliver relief to the people living in the delta and reached out to international networks among donors living abroad to help in the relief effort. U Nyanissara's ability to raise funds abroad and set up relief clinics was especially prominent. Initially, the regime hesitated to permit monks to organize relief efforts. However, as the scale of the disaster became apparent, the regime eventually gave its tacit consent to monks who mobilized local resources and delivered food and other aid to victims of the catastrophe.

Social activism has connected some Burmese monks with similar efforts elsewhere in the Buddhist world and allowed them to share strategies for mobilizing an international audience for their cause. Through its links to the Theravada diaspora in Asia and in the west, the Burmese sangha has internationalized local Burmese concerns, while localizing an engaged Buddhist discourse about modernity in Burma. This discourse implicitly juxtaposes the nation of Myanmar with other modernizing nations in the region. It also speaks to Myanmar's transnational and multiethnic diaspora communities, which generally favor a socially engaged form of Buddhism and are in regular contact with families back home.[22] The suppression of monks in 2007 helped initiate the formation of an international organization of Burmese monks living abroad, the Sāsana Moli. Its mission is to generate transnational awareness about the safety and well-being of monks in Burma and to collaborate with organizations of different faiths to ensure the well-being of all Burmese citizens. It issued a special appeal for the release of monks detained in prisons or labor camps. It demanded a public accounting of monks who perished in the Saffron Revolution and proclaimed that "killing monks is an unpardonable crime leading to hell."[23] It called for the withdrawal of the military forces that continued to control access to major monasteries. It urged that the Sangha Mahanayaka Council not be forced to collaborate with the regime. The leaders of Sāsana Moli admonished that the teachings of local abbots and village administrators should be respected and asserted that monks who participated in the boycott should not suffer persecution by the state.

Yet, the sangha's moral imperative to speak truth to political power predates the emergence of socially engaged Buddhism. At least since Buddhist resistance movements to colonial rule and their charismatic leaders, which included Saya San and monks like U Wisara and U Ottama, members of the sangha have articulated their moral obligation to speak out against unjust government. The moral thrust of the sangha's public opposition to the authority of the secular state rests on Buddhist ethics and the notion that monastic law empowers the sangha to withhold merit and legitimation from undeserving members of the laity. This interpretation justifies the sangha's contestation of the secular state and its intervention in public politics. At the same time it enables the sangha to claim that its boycotts are not motivated by a desire for political power, but follow from a strict observance of monastic law.

Contestations of Monastic and Secular Law

The *vinaya* constitutes the source of moral authority that empowers the sangha's public protests. From a Burmese perspective, it also authorizes ritual sanctions, such as the *pattam nikkujjana kamma* that was imposed on unworthy lay supporters in the course of the events of September 2007, when monks claimed that, as moral guardians of good governance, their observance of monastic discipline (*vinaya*) empowered them to invoke the nationwide ritual boycott of the regime. However, such claims also invite debates about the extent to which monks incur potential liabilities as political actors. Aung Zaw, a commentator known for his critical stance on the regime, speaks to this ambiguity when he observes that "monks, considered 'sons of Buddha,' are the strongest institution in Burma after the armed forces. History has shown that monks have long played a pivotal role in Burmese politics. But there is continuing debate on whether they should involve themselves in politics."[24] In strictly legal terms, the behavior of Burmese monks is governed by the *vinaya* and is not subject to civil laws unless extreme transgressions (*pārājika*) trigger an automatic expulsion of a monk from the sangha that would also prompt his return to the social status of a lay person subject to the laws of the state. Unlike their Sinhalese counterparts, Burmese monks cannot hold public office or lead political parties.[25] Nor do they have the right to vote in political elections like the referendum on the proposed new state constitution in May 2008.

Many monks, particularly younger ones, saw the boycott in 2007 as an extreme, but appropriate response under the circumstances. They claim that the Buddha's teachings are consonant not only with invoking the boycott, but, more generally, with the democratic movement and its ideology. One Burmese monk living in exile explained: "The monks' boycott of donations was, in fact, the most extreme political action they have done in the history of their political involvement." He stressed that the boycott of donations by members of an unjust regime strengthened the democratic movement and should not be misconstrued, because "Buddhism rejects terrorism and other extreme forms of political action, such as violence. . . . The *dhamma* in Buddhism's Tipitaka textbooks prohibits every Buddhist [from committing] violence."[26] Rather, the boycott was enacted on account of the monks' moral obligation to challenge the regime's practices in a nonviolent manner. In their media interviews, monastic organizers have emphasized the peaceful, disciplined, and nonviolent conduct of the monks during the protest.

A range of interpretations characterize the debates about the public conduct of monks. In 2006 a young monk in Mandalay explained to me that the sangha has an obligation to rise up against an unjust regime in order to protect lay people from suffering. "Who else would be in a better position to do this, since monks are not vested in worldly assets and family responsibilities like lay people," he asked and added, "We monks have nothing to lose." This socially oriented interpretation of the *vinaya* has grown more prominent throughout the modern Theravada world and emphasizes that monastic practice entails a responsibility toward the welfare of lay people in *samsāra* and toward the protection the Buddha's dispensation.[27] In actuality, monastic discipline is continually subject to interpretation. These debates may concern the appropriateness of monks studying a foreign language like English or other secular subjects, attending movies or watching television, being informed about world affairs, benefiting from modern conveniences like driving cars, and so on. While the orthopraxis of monastic discipline always claims purity, the interpretation of what constitutes a monk's pure practice remains subject to validation by Buddhist communities.

The discourse about monastic legitimacy reiterates past confrontations between the sangha and the state and underscores the contested authority of monks in the secular state. The regime contended that the monks who participated in the boycott were not legitimate members of the sangha. It alleged that "bogus ringleaders" had organized the boycott and protest marches, which would render them subject to civil, rather than monastic, law on account of their status as imposters. Following the government raids on monasteries in Yangon, the state-run media announced that explosives and pornography were found among the personal possessions of protest leaders.[28] Many saw this as a rhetorical strategy by the regime to discredit the religious status of monks and diminish the moral authority of the protesters. The regime's public questioning of the legitimacy of the monastic protest inflamed the conflict further, evoking the social memory of monks who were forced to disrobe and then imprisoned on account of their political activity during colonial rule.

The *New Light of Myanmar* reported that "monks had been defrocked during interrogation," so they could be questioned as ordinary citizens and then be reordained and sent back to their monasteries. The fact that agents of the state disrobed monks for interrogation demonstrates the secular state's disrespect for monastic authority. It also undermines the sangha's power to enforce *vinaya* rules against transgressions within its own ranks. The leader of the Saffron Revolution, U Gambira, was convicted of treason against a state of which he is not, strictly speaking, a citizen. The discourse on moral and legal authority epitomizes for many the ways in which the state coerced the sangha in the conflicts of 2007. In their conversations with me, monks voiced their outrage about the restrictions the state imposed on the status of monks and affirmed that civilians did not have the authority to defrock monks. Reports circulated after September 2007 that some monks commenced hunger strikes in detention. In response to their defiance, their captors were said to have threatened that "we will beat you until you eat." Such rhetoric evokes vestiges of the colonial state and recalls the martyrdom of U Wisara, the Buddhist monk and hero of the struggle against the British, who protested his treatment in prison with a prolonged hunger strike that eventually led to his death.

The confrontation between Buddhist and secular authority also exposed tensions within each of these important institutions, the sangha and the armed forces. The protests revealed fragmentation within the hierarchy of sangha, which weakened its legal claim of implementing a formal boycott as an undivided community bound by *vinaya* law. The conflict pitted senior monks in the state's Sangha Mahanayaka Council against the authority of local abbots and the young monks they supervised at monastic universities and in monasteries that maintained social welfare and public health programs. Even well-established, elite teaching monasteries like Mahagandhayon and Mahsoyin Kyaundaik were targeted in night-time raids and continue to be closely watched by military guards. The regime attempted, and initially failed, to pressure the Sangha Mahanayaka Council into exercising its authority and acting on behalf of the state to end the protest marches and accept donations from members of the military. Following the military reprisals to the events of September 2007, many local communities cancelled their customary rituals of making donations to monks during the Buddhist Lent to avoid risking additional public boycotts by members of the sangha.

However, rumors also circulated about fragmentation in the armed forces. Various reasons for divisiveness are cited that range from corruption to religious concerns about the military's role in putting down the monastic revolt. Within the ranks of the armed forces, some expressed concern about the karmic implications of the orders they received to intervene against the monastic protestors. "Most of the commanders disagree about attacking monks, but they obeyed the order."[29]

After the public marches, the secular state succeeded in dispersing many of the protesting monks, who were now bereft of their leadership, and so created a public appearance of having succeeded in returning the country to a status quo ante and having dispelled popular unrest through coercion. Yet the superficial calm only submerged from the public arena continuing tensions that had impelled the protests in the first place. Signs of potential unrest and covert resistance still emerge suddenly. Monastic examinations and the conferring of titles, the mechanisms by which the state recognizes the individual achievement of monks, have become sites of passive resistance. To protest the referendum on the proposed new constitution, monks issued a call to boycott the annual monastic examinations, which are sponsored by the state and which offer monks the opportunity to advance within their scholastic ranks. Fewer monks registered to sit for the examinations than in previous years. One year after the protests of 2007, monks and police in Sittwe jointly protested their difficult economic conditions. Nevertheless, despite such signs of internal dissent, global economic forces seem to be the wind behind the sails of the generals and have rendered them immune to international pressure. If, for the moment, the secular state has won the moral challenge posed by Buddhist forces through coercion, it has yet to remedy the economic disparity that fueled public tension and the monastic boycott in the first place.

Like other religious communities throughout history, Buddhists have been both victims and perpetrators of violence. In *Colors of the Robe,* Abeyesekera offers a critical examination of the Buddhist discourse about violence and nonviolence in the Sinhalese tradition, and he shows that this history had included Buddhist advocacy of and involvement with violent incidents. He argues that this history of violence does not negate the authenticity of the tradition or ideal of nonviolence. Rather, it is the legacy of an orientalist vision of a "nonviolent, mystic east" that nourished the expectation that Buddhists are immune to the universal human propensity for violence. Nonviolence, like world renunciation, constitutes a normative ideal for monks in the Theravada tradition. It is a mistake to confuse normative Buddhist ideals about transcending conditions of violence with the cultural practices that shape the historical realities of lived experience.[30] The cultural emphasis on nonviolence as a normative ideal does not negate, but instead empowers, the hegemonic discourse about a ritual economy of merit in which social status in traditional and modern Southeast Asian polities continues to be negotiated.[31]

The Colonial Discourse about "Political Monks"

The 2007 protests showed that modern interpretations of the *vinaya* that empower the sangha to intervene in the politics of the state by invoking *pattam nikkujjana kamma* against lay people whose behavior has been judged to harm the *sāsana* has earned some members of the sangha the pejorative designation "political monks." Interventions like this are used by those in power to impute that monks who resist the political center are vulnerable to allegations of *vinaya* transgressions. While Buddhist practice in social contexts is not readily separated from its political import, contemporary scholars must be cognizant of the hegemonic discourse that portrays the political implications of monastic

Observing Buddhist rites. Drawing by Harn Lay, *The Irrawaddy*, September 24, 2008. WITH PERMISSION FROM *THE IRRAWADDY*.

behavior as a transgression against the *vinaya.* The scholarly project must avoid complicity in the construction of such hegemonic inflections and chronicle instead the diversity of interpretations Buddhist monks and their lay supporters present in their engagement with the religious and political contexts of the modern world. Commenting on the events of September 2007, Jordt cautioned that labeling Burma's monks as political made scholars complicit in the hegemonic discourse of the state.[32]

Decades earlier, Mendelson voiced similar hesitations about the use of this label, for it affirmed the critique by the modern Burmese state and its claim that political action was transgressive conduct unworthy of disciplined monks. Commenting on the relative ease with which men move in and out of the sangha, Mendelson noted several instances during the nineteenth century when monks and former monks led rebellions.[33] The permeability of social boundaries between lay and monastic status further increases the potential of Buddhist communities to contest the power of the traditional polity. The easy movement in and out of the sangha by individuals like Saya San presented a challenge to the colonial administration, but even early Burmese history contains several instances in which the traditional boundary between ascetic and coercive power was blurred. For example, Harvey states that monks led several revolts in the precolonial era.[34] The military leadership of monks and their knowledge of martial arts are well known, but these subjects still await systematic study.

The construction of "political monks" emerged from the practical contexts and academic discourse of colonialism. Its pejorative connotations were first articulated to criminalize monastic resistance against the Government of India and its policies.[35] The label of "political monks" was part of a discourse intended to diminish the legitimacy of the anticolonial struggle of monks like U Ottama, U Wisara, *dhammakathikas,* and other monks who worked in organizations such as the *wunthanu athin,* the General Council of Buddhist Associations (GCBA), or the General Council of Sangha Sammeggi (GCSS).[36] It implied that monks who engaged in politics not only opposed the colonial government but also, by definition, transgressed against the monastic code of conduct, the *vinaya,* denigrating their religious authority and compromising their legal status as world renouncers. As the historical record makes evident, these monks saw themselves as practicing their vocation by mobilizing the public to boycott the British colonial government. Historians trained during the late colonial era, however, participated in the construction of Burma's "political monks" and articulated the view of the Government of India, which was antagonistic toward Buddhist nationalist movements and their monastic leaders during the late nineteenth and early twentieth centuries. Max Weber's view of Buddhism as a religion that advocated ascetic renunciation of the world emerges out of this colonial rhetoric.

The colonial insertion of secular power into the public domain precipitated a weakening of central monastic authority. It forced an eventual redefinition of monastic life in the emergent social spaces of a modern nation-state, where political power was no longer based on the economy of merit that had characterized the Burmese Buddhist court. Appointing a monastic patriarch (*thathanabain*) and ensuring his central authority in the sangha had been an important function of the Buddhist court. In the absence of a Buddhist court in Lower Burma after 1825 and in light of the British decision to treat religious matters as merely local matters that did not concern the Government of India or the British Crown, the prelate's influence on the sangha as an institution waned throughout Burma, which was exacerbated by prolonged vacancies in the office at the end of the nineteenth century. During Mindon's reign, the sangha was engulfed in fragmentation and began to collapse, especially as it faced the rise of new reformist lineages. These new communities included lineages like the Shwegyin and Dwara Nikāya, which emphasized internal reforms and strict observance of the *vinaya.* When the last *thathanabain* passed away in

1938, his office was transformed into the Thudhamma Council, an institution that harkens back to the reign of Bodawpaya, when it also did not wield power cohesively.

One consequence of this process was a proliferation of charismatic monastic communities, who constitute a modern phenomenon that emerged during the colonial period. In response to colonialism and modern political structures, the ritual structures that had traditionally conferred status on political actors now devolved into decentralized patterns of patronage composed of diverse local communities and new social classes. As monastic authority became decentralized, charismatic monks with local or regional influence arose to regional and at times even national prominence empowered by the rise of communities that formed around them. Colonial history thus diminished the central authority of the sangha in favor of local monastic communities and charismatic monks who were able to mobilize supporters around particular causes.

The late colonial period saw conflict over the legal precedence of *vinaya* over secular colonial law, a contest that inflamed the sangha's anticolonial stance and fanned nationalist sentiments. At local levels, the sangha agitated to limit the power of civil courts under colonial authority by claiming it had the right to settle legal disputes involving monastic concerns. In the opinion of most monks, the colonial government lacked the moral authority to control either the public or the internal affairs of the sangha. The GCSS demanded that monks be empowered to settle legal matters in local civil disputes in order to limit colonial involvement, a stance that became a factor in the GCSS's eventual call to boycott the Government of India. British involvement in religious matters not only contravened the self-regulation of monks according to the *vinaya* rule, but it also contradicted Britain's own policy of noninvolvement in the religious affairs of Burma. The legal status of monks under colonial rule was, in addition, ambiguous, for monks were traditionally not subject to civil laws or taxation.

Many who had subscribed to theories of modern progress during the twentieth century mistakenly assumed that religion would become irrelevant to public life and to the politics of the modern nation-state. British administrators, like J. S. Furnivall, who established the Burma Research Society in 1910, saw themselves as agents in a modernizing project. Many of them assumed that Buddhism as a factor in the political process would soon be eclipsed by modern political institutions. But in the absence of continued nation-building and strong foundations for civil institutions, the secular state did not displace the role of Buddhism in public life, and new conjunctures emerged to reshape modern alliances of political and Buddhist power. Buddhist practices remained, and remain to this day, a readily accessible source of power for supporters of the state as well as for those who contest, implicitly or overtly, the authority of the secular state.

The conflict between secular and Buddhist authority emerged from multiple conjunctures to produce an ongoing colonial legacy. Colonial discourse appropriated those Buddhist notions that affirmed an orientalist construction of this tradition's presumed otherworldly focus. Colonial rule firmly rejected the public, ritual, and political role the sangha had played in the traditional polity and introduced in its place its own construct of political power in the form of a secular state that was subject to the Government of India and functioned independently of monastic validation. This reconfiguration of political and religious power challenged traditional expressions of monastic authority and it also opened up new social spaces in which monks could claim a public role. The British colonial and later Burmese governments defined the public role of the sangha implicitly through a reading of the *vinaya* that served the interests of the modern state. They sought to bring the institutional authority of the sangha under state control and to limit the activities of local charismatic leaders to the private domain. But these attempts undermined the religious status of the sangha as validating the authority of political power and also the legal status of the sangha as a self-regulating institution beyond the authority of the state.

To enforce the state's control over the sangha, the state must, at a minimum, maintain a national economy of merit. Earlier chapters have examined the state's ritual economy during the U Nu era and during SLORC's nationalist patronage of Buddhism. This contradiction remains a political dilemma for the modern state in Myanmar, where alternatives to the authority to the sangha or the military—for instance, an independent judiciary, higher education, and other civil organizations—have not been sufficiently developed. Consequently, the crisis of authority in the modern nation-state in Myanmar remains confined to contestations between the sangha and the military.

The events of September 2007 reiterated that Buddhist practice, including the practice of monks, can be simultaneously religious and political. The Buddhist contestation of the state's authority was effective precisely because social status continues to be validated by a moral economy of merit that confirms the legitimacy of monks and rulers. Public Buddhist practice involved the mobilization of fields of merit to bring about political transformations. Since independence, the state has sought to control the institution of the sangha and its members in a variety of ways. A mass meditation movement initiated during U Nu's Sixth Buddhist Convocation, the Sanghāyana, and Ne Win's reforms in the 1980s, and later state-sponsored rituals venerating relics of the Buddha were all designed to solicit, patronize, and appropriate the public and political agency of monks as sources of merit. Through the Sangha Mahanikaya

Council, regimes like the SLORC and SPDC similarly sought to ensure that "good" monks conform to the Weberian ideal of political agnosticism, but in fact, the modern state does not rebuke, but actually encourages the sangha's legitimation of politicians.

The conjunctures of Burmese Buddhism and politics demonstrate that modern Buddhism has not been relegated to the private domain of civil society, but retains the potential to bring about political transformations. Buddhist practice continues to harbor political potential because it is required for public validation of the ritual exchanges between the sangha and the laity. The practice of monks is still not subject to the secular law of the modern nation-state. This fact has enabled Buddhist actors to elude or contest the authority of the state and take public positions on political issues in contexts like sermons and other merit-making activities. When the state intervenes against Buddhist protestors, it has to negate the separate status of monks. This disregard for monastic authority, in turn, not only inflames the conflict between the state and the sangha, but also diminishes the moral authority of the state in the eyes of many Burmese Buddhists.

Monks have been imprisoned and disrobed to render them subject to civil authority and to enable the state to bring them to trial for crimes they allegedly committed. Forcing monks to disrobe in prison is generally seen as an inflammatory practice that evokes the subjugation of Burmese monks during the British colonial era. In particular, it evokes the cultural memory of U Wisara, who was disrobed in the 1930s by the Government of India. His resistance to this colonial demonstration of disrespect for the Buddha's robes impelled him to take up hunger strikes that eventually caused his death and made him a martyr of the nationalist struggle in Myanmar. The disrobing of monks for the purpose of interrogation by agents of the secular state in the wake of political unrest in 1988 and 2007 was generally seen as a blasphemous incursion against monastic authority of *vinaya* law that regulates, first and foremost, the ordination and excommunication of monks. The state's blatant disregard for the sangha's authority riled many in their fight for moral and economic justice. Against this background of potential and actual contestations between monastic and civil law, many Burmese felt that the treatment of U Gambira, one of the leaders of the All Burma Monks Alliance, was especially harsh. He was disrobed during his arrest, convicted of treason by a secular court, and given a lifelong prison sentence.[37]

This social dynamic reveals the cultural authority that modern Buddhists continue to attach to the notion of fields of merit, on which traditional Buddhist theories of power are based. The discourse about political monks, therefore, confounds normative ideals about religious traditions, such as ascetic detachment from society, with normative Buddhist cultural practices like merit-making, which require public validation. The potential for conflict between secular and religious authority is therefore unlikely to be dispelled by any secular government in Myanmar, whether a military dictatorship or a representative democracy. As long as the political process invokes Buddhist concepts of power in the national discourse, it is difficult to imagine that public power will be transacted and negotiated in entirely secular terms. In the face of a crisis of authority, such as a rebellion, a transition struggle, or a popular protest, the social and legal boundaries between the monastic and the civil domains in Burmese society have frequently been transgressed. Although the *vinaya* prohibits ordinations that are motivated by a desire to neglect social responsibility, by illness, or by criminality, the sangha has nonetheless been a refuge for those who have sought to evade the state's legal authority and coercion. During the popular uprising in 1988, many student demonstrators from the authorities in monasteries under the guise of monastic robes.

Today, Myanmar's two most powerful institutions, the sangha and the military, are embroiled in a confrontation that unfolds in a variety of cultural locations. Each institution is structured in a way that allows it to mobilize its members in support of public causes and in the service of the nation. A comparison of their respective organization and characteristic membership reveals insight into the dynamics of this national conflict. Both institutions are nearly matched in size, age groups of its members, and in their hierarchical structures of authority, which inculcates a strong sense of identity. In 2007 the sangha reportedly included approximately 400,000 monks. The number of young men in the military has increased in recent years, and the military forces in Myanmar are now said to comprise about 500,000 recruits.

The young men in each institution are set apart from ordinary social life and identify with a group that functions on the basis of disciplined action under the authority of their senior leaders, who are expected to enforce hierarchy and exercise their authority. Each institution inculcates its recruits with a definite sense of belonging and shapes a new identity that sets them apart from their previous social roles. Each trains its recruits to observe specific practices, though the educational focus and intellectual orientations sharply differ. Many of the young monks are more literate and better educated than their peers in the armed forces. By contrast, military recruits are often poorly educated and have few alternatives to military service or conscription. While monks are called upon to preserve the moral ground of *sāsana*, the dispensation within which the nation-state exists, soldiers are taught to guard the safety and prosperity of the nation-state.

Most Burmese are of the opinion that both the sangha and the military can make important contributions to the future prosperity of the nation-state. The sangha is seen as embodying the moral authority (*oza*) that empowers a field of merit that the present government seeks to control. While the sangha has a seemingly endless potential for nourishing charismatic leaders outside the purview of the state, this kind of popular appeal has been absent among the ranks of the military leadership since the martyrdom of Aung San. The military, however, controls arms that monks do not possess and embodies, in the Burmese cultural terms, coercive power (*ana*). From this colonial history emerged two social classes, namely, the sangha and the military, that were locked in competition for the moral and political authority to determine the nation's future. In contrast to many military recruits, monks are trained to reflect upon the workings of *samsāra*. Having chosen to devote their lives to a monastic vocation, many young monks are keenly aware of the limited options for the younger generation working toward the nation's future. Some stress that, unlike their married age cohorts, who struggle to support their families, monks are free to resist the regime and fight for justice. Such statements signal their awareness of the sangha's ability to mobilize its institutional power to resist secular control and claim for itself the moral authority to challenge the modern nation-state on behalf of the disempowered poor.

Collaboration between the sangha and the state could perhaps create overwhelming social and political synergies, but their mutual contestations certainly harbor the potential for divisive conflicts. These potentialities challenge the purportedly inevitable secularization of the modern state and illustrate how religious practice continues to empower the imagination of political futures. Burma's colonial legacy has survived into its contemporary political and religious transformations and has given rise to a coercive military regime that rules despotically over the independent state in disregard of the civil values, rights, and liberties to which its citizens aspire. Monks and secular activists, including social workers, labor organizers, and students who are aging beyond their youth, continue to mobilize resources to resist the colonial hegemonies in a supposedly postcolonial nation. As a Burmese monk living in exile, U Pandavamsa, has observed, monks "are always involved in every process of social change. Only maybe, the action or organization is different."[38]

8 Potential Futures

In Southeast Asia, Buddhist encounters with modernity unfolded in the context of wider engagements of traditional polities with the economic networks of the colonizing west. Partly in response to the encroaching west, modernizing reforms were initiated in 1851 by the Thai King Mongkut (r. 1851–1868) and in 1872 by the Burmese King Mindon (r. 1853–1878). These reforms led to significant revisions of Buddhist institutions, practices, and texts and stripped the Theravada tradition of many of its cosmological and mythic articulations. Equally significant was the fact that these reforms made possible changes that, until then, had been unimaginable. They gave rise to new Buddhist conjunctures that came to range from traditional forms of resistance against colonial rule to debates about the moral authority of the state, monks, and lay people, respectively. The advent of modernity in Southeast Asia clearly triggered profound changes in the social, political, and intellectual expressions of Buddhism.

The colonization of Burma and its subsequent annexation into the Government of India in 1886 led to a long trajectory of conflict between Buddhist institutions and the modern state. For instance, colonial attempts to displace Buddhist education and the affinity of Burmese colonial politicians to seek out alliances with members of the sangha eventually gave rise to anticolonial Buddhist millennialism. The British refusal to carry out the responsibilities that traditional governments had toward the Buddhist sangha also gradually fomented strong anticolonial sentiments. Many Burmese were suspicious of the intentions of the secular colonial government and sought to resurrect some form of Buddhist governance. Buddhist monks mobilized resistance against a colonial state and against non-Buddhist others, especially Indian Muslims, who were competing for their livelihoods with Buddhists. Military strength silenced Buddhist political activism at several conjunctures. However, the colonizing use of religion as a hegemonic practice has continued in some forms up until the present regime.

In Myanmar the discourse about Buddhism and politics has remained confined within the conceptual parameters of colonialism, even though the British colonial period ended more than six decades ago. The description of colonial scholars of Buddhism as either a philosophy or an "otherworldly" religion, obscured much of its religious relevance in contemporary practices. Both descriptions take their departure from the colonial project and its hegemonic interventions in Buddhist forms of resistance to the modern, secular state. Previous chapters traced the cultural discourse about colonial modernity and iterated social tensions surrounding nationalism, education, secularism, access to modern knowledge, and the formation of a civil society that emerged at particular historical moments. These tensions surrounding issues of modernity are yet to be resolved and will likely shape the future of this nation. Consequently, for much of Burma's modern history, Buddhist discourse about power has been articulated through genealogies of resisting the power of the state, or, alternatively, through validation of the state's patronage over Buddhist sources of power.[1]

Secularism entered the Burmese cultural lexicon as part of this colonial discourse and proved to be a major challenge to the power of the modern state in Burma. As a modern paradigm of political power, secularism has not been successful and has yet to demonstrate its long-term viability and acceptance in the civil society of contemporary Myanmar. For most Burmese, secularism is not synonymous with good governance; for them, secular government often implies an abdication of political ethics and justice, for they consider worldly matters (*lokiya*) to be subject to Buddhist Universal Law, which is manifest in all human events.[2] Since independence, the Burmese state has espoused secular political ideologies in several guises, including democracy, socialism, and militarism. None of them have been entirely successful and all their proponents eventually reverted to the use of Buddhist paradigms of power. For instance, during the democratic government of U Nu and later military regimes, various elites employed Buddhist constructions of power to legitimate their political claims. The idea that the development of the nation mirrored the stages of the Eightfold Noble Path in the attainment of perfection (*nibbāna*) was articulated first by nationalists in the 1920s and later by the democratic, socialist, and military regimes that followed. This return to a Buddhist discourse of power frequently resulted from the insurmountable tensions of modernity and most particularly from weak institutions in civil society.

At many conjunctures our received categories for understanding Buddhist practices and communities offer only inadequate descriptions and compel us to rethink earlier approaches to the study of Buddhism and society. Specifically, scholarship that takes its departure from Max Weber's characterization of Buddhism as otherworldly must be reappraised in light of the political agency of modern Buddhist practices, communities, and institutions. His description implied, wrongly, that the engagement of monks with public concerns undermines the authenticity of their practice. Weber's views thus echo a strict reading of the *vinaya* that privileges some Buddhist interlocutors at the exclusion of other voices in this tradition. Yet contemporary scholarship recognizes that the valuation of practices as "pristine" or "defiled" belongs to a colonial discourse in which scholars endeavored to define an "original" Pāli canon. The works on Burmese Buddhism, culture, and the state by scholars such as Spiro, Manning Nash, and Trager similarly reproduce a valuation of Burmese Buddhist practice as a "veneer" covering more pervasive and historically rooted impurities of religion. More recent scholarship is cognizant of the fact that the voice of authenticity belongs to religious communities and that the history of Buddhist traditions is far more complex than colonial imaginings had envisioned.[3]

Equally compelling is the need to rethink Weberian theories of reforms in a Buddhist context.[4] Many theorists writing on modernity and civil society presume that the western model of religion in modern, civil society applies equally to non-western cultures and their religious traditions. Yet modernizing reforms of religion do not inevitably engender individualism, a Protestant ethnic, the development of capitalism, and the relegation of religion to the private sphere. Nor is the Buddhist tradition inevitably incapable of embracing a capitalist middle class and its patterns of consumption. Weber's ideas about Protestant ethics as a hallmark of modernization, the privatization of religion in civil society, and the secularization of the state simply do not unfold in the same way in Theravada Buddhist contexts where colonial hegemonies have altered the distribution of power from the start of the modern era.[5] The modernizing reforms of Theravada Buddhist communities since the mid-nineteenth century have not, as Weberian theories would predict, relegated Buddhist practice to the private domain. Previous chapters have traced the interventions of Buddhist institutions, communities, and symbols into the politics of the state. While some instances, such as the Thai Dhammakay movement, exemplify the privatization and commercialization of religion in a capitalist society, these features are not universal to all modern contexts.

David Steinberg observes that the weakness or nonexistence of the institutions of civil society have inevitably strengthened military rule in Burma.[6] The suppression of democratic practices since 1962 by successive military regimes inevitably undermined such institutions of civil society as an independent judiciary, a free press, and access to higher education. Their absence has curtailed the development of democratic institutions and nurtured an authoritarian ethos for more than half a century. Operating without a national constitution between 1990 and 2008, the military state has become the most salient form of secular power in Burma today. Ethnic wars at the nation's periphery, an economically lucrative cross-border trade in narcotics and weapons, and the centrifugal forces of the Chinese economy during the twentieth century further challenge the state and strengthened military rule.

The regime has succeeded in dispersing most of its internal enemies, and many leaders of democratic reforms remain imprisoned.[7] An important aspect of its strategy to silent dissent involves higher education and the dispersal of university campuses. One prominent member of the Union Solidarity and Development Association (USDA) explained that the opening of new regional campuses has increased access to higher education. Others said that daily commuting to distant campus was exhausting and directly impacted the students' academic performance.[8] It is likely that the development of dispersed commuter campuses was intended to forestall potential student-led unrest and control, rather than disperse, access to higher education among Myanmar's younger generation.

Potential roles for Buddhist communities in shaping Myanmar's political future can be gleaned against these weak markers of civil society. New forms of Buddhism are closely linked to political visions of the Burmese nation and its continuing struggle to resolve tensions surrounding the concerns of modernity, which will necessarily have to include developing modern institutions and their roles in negotiating the future of Burmese society. Other than the sangha, few segments of Burmese society will be able to challenge the military. The emphasis on socially engaged Buddhist practice and the public demonstrations of the sangha's moral authority as a challenge to the military state in 2007 may only indicate one among several possible future directions.

Although general elections are planned for 2010, a new constitution adopted in 2008 ensures decisive participation by the military in the political process, thus making major social changes difficult to implement. Observers have noted efforts to create new parties that are friendly to the regime and to position former military and leading members of the USDA as candidates for the 2010 elections.[9] This organization is well integrated into the fabric of local communities and some experts suggest that it will become a political party in support of the status quo. The 2010 elections will supersede the electoral victory of the National League of Democracy in 1990 and create an appearance of democracy and national reconciliation. This strategy may help ease the economic sanctions imposed by the United States and Europe to protest the regime's human rights violations.

Since the early 1990s, the state's policy of economic liberalization produced invitations for joint ventures with foreign capital from which the government and private business parties benefited directly. The new economic climate favored individuals with access to political influence at home and connections abroad; it enabled some Burmese to open highly profitable businesses with foreign financing. Members of the USDA benefited from these investment opportunities by helping agricultural cooperatives attract foreign investors and gain access to export markets. Within a few years numerous state-initiated organizations, ministries, and military organizations also took advantage of joint ventures. Their collaborations have permitted foreign business to extract resources and profit from cheap labor, while their Burmese counterparts have benefited financially from these lucrative projects and gained access to foreign currencies and investments. Joint ventures have thus become the entry point into global markets for some Burmese cliques, allowing them to diversify their wealth and invest in multiple strategies for the future.

Economic liberalization has directly and indirectly influenced the potential futures of Buddhist communities in Myanmar. Opening the economy to foreign investment has provided access to foreign monies, goods, and information and accelerated social transformations of lifestyle, as can be seen in cities like Yangon and Mandalay. As the main financial and economic center, Yangon looks to Singapore and other economies in Southeast Asia and East Asia. By contrast, Mandalay's economic focus is interior, and trade moves overland on a new highway in and out of China. While luxury goods and hi-tech items stand out in Yangon's consumer economy, heavy machinery and farm and industrial equipment lead trade in Mandalay: motorcycles, washing machines, refrigerators, and manual sewing machines entered the country from China and were resold from Mandalay to less-developed regions in Upper Burma.

As the country's premier mercantile center, Yangon has undergone a considerable economic boom. Signposts of a new affluence and conspicuous consumption fuel the expansive lifestyle of a growing middle class and its desires to consume modern fashions and luxury goods. While private property was inconspicuous during the socialist Ne Win era, economic liberalization has created considerable quite-visible wealth for the new cosmopolitan urban elite engaged in joint ventures. Upscale businesses quote prices in U.S. or Singapore dollars, with Singapore dollars now the informal currency of the country.[10] Individuals with privilege and access to the regime have benefited from foreign currency and Myanmar's participation in China's emergent consumer economy. This new access to foreign investment has allowed members of the elite to secure assets abroad, travel, and educate their children at universities in Asia, Europe, and North America, while retaining strong social and financial ties to their communities back home.

The state has restructured its fiscal policies and encouraged ministries to act as economic agents in collaboration with foreign investors. While this policy has helped to ease financial pressures on the state by increasing revenue for particular ministries, it has also turned state agencies into participants in a market economy and rendered them dependent on a seemingly limitless need to attract more foreign investment. With the increasing reliance of government agencies on revenue generated by foreign capital, economists estimate that currently 60 percent of the military's budget comes from its investments in joint ventures.[11] These policies have a detrimental effect on public funds and private practices, for economic liberalization has disenfranchised a significant part of the population who have no access to foreign monies. The distinction between private and public property has become blurred as a consequence of government involvement in these joint ventures. With the expansion of the government's informal role in commerce, private businesses have become vulnerable to interventions by those representatives of the state who issue permits for importing and exporting goods, such as cars or raw materials. The obligations acquired in these transactions became part of traditional social hierarchy and patterns of patronage.

At the start of the twenty-first century, construction of the new capital, Naypyidaw, became a new focus of the regime's planning and expenditure. Relocation of the capital and the opening of the Burmese economy to global markets recall earlier conjunctures in Burmese history, when King Thalon moved capital from Pegu, Lower Burma, to Ava in Upper Burma to signal a shift in his polity's renewed focus on trade with other polities in the Southeast Asian mainland. The contemporary developments clearly also signal a new orientation for the nation. In late 2005 core ministries moved from Yangon to their new location in the geographic center of the country. Few outsiders have been granted access to Naypyidaw. Popular opinion speculated that the remote location was chosen to insulate the regime strategically from potential unrest. At the same time the state's preoccupation with Buddhist nationalism ceased, along with its construction and restoration of major religious centers. No longer visible were the columns of workers who had labored to widen the road and reconstruct the moat of the Mandalay Palace. A shift in public rhetoric signaled an embrace of modern technology and science, which now portrayed Myanmar as a modern nation within a global network of Asian nations.

The regime's agenda began to emphasize economic and technological development. Government media focused on technological and scientific discourse. News media reported extensively on science, health care, technology, and the influx of foreign investment and debated Myanmar's preparedness for climate change; all this was to show that the state actively participated in technological progress.[12] Slogans on public billboards, on television, and in the print media advertised the regime's new agenda for development. Its political, economic, and social objectives conveyed both the goals and limitations of the regime's vision for the future. The state urged its citizens to work toward political stability, national reconciliation, a new constitution, and national development. The state also emphasized expanding the agricultural market and developing a market economy, technical capacity, and foreign and Burmese investments through state initiatives. Its social objectives focused on patriotism, morality, national character, cultural heritage, and improvements to public health and education.[13] Many Burmese have memorized these widely publicized objectives.

It is not evident to an outside observer that the military's vision for the future of the country transcends its paramount interest in self-preservation. Revenues generated from the sale of energy resources, including natural gas reserves, to Thailand, China, and India generate considerable returns, estimated to be around US$2 billion annually. While it is likely that some of the revenue supports the construction in Naypyidaw, a sprawling network of underground tunnels and various military stockpiles, much-needed investment in the country's infrastructure is less evident. Public spending in support of education, public heath, and related infrastructure does not match the need in these areas. The government's insufficient response to Cyclone Nargis speaks directly to these concerns.

In contrast to those who make a public display of their newfound wealth, those Burmese without access to the new economy have been increasingly pushed to the margins of subsistence. Sacred sites like stupas, pagodas, and monasteries have long been a refuge for the destitute, such as the poor and homeless people living at the Mindon pagodas in Mandalay. The social margin between petty traders, food-stall vendors, guards, and the homeless appears fluid at these places. Some adults spend their days sleeping in the shade of Buddhist monuments and looking upon visitors with a hazy glance. Children are particularly vulnerable victims of poverty and a surprising number of sickly, neglected children live in the shadow of pagodas. On one of my visits to Bagan, I witnessed a baby boy, too young to crawl, who had been left at a pagoda during the night, according to the workmen. In the morning a young shop girl picked up the baby hesitantly and said, "Don't cry any more." Some of the children worked for vendors at the pagodas, waiting for tourists whom they would ask for "lucky money," the first sale of the day of trinkets and cheap souvenirs.

For many, this is a major source of family income. A ten-year-old girl explained that she came to the pagodas to sell tourist souvenirs after school each day until the sun set. These children were part of a low-wage workforce with few alternatives. Their future belongs to a marginalized segment of Burma's population with few resources for improving their standard of living. In the absence of a social safety net, the role of providing for the disenfranchised and poor has fallen, in a traditional manner, upon the sangha and its monasteries. These economic pressures are precisely the ones that became a flashpoint in the Saffron Revolution in September 2007, when monks marched in public demonstration to protest the economic pressures under which their lay supporters labored.

The impact of globalization affects Myanmar and its Buddhist communities mostly through two venues, the need for energy and the patterns of its consumption, and access to digital information and the knowledge structures it produces. From these two trajectories of globalization, new Buddhist contestations are emerging concerning social justice, the moral discourse of Buddhist social engagement, and the rights of citizens of the state. Myanmar's engagement with the global economy is fueling renewed tension between Buddhist and political institutions. The need for sources of energy, including the natural gas that the junta is able to supply to the global market, has strengthened its hegemonic position within Myanmar's political structure. Sudden fluctuations in the cost of gasoline for citizens, however, have also fueled public dissent with the junta's policies and even inflamed the protests led by monks in 2007.

Equally significant has been access to digital information. Like all media, internet access is closely monitored, and the government exercises considerable control over the flow of information through such networks. In internet cafes, young people know how to circumvent the communication barriers, chat feverishly with conversation partners around the world, and seek out foreign entertainment and news. By contrast, e-mail and phone calls between Burmese and others abroad are more closely monitored. A recent verdict under the Electronics Act, resulting from one of the many charges leveled against U Gambira, the monastic leader in the 2007 uprising, illustrated how the use of digital information can be construed as a hostile act against the state.[14] The internet has been an important medium for Buddhist activists who propagate the message of social engagement among Buddhist communities. Such new economies of knowledge bring local interlocutors into conversation with others, who implement similar agendas elsewhere and carry conversations about Buddhist social engagements into a disembedded, virtual reality. These possibilities underscore the democratizing forces of the digital information age.

The intellectual tenets of socially engaged Buddhism, a decidedly modern formation of Buddhism, have been inspired by grassroots politics in multiple locations across Asia. It emerged initially as a voice against war in Vietnam. Through the work of Buddhadasa Bhikkhu and social innovators like Sulak Sivaraksa in Thailand, socially engaged Buddhism has been the platform for formulating a renewed Buddhist relevance and alleviating social and economic injustice. This advocacy for a Buddhist engagement in the world as a way to envision a future has found appeal among many Buddhist communities in diverse transnational contexts. These new Buddhist voices have come into conflict with the policies of the modern state in many places, among them Myanmar in 2007 and Tibet's resistance to Chinese immigration in 2008.

Global realities influence Buddhist formations in Myanmar. They open up new social spaces for Buddhist communities to voice their visions of moral authority. They also prompt the state to intervene in the public discourse of Buddhist actors and institutions. It is unlikely that the genealogies of Buddhist resistance and the state's attempt to control them will fade as Myanmar struggles to overcome its colonial legacies. As long as the tensions of modernity remain unsolved, and Myanmar's social resources and viable options remain limited, debates about the future of civil society at the interstices of pragmatic politics and Buddhist visions of potential futures are likely to continue.

CHRONOLOGY

1531–1752	Restored Taungoo dynasty rules Burma.
1635	King Thalon moves capital from Pegu to Ava.
1752–1885	Konbaun dynasty.
1755–1760	Reign of Alaungpaya, founder the Konbaun dynasty
1782–1819	Reign of Bodawpaya.
1824–1826	First Anglo-Burmese War leads to the Treaty of Yandabo and the establishment of British colonial rule is Lower Burma.
1852-1853	Second Anglo-Burmese War leads to the British annexation of Pegu.
1853–1878	Reign of Mindon.
1857	King Mindon moves capital to Mandalay from Ava.
1868	King Mindon convenes the Fifth Buddhist Council.
1871	Buddhist Tipitaka and commentaries inscribed on stone slabs at Kuthodaw Pagoada in Mandalay; restoration of Shwedagon Pagoda in Rangoon.
1878–1886	Reign of King Thibaw.
1885	Third Anglo-Burmese War.
1886	The British abolish the Konbaun court and annex Burma, placing it under the Government of India. A brief rebellion against the British takes place in which monks participate; sangha accepts British rule, with the expectation that the British will assume royal duties. Strong anti-Thibaw sentiments exist among the sangha.
1895	Taungdaw Thathanabain dies; his office remains vacant until 1903.
1897	Buddha Sāsana Noggaha Association founded.
1903	Lieutenant Governor Barnes agrees to recognize, but not appoint, the Taunggwin Sayadaw as *thathanabain* for Upper Burma only.
1906	Young Men's Buddhist Association founded.
1917	Burma excluded from constitutional reforms of Government of India; becomes a province of India.
1920	General Council of Burmese Associations (GCBA) founded.
1920	Rangoon University founded; Rangoon University students go on strike.
1921	U Ottama returns to Burma, influenced by Gandhi's ideals, and links Buddhism to ideals of freedom from colonial rule; Ottama asserts that independence constitutes *nibbāna*.
1921	General Council of Sangha Sammeggi established. British administration permits creation of a partially elected legislative council in Burma.
1929	U Wisara dies in prison at age 41 from hunger strike.
1930	Dobama (We Burmans) Association founded; has Marxist leanings. Members address one another as *thakin* (master).
1930–1931	Tharrawaddi or Saya San Revolt, led by the Thupanna Galon Raja, starts in Pegu Yoma and spreads to the economically depressed Irrawaddy Delta.
1930s	More than 1 million Indians live in Burma; more than half of population of Rangoon is Indian.

1932	Anti-Indian riots erupt; Young Monks Association promotes anti-Indian sentiments.
1936	Rangoon University students strike.
1937	Burma administered separately from India.
1938	Anti-Indian riots.
1938	Taunggwin Sayadaw dies; the office of *thathanabain* lapses for half a century.
1938	All Burma Young Monks Association forms as result of anti-Muslim sentiments; headquartered in Mandalay; founder U Zawtika.
1938, 1939	Anti-Indian riots.
1941	Indians own two-thirds of rice-producing fields in the Irrawaddy District.
1941	Burma Independence Army (BIA) formed, led by Bogyoke Aung San; Burma Defense Army (BDA) formed, which transforms into the Burma National Army (BNA), then becomes the Patriotic Burmese Forces (PBF).
1945	Regular Burmese military forces (Tatmadaw) formed.
1947	British leave Burma.
Jan. 4, 1948	Burma becomes independent under U Nu as prime minister; U Nu seeks to restore Buddhism, blaming western values and colonialism for a decline in Buddhist piety.
1949	Ecclesiastical Courts Act.
1950	Pāli University and Dhammacariya Act.
1951	U Nu starts preparations for Sixth Buddhist Council.
1952	Pāli Education Board Act.
1954–1956	Sixth Buddhist Convocation in Rangoon; key architects are Attorney General U Chan Htoon and Minister of Home and Religious Affairs U Win.
1955	New edition of Buddhist Tipitaka produced by All Burma Monks Association.
1958–1960	Monastic registration efforts begin.
1958–1960	Army employs Buddhist concepts in its rhetoric against communism.
1960–1962	U Nu abolishes the slaughter of cattle, introduces lunar Buddhist calendar, and commutes death sentences; he considers federalism to appease minorities and the threat of ethnic secession.
1962	Yahan Pyo Apwe pressures U Nu's government to prohibit non-Buddhist religious education in public schools. Some members form a splinter group, Yahan Nge Apwe.
1962	Ne Win's military coup topples U Ne's government, abolishes the federal system, and inaugurates "the Burmese Way to Socialism." He nationalizes the economy and forms a single-party state, with the Socialist Program Party as the sole political party. All independent newspapers are banned.
1965	All Sangha All-Sect Convention is unable to implement monastic registration.
1974	Student protest at the funeral of former United Nations General Secretary U Thant.
1974	New constitution transfers power from the armed forces to the People's Assembly headed by Ne Win and other former military leaders.
1975	The National Democratic Front formed by regional minority groups, who conduct insurgencies against Ne Win's government.
1980	Sangha Mahanayaka Council convened under the supervision of the Ministry of Religious Affairs; 1,200 selected monks convene to implement monastic registration; constitution of centralized administration (village, ward, district,

	state/division). 300 monks comprised the Central Working Committee; 47 monks made up the Sangha Mahanayaka Committee; this structure parallels the state's political administration.
1980	Ne Win begins construction of Mahāwizaya Pagoda in Rangoon.
1982	People of non-indigenous background are made "associate citizens" and barred from holding public office.
1985	The Sangha Mahanayaka Council ratifies the sangha act and constitution.
1987	Currency devaluation wipes out savings and triggers antigovernment riots.
Aug. 8, 1988	Thousands killed in antigovernment riots. The State Law and Order Restoration Council (SLORC) comes to power.
1988	Ministry of Religious Affairs expands mission to propagating Buddhism in tribal areas.
1989	The SLORC declares martial law.
1989	National League for Democracy (NLD), Aung San Suu Kyi's party, wins landslide victory, but election results not honored by the military.
July 20, 1989	Aung San Suu Kyi arrested for the first time.
Aug. 8, 1990	7,000 monks in Mandalay commemorate the NLD election anniversary and refuse donations from military families. Protesting monks are attacked by military forces.
Aug. 27, 1990	20,000 monks participate in donations boycott against military and families; proscription eventually lifted under pressure from SLORC.
1992	About 6,000 monks live on Thai border. Exile organizations such as the All Burma Young Monks Association and the All Burma Students Democratic Front (ABSDF) formed.
1994	The Mingyan Sayadaw elected *thathanabain* by the State Central Committee of the Sangha. A nationwide hierarchy of monastic courts is created to adjudicate *vinaya* cases. Ministry of Religious Affairs administers annual Dhammacariya and monastic exams.
1990s	Era of Buddhist nationalism; state officials sponsor restoration of many sacred sites.
Dec. 1996	University student protests.
1997	SLORC renamed the Solidarity, Prosperity and Development Council (SPDC).
March 1997	Anti-Muslim riots sparked by rumors of damage to Mahamuni Buddha image.
Feb. 2001	Burmese army clash with Shan rebels on Thai border.
Sept. 2001	Intelligence chief Khin Nyunt visits Thailand. Burma pledges to eliminate drug trade in Golden Triangle.
May 2003	Attacks at Depyin on Aung San Suu Kyi, who is forced into "preemptive" house arrest.
Nov. 2005	Capital moved to Naypyidaw in central Myanmar.
June 2006	The 88 Generation begins prayer campaign.
Sept. 2007	The Saffron Revolution sweeps through the country.
May 2008	Constitutional referendum passes, ensuring military control of future parliament.
2010	Multiparty elections are planned.

NOTES

Introduction

Bellah and Hammond, *Varieties of Civil Religion,* 1980: iv.

1. I use the linguistically related terms of Burma and Myanmar interchangeably throughout my writing. In doing so, I do not want to disrespect Burmese national sentiments that stress the colonial heritage of the name "Burma." In the same way, I want to distance myself from the practices and ideology of the State Law and Order Restoration Council (SLORC) and its successors that changed the country's official name in 1989 to "Myanmar," a formal term that is linguistically related to its previous designation, Burma. Although this change was intended to express a postcolonial national identity, many who remain opposed to the regime continue to use "Burma" to refer to this Southeast Asian nation. Without wishing to engage the politics of terminology, I continue to use "Burma" and "Burmese" in most of my writing, reserving the term "Myanmar" for social and cultural realities specific to the identities constructed by the military in the aftermath of the pro-democracy uprising in 1988.

The country of Burma/Myanmar, surrounded by Bangladesh and India to the west, China to the north, and Laos and Thailand to the east and southeast, today comprises about 52 million people. About 80 percent are ethnically Burman, and nearly 90 percent of the state's citizens are Theravada Buddhists. This religious tradition is also prominent among some of Burma's many ethnic minorities, notably the Shan, Karen, Pao, Arakanese, and Mon. Muslim, Hindu, Christian, and tribal communities account for about 10 percent of the population, although some put this percentage considerably higher and argue that the census is outdated or deliberately skewed by the state. The national language is Burmese, which belongs to the Tibeto-Burman groups of languages. The languages of the ethnic minorities, although not always taught in government schools, are spoken within the ethnically diverse regions of the country.

2. In my use of the notion of conjuncture, I follow David Scott who defines it as a pivotal historical moment in which potential developments are circumscribed by cognitive, cultural, and political contingencies (*Refashioning Futures*, pp. 4–5, 18–19). In *Colors of the Robe*, Abeysekara also employs this concept to analyze Buddhist modernity in Sri Lanka.

3. This study takes as its departure earlier work by Michael Mendelson (*Sangha and State in Burma*), John Ferguson ("The Arahat Ideal"), and Michael Aung-Thwin (*Pagan*), who have debated the relative strengths of the Burmese polity to control the sangha. Justin McDaniel ("Buddhism in Thailand") characterizes modern Thai history as also being shaped by Buddhist contestations of and support for the state.

4. See Lieberman, *Strange Parallels*, pp. 196–199; see also Leider, "Text, Lineage and Tradition" for further discussions of the hierarchical nexus between social hierarchy and Buddhism at the Burmese court.

5. Traditional Burmese military science used battle formations in the shapes of astrological zodiac signs deemed to be auspicious omens that would affect a victorious outcome. For instance, a commander might lead his soldiers into battle in a formation that resembled the shape of a scorpion. The aim of warfare also differed greatly. While European colonial expansion aimed to control strategic territories from which to extract resources and protect global trade networks, the traditional goal of Burmese warfare was to take prisoners, who were usually enslaved in labor projects at the center of the polity.

6. See Thant Myint-U, *The Making of Modern Burma*; Cohn, *Colonialism and Its Forms of Knowledge*; Furnivall, *Colonial Policy and Practice*; and Moscotti, *British Policy*.

7. The designations of Lower and Upper Burma gained particular currency as a result of colonial history and the territorial divisions of the Anglo-Burmese Wars. Jan Bečka (*Historical Dictionary of Burma*, pp. 127, 210) points out that prior to 1886, Lower Burma referred to the southern regions under British administration, namely, the Irrawaddy Delta, Pegu, the Tenerassim, and Arakanese districts, while Upper Burma designated territories under the control of the Mandalay court. Following the British annexation in 1886, Upper Burma comprised the administrative division of central and northern Burma, including Magway, Mandalay, and Sagain. However, Michael Aung-Thwin (personal communication) has also noted that the designations of Upper and Lower Burma are indigenous to the precolonial discourse in Burma.

8. This suggestion has been made by Helen James, *Governance and Civil Society*.

9. Gravers, *Nationalism as Political Paranoia*.

10. The remainder of this section was published in slightly different form as a part of "Buddhism and Modernity in Myanmar," in *Buddhism in World Cultures*, pp. 73–100.

11. My use of religion follows the definitions Bruce Lincoln set out in *Holy Terrors*, pp. 4–8. Religious discourse, then, is an engagement not only with the practices, institutions, and communities that are Buddhist in Burma. More broadly, religious discourse may engage any subject in mythic terms. By this I mean that religious discourse, by definition, refers to atemporal and mythic realities, values, narratives, ideals, utopias, beliefs, and similar culturally constructed and imagined ultimate realities in order to authorize agency at specific historical moments. By politics I mean, most broadly, the transaction of power in human relationships. Like the religious discourse, the political discourse about power is rarely absent from the context of social relationships. However, it may or may not be the dominant feature of any particular discourse.

12. The notion of a Protestant Buddhism has been specially debated in the literature on colonial Buddhism in Sri Lanka, where the term has been applied to a Buddhist revival after centuries of strong Christian influences. Anthropologists like Abeysekara

(*Colors of the Robe*) and Seneviratne (*The Work of Kings*) have been critical of applying Weber's notion to modern Buddhist history in Sri Lanka, and its applicability to the Buddhist traditions of Southeast Asia is equally wrought with conceptual problems.

13. See in particular Choompolpaisal's "Constrictive Constructs," Gellner's "The Anthropology of Buddhism and Hinduism," Keyes' "Weber and Anthropology," and Kitiarsa's "Beyond the Weberian Trials."

14. This task has already been accomplished. For instance, meditation constitutes a significant conjuncture in modern Burmese Buddhism, and Ingrid Jordt's *Burma's Mass Lay Meditation Movement* offers unrivaled insights into the mass meditation movement. I also want to point to Alicia Turner's work on Buddhist missionizing (*thathana pyu thi*) during the era of the YMBA ("Buddhism, Colonialism, and the Boundaries of Religion") and Maitrii Aung Thwin's focus on the colonial criminalization of traditional culture during the Saya San uprising ("Genealogy of a Rebellion Narrative"). See also the valuable work of Penny Edwards ("Grounds for Protest"; "Relocating the Interlocutor"); and Chie Ikeya ("Gender, History, and Modernity").

15. See Gravers, *Nationalism as Political Paranoia.*

16. See Cohn, *Colonialism and Its Forms of Knowledge*; Furnivall, *Colonial Policy and Practice*; and Moscotti, *British Policy.*

Chapter 1: Theravada Cultural Hegemony in Precolonial Burma

1. Hall, *Burma,* p. 66.

2. For my discussion of the ways in which Buddhism shaped the administrative rationale and policies in precolonial Burma, I am indebted to Lieberman, *Strange Parallels,* pp. 187–202; Leider, "Text, Lineage and Tradition in Burma," pp. 82–129; Pranke, "Treatise on the Lineage of Elders"; and Mendelson, *Sangha and State in Burma.*

3. See Lieberman, *Strange Parallels,* p. 196.

4. Ibid., p. 192.

5. See Than Htun, "December 3, 1807," *Royal Orders of Burma*; and Leider, "Text, Lineage and Tradition in Burma," p. 95.

6. See Tambiah's essay on Buddhist galactic polities in *Culture, Thought, and Social Action.* Steven Collins critiques Tambiah's model for its use of the notion of "total social fact" and argues for a less static model for cultural systems of literate societies, such as those shaped by the Pāli Imaginaire (*Nirvana and Other Buddhist Felicities,* p. 466, fn. 70).

7. During the third century BCE, the Mauryan emperor Aśoka converted to Buddhism and used his new religious identity to consolidate his rule over a vast and ethnically diverse region of South Asia. He is credited with constructing pillars with inscriptions that recount his conversion, with building 84,000 stupas, and with acting as the royal patron of the Third Buddhist Council. See Strong, *The Legend of King Aśoka.*

8. In Burma, both the state and the sangha draw upon multiethnic and overlapping constituencies. Unfortunately, our record of how ethnicity crosscuts these major institutions still awaits further documentation of local traditions and their articulation with the Pāli textual tradition. In his essay "On the Very Idea of the Pāli Canon" (pp. 89–126), Steven Collins points to the cultural value of the Theravada canon as a symbol that represents the entirety of the Buddha's teachings. As a body of texts that is grounded in historical contexts and maintained in several vernacular languages, it shows that variations have occurred in the course of its transmission.

9. However, historical evidence suggests the presence of Theravada institutions as early as the sixth century CE, indicating that the genealogy of the Myanmar state is intentionally constructed. See Stargardt, "The Oldest Known Pāli Texts."

10. See Aung-Thwin, *Pagan*.

11. See Lieberman, *Strange Parallels*, p. 121.

12. Often translated as "religion," the connotations of the term are much broader. *Thathana* (Burmese) or *sāsana* (Pāli) denote the extent in time and space of the Buddha's dispensation. I have always been perplexed by the fact that textbooks rarely discuss or even index the term, which, in my view, is as central to the tradition as Buddha, *dhamma*, and sangha.

13. Such icons were usually placed in large public monuments and included Buddha images and stupas, i.e., reliquaries containing remains of the Buddha or ritual substitutes.

14. Collins explores the royal potential for demerit in *Nirvana and Other Buddhist Felicities*, pp. 414–496.

15. See Weber, *The Religion of India*.

16. See Schober, "Venerating the Buddha's Remains."

17. Ibid.

18. For an excellent discussion on the bodies of the Buddha, see Strong, *Relics of the Buddha*, 2004. For a discussion of Burmese cultural conceptions about the ways in which relics organize communities, see Schober, "Venerating the Buddha's Remains."

19. See Schober, "Mapping the Sacred."

20. See Schober, "In the Presence of the Buddha," pp. 259–288; and "Venerating the Buddha's Remains."

21. See Lieberman, *Strange Parallels*, p. 190.

22. See Lieberman's discussion on the mediating role of monastic education in ibid., pp. 188–189. He notes that the earliest extant palm-leaf manuscript dates to 1680. It was already written in the rounded script of the contemporary Burmese alphabet, rather than the edged lettering found on earlier stone inscriptions.

23. The texts of the Tipitaka constitute a rather large canon of the Pāli Theravada tradition. They are divided into three baskets, namely, the rules for monastic discipline (*vinaya pitaka)*; the *sutta pitaka* containing narratives about the Buddha and his

preaching; and the *abhidhamma pitaka*, which is a collection of Theravada philosophy concerning the causality that governs the path to enlightenment. Because these texts are believed to contain all of the Buddha's original teachings, much effort has been invested throughout the history of the Theravada tradition to preserve the purity of the texts. At various Buddhist councils, kings commissioned literati to remove any accretions that might have crept into the text. Pointing to the actual textual diversity that does exist within the Theravada tradition, Collins ("On the Very Idea") notes the use of the canon as a symbol around which Theravada "orthodoxy" has been constructed. Indeed, the claim to textual purity is critical to Theravada political theory and to the role and office of a righteous king (*dhammarāja*).

24. For a discussion of ethnographic constructions of *pativedha sāsana* as a Buddhist utopian ideal, see Schober, "Paths to Enlightenment."

25. In contrast to other places in the cultural complex of the Pāli Imaginarie, Buddhist millennialism in Burma rejected the expectations tied to the coming of the next Buddha, Metteyya.

26. Pranke, "Treatise on the Lineage of Elders," p. 6.

27. In his essay "Text, Lineage and Tradition in Burma," p. 113, Leider points out that one day after pronouncing his severe punishment, the king reversed himself and commuted the sentence he had imposed upon Atulayasa, his monastic disciples, and his lay supporters. One may speculate about the king's motivations as to whether they demonstrated his compassion, volatile personality, or contestations internal to the court. Regardless, the reversal complicates the uniform, orthodox stance of the court that is projected in the chronicles and reveals at the very least a multiplicity of voices seeking to shape the reform process.

28. Cady ("Religion and Politics in Modern Burma," p. 152); and Myo Myint ("The Politics of Survival in Burma," p. 175) contain further discussions of the court's supervisory role over the office of the *thathanabain* and his advisory Thudhamma Council. It is noteworthy that the Ministry of Religious Affairs in the contemporary state carries out very similar functions in its work with the Sangha Mahanayaka.

29. Than Htun, "December 26, 1812," *Royal Orders of Burma*.

30. See Pranke, "Treatise on the Lineage of Elders," pp. 7–9.

31. According to Pranke, ibid., p. 1, the name of this lineage derives from the name of the celestial pavilion, Thudhamma-zayat, in Tāvatimsa Heaven, where the Buddha taught the Abhidhamma to his mother.

32. Leider, "Text, Lineage and Tradition in Burma," p. 115.

33. Ibid., pp. 82–129.

34. See Pranke "Treatise on the Lineage of Elders"; also Leider, "Text, Lineage and Tradition in Burma."

35. See Pranke, "Treatise on the Lineage of Elders," p. viii.

36. See Than Htun, *Royal Orders of Burma*.

37. See Pranke, "Treatise on the Lineage of Elders, p. 5.

38. See Schober, "In the Presence of the Buddha."

39. See Symes, *Journal of His Second Embassy,* p. 212.

40. For a discussion of Mindon's challenges, see Myo Myint, "The Politics of Survival in Burma."

41. Mendelson, *Sangha and State in Burma,* p. 87.

42. Ibid.

43. Although local traditions like the monastic practice of martial arts (*pwe kyaun:*) or the veneration of spirits (*nat*) have been discouraged for failing to comply with the reforming institution's view of orthodoxy, they have continued to be popular among some local communities. A great deal of scholarly collaboration will be required to document the diversity of local, regional, and ethnic Buddhist traditions throughout the region.

Chapter 2: The Emergence of the Secular in Modern Burma

1. See King, "Colonialism and Buddhism," pp. 162–165.

2. Keyes, "Buddhist Economics and Buddhist Fundamentalism"; and Keyes, Kendall, and Hardacre, "Contested Visions of Community in East and Southeast Asia."

3. Furnivall, *Colonial Policy and Practice.*

4. See Schober, "Buddhist Just Rule and Burmese National Culture"; and "Buddhist Visions of Moral Authority and Civil Society."

5. See Thant Myint-U, *The Making of Modern Burma.*

6. Schober, "Buddhist Visions of Moral Authority and Civil Society."

7. Cohn, *Colonialism and Its Forms of Knowledge.*

8. Thant Myint-U, *The Making of Modern Burma,* p. 101.

9. Burmese chronicles and other texts also use the concept of *auk myi',* meaning "down river," to refer to the region of Lower Burma that had been developed prior to the arrival of the British.

10. In his essay, "Rural Monetization and Land-Mortgage Thet-Kayits in Konbaung Burma," Truiko Seito provides statistics on the mortgaging of property to moneylenders from the late eighteenth century to the early twentieth century. Following a sharp increase in debt after 1791, mortgaged wealth flowed into the expanding colonial economy along the coastal regions of Lower Burma, thus contributing to growing British mercantile interests.

11. Thant Myint-U, *The Making of Modern Burma,* pp. 130–153.

12. For a discussion of the growth of lay influence in modern Theravada traditions, see Schober, "Buddhism and Modernity in Myanmar"; Keyes, Kendall, and Hardacre, "Contested Visions of Community in East and Southeast Asia"; Maung,

From Sangha to Laity; Sarkisyanz, *Buddhist Backgrounds of the Burmese Revolution;* and Swearer, "Fundamentalistic Movements in Theravāda Buddhism."

13. See Ling, *Buddhist Trends in Southeast Asia.*

14. See Cohn, *Colonialism and Its Forms of Knowledge.*

15. The colonial networks that reached from Sri Lanka to Burma and beyond are discussed by Frost in his essay "Wider Opportunities."

16. A series of millenarian Buddhist revolts against the British presence that fostered expectations of the imminent appearance of a universal monarch (*setkya*) developed in Upper Burma in 1906, 1910, and 1916. It finally culminated in the Saya San Rebellion of the 1930s. See Bečka. "The Role of Buddhism," p. 397; and Sarkisyanz, *Buddhist Backgrounds of the Burmese Revolution.* See also Maitrii Aung Thwin, "Genealogy of a Rebellion Narrative." A re-examination of British sources on the Saya San Rebellion calls for a complete rethinking of the place this rebellion holds in the history of the Burmese struggle for independence. Aung Thwin's study reveals colonial preconceptions about Burmese cultural practices that led to misinterpretations of the rebellion and its leader as well as a general criminalization of Burmese culture. Aung Thwin suggests that Bengali independence fighters with whom U Ottama was acquainted may have crossed the border to create these insurgencies.

17. See Schober, "The Theravada Buddhist Engagement with Modernity"; and "Mapping the Sacred."

18. See Sarkisyanz, *Buddhist Backgrounds of the Burmese Revolution,* pp. 149–165.

19. See Herbert, *The Hsaya San Rebellion.*

20. Frost discusses the ways in which Sri Lankan Buddhists constructed a transnational Buddhism to contest colonial hegemonies in "Wider Opportunities."

21. See Sarkisyanz, *Buddhist Backgrounds of the Burmese Revolution,* p. 128.

22. See Erik Braun, "The Birth of Modern Buddhism."

23. Chapters 3, 4, and 6 discuss these modern Buddhist groups.

24. See Singer, *Old Rangoon.*

25. By 1936 Aung San, U Nu, and others began to refer to themselves as *thakin* also, in order to voice their anticolonial sentiments.

26. In her essay on the "Intellectual Life in Burma and India under Colonialism," Aung San Suu Kyi indicates the absence of an intellectual renaissance in Burma that enabled the intelligentsia in India to integrate modern values with aspects of traditional culture. See Aung San Suu Kyi, *Freedom from Fear and Other Writings.*

27. Similarly, scholars have noted that the concept of the secular in the west emerged from a Protestant ethos.

28. See Turner, "Buddhism, Colonialism, and the Boundaries of Religion" on Buddhism during the colonial period in Burma.

29. Scott, *Refashioning Futures.*

Chapter Three: Educating the Other

1. Cohn, *Colonialism and Its Forms of Knowledge,* pp. 1–15.

2. Altbach and Kelly, *Education and the Colonial Experience*, p. 1.

3. See Taw Sein Ko, *Burmese Sketches,* p. 242; see also Edwards' essay on his role in brokering local and colonial knowledge, "Relocating the Interlocutor."

4. Taw Sein Ko notes in *Burmese Sketches*, p. 224, that basic multiplication was taught in monasteries alongside the study of classic texts. Khammai Dhammasami, "Idealism and Pragmatism," also points to the use of basic math as an aid in memorizing Pāli texts. The monastic curriculum also incorporated subjects such as Burmese traditional law, history, astrology, military skills, and archery, which were taught by court Brahmins of primarily Manipuri descent to children of the elite. However, these subjects were presented as part of an encompassing Hindu-Buddhist worldview, and only during colonial modernity would they be separated from that context and be labeled as secular.

5. See Cohn, *Colonialism and Its Forms of Knowledge.*

6. See the introduction by Nicholas Dirks to Cohn's *Colonialism and Its Forms of Knowledge,* p. xi.

7. Schober, "The Theravada Buddhist Engagement with Modernity."

8. Donald Lopez has recently published an insightful discussion on *Buddhism and Science,* in which he takes up their interconnections in greater detail.

9. See Rives, "The Teaching of English in Burma (Myanmar)," p. 106. Bishop Calchi, who was the Vicar of Ava and Pegu (Bishop Bigandet's predecessor, see below), began to compile the first Burmese dictionary, which later provided Adoniram Judson with the foundation for his own work on the *Burmese-English Dictionary,* 1953.

10. Thant Myint-U, *The Making of Modern Burma,* p. 101.

11. While elite monasteries promoted textual study and Buddhist learning, royal subjects seeking erudition beyond their social position risked being suspected of aspirations to power and possibly intending a revolt against the prevailing hegemony.

12. In "The Development of Education in Burma," p. 108, Ono Toru reports that a British survey taken in 1869 counted nearly 3,500 monastic schools in Lower Burma alone, with nearly 16,000 resident monks and almost 28,000 lay (male) students enrolled.

13. Taw Sein Ko, *Burmese Sketches,* p. 224.

14. Spiro, *Buddhism and Society,* p. 362.

15. Taw Sein Ko, *Burmese Sketches,* p. 248.

16. Ibid.

17. These designations refer to examination levels within the monastic education system. *Pahtama-nge* designates the lowest examination level to test knowledge of Buddhist texts. *Pahtama-lat* is the intermediate level; *pahtama-gyi:* refers to an advanced level of examination; and *pahtama-gyan* refers to achievements beyond the advanced level of examination. This last is comparable to the level of doctoral work.

18. In *Sangha and State in Burma,* p. 367, Michael Mendelson lists Buddhist texts used for study at each level of monastic examination, beginning with basic *vinaya* rules and progressing to include Pāli grammar and selected canonical texts from each of the three baskets, including the Abhidhamma.

19. Taw Sein Ko, *Burmese Sketches,* p. 230, mentions these Burmese texts as constituting a part of the monastic curriculum. They contain ethical and moral instructions on matters of lay life, law, and government; they have been translated by Bechert, Su, and Myint in *Burmese Manuscripts.*

20. See Mi Mi Khaing's discussion of Buddhist and secular education in her memoir entitled *Burmese Family,* pp. 75–85.

21. See Charney, *Powerful Learning,* on monastic intellectual communities and Buddhist learning during the Konbaun dynasty. In this work he discusses some regional variations in Burmese traditions of learning.

22. See Than, "December 1864," *Royal Orders of Burma,* p. xx.

23. According to Bečka, *Historical Dictionary of Burma*, p. 166, the *Maulmain* [sic] *Chronicle* commenced publication in 1836.

24. See Cuttriss, "Early Newspapers in Burma," p. 47. According to Cuttriss, p. 45, the *Rangoon Chronicle* began publication in 1853 and was renamed as the bi-weekly *Rangoon Times* in 1858.

25. Bečka states in his *Historical Dictionary of Burma,* p. 166, that an English gloss would be "The Mandalay Citizen," referring to the city's the classical name, Yatanabon.

26. Mendelson, *Sangha and State in Burma,* p. 158, writes that in "1867–1868, only 41 monastic schools were using the new textbooks, and only 91 students nominally studying them. In 1868–1869 . . . 170 books were distributed and 82 pupils were studying them."

27. Colonial sources report that basic literacy rates exceeded those of India and matched those of Italy, Ireland, and North America in the mid-nineteenth century.

28. Rives, "The Teaching of English in Burma (Myanmar)," p. 122.

29. Sir Arthur Phayre (1812–1885) resided in Burma from 1834 until 1867. He was chief commissioner from 1862–1867 and headed several missions to Mandalay between 1862 and 1866.

30. Ono Toru, "The Development of Education in Burma," p. 111.

31. D. E. Smith, *Religion and Politics in Burma,* p. 59.

32. Ono Toru, "The Development of Education in Burma, pp. 108–109. Ono Toru reports that according to an 1869 government census, 15,980 novices and 27,793 students attended 3,438 monastic schools in Lower Burma, while 5,069 students attended village-based lay schools. Mendelson, in *Sangha and State in Burma,* p. 159, reports that in 1891 there were 2,343 monastic schools and 757 registered lay schools, whereas in 1938 the numbers had shifted to 976 monastic schools and 5,255 lay schools. The most comprehensive account on the types of schools in colonial Burma is found in Furnivall, *Educational Progress in Southeast Asia,* pp. 25–30. While the specific statistics differ in

various sources, they concur in demonstrating a trend of decline in monastic education and disproportionately greater growth in demand for a curriculum delivered in English.

33. See Taw Sein Ko, *Burmese Sketches.*

34. Ibid., pp. 249–253, writes about the cultural debates on appropriate demonstrations of respect for lay teachers. This aptly illustrates the ways in which the authority of lay teachers was initially contested.

35. See Mendelson, *Sangha and State in Burma,* p. 161.

36. See Cady, *A History of Modern Burma;* and Cohn, *Colonialism and Its Forms of Knowledge.*

37. See the *Report on Public Instruction in Burma, 1891–1892, Resolution,* pp. 9–10; *Upper Burma,* pp. 12, 24, 35–36, 43–44, 48–50.

38. Following the British annexation, the Taungdaw Sayadaw was the monastic patriarch or *thathanabain* who had been appointed by Thibaw, the last king of the Konbaun dynasty. Although he resided in Mandalay, he assumed at least nominal authority over the entire Burmese sangha. When he passed away in 1895, the office was left vacant until 1903, when the British finally confirmed his successor, the Taunggwin Sayadaw, who resided in Rangoon.

39. It is noteworthy that already in April 1855, two "American missionaries, Kincade and Dawson, presented King Mindon with history and arithmetic books written in Burmese," according to the Burmese historian, Dr. Than Htun who compiled the *Royal Orders of Burma*, vol. 9, p. xvi. It is unclear why the instruction of arithmetic, given its general level of abstraction and potential affinity to mathematical calculations employed in astrology and related Indian forms of knowledge, should be especially objectionable to the Buddhist sangha. A plausible explanation may be its application to geography and colonial land-surveying techniques. Modern conceptions of geography were in clear contradiction to traditional Buddhist cosmology. Buddhist cosmology not only formed the conceptual foundation for a Buddhist understanding of the structure of the universe, it was also the basis for calculating the positions of constellations to foretell the future. Astrological signs also informed military formations in battle. Given such radical divergence in conceptualizing the universal order, it is not surprising that Buddhist monks objected to the teaching of modern geography and drawing techniques, such as those used in land surveys.

40. See Ono Toru "The Development of Education in Burma," pp. 107–133; and D. E. Smith, *Religion and Politics in Burma,* p. 59.

41. Taw Sein Ko, *Burmese Sketches,* pp. 263–268, offers the minutes of a meeting in August 1911, which was attended by the *thathanabain* and his council, representatives of the Education Department, and the commissioner of Mandalay, Colonel Strickland, and his entourage.

42. Cohn, *Colonialism and Its Forms of Knowledge,* p. 61, notes the important place modern land-surveying techniques held in colonial knowledge; they were central

to the colonial project. Traditional Buddhist cosmology imagined the geographic order of the universe in entirely different terms, with Mt. Meru at the center surrounded by great walls that contained the Southern island on which human beings were thought to live. For a particularly helpful discussion of Burmese cosmological representations, see Herbert, "Burmese Cosmological Manuscripts."

43. Taw Sein Ko, *Burmese Sketches,* p. 268,

44. See Cady, *A History of Modern Burma,* p. 179, where he writes: "In 1891–1892, government-recognized monastic schools numbered 4,324 compared to 890 lay schools. The numbers were: 3,281 monastic to 1,215 lay in 1897–1898; 2,208 to 2,653 in 1910–11; 2,977 to 4,650 in 1917–1918. Lay schools were obviously taking over."

45. Mendelson, *Sangha and State in Burma,* p. 159.

46. Schober, "Mapping the Sacred."

47. Robert Taylor, *The State In Burma,* p. 177.

48. Ibid., p. 162.

49. See Bečka, "The Role of Buddhism."

50. This occurred largely because of the rush toward the economic benefits that a modern, secular, or Christian education made possible. It was also a reaction to the malaise that characterized monastic education, its retreat to rural areas, and, finally, the decline in monastic educational expectations and levels of performance that had resulted from monastic refusal to integrate scientific subjects, particularly geography and mathematics, into their curriculum.

51. Singh, *Growth of Nationalism in Burma,* pp. 30–31.

52. Maung Maung, *From Sangha to Laity,* p. 5.

53. McMahan, "Modernity and the Early Discourse of Scientific Buddhism."

54. Hallisey, "Roads Taken and Not Taken."

55. Among them can be listed the Young Men's Buddhist Association, the Mahasi Meditation movement, U Ba Thein's Meditation Center, the World Peace Congress, the Buddhist Peace Fellowship, the Mahabodhi Society, and others.

56. Shwe Zan Aung, "Some Key Buddhist Concepts."

57. Chan Htoon, "Address to the Conference on Religion in the Age of Science," p. 29.

58. Student strikes have been important junctures in the struggle for national independence in Burma. Because student strikes revolve primarily around issues of secular education, they have been largely left out of this discussion. It is worth noting, however, that during the late colonial period and since independence, student strikes have become an increasingly powerful instrument of political mobilization. Many of the leaders of the nationalist struggle emerged from student strikes at Rangoon College, later Rangoon University, and they went on to become prominent politicians. The threat of student strikes continues to be perceived as a major threat to governance.

59. See D. E. Smith, *Religion and Politics in Burma,* pp. 140–185.

60. See "Burma Human Rights Year Book 2002–2003: Rights to Education and Health."

Chapter 4: Civil Buddhism in a Colonial Context

1. Robert Taylor, *The State in Burma,* pp. 112–115.

2. Thant Myint-U, *The Making of Modern Burma.*

3. See Cohn, *Colonialism and Its Forms of Knowledge*; Furnivall, *Colonial Policy and Practice,* 1948; and Moscotti, *British Policy and the Nationalist Movement in Burma.*

4. The YMBA has been resurrected several times since its demise in 1920 and currently continues to function in Rangoon as a social and religious organization that is very much at the service of the present regime. The organization celebrated its centenary in 2006. A new edition has appeared recently of one of the YMBA's most popular publications. *The Illustrated History of Buddhism* contains modern drawings by the famous artist U Ba Kyi and text, in Burmese and English translation, by the late Sayadaw Ashin Janakabhivamsa, a well-known scholar of Burmese and Pāli works.

5. Rhys Davids established The Pāli Text Society in 1881 in Sri Lanka. Henry Olcott and Anagarika Dharmapala (1865–1933) worked to revitalize and reform Buddhism in Sri Lanka. Olcott, in particular, strove to create a unified and universal Buddhism. To promote this he developed a Buddhist Catechism and gained universal support among Buddhist lineages for his Buddhist Platform, which declared an "essential" doctrinal and ethical coherence that all Buddhists could subscribe to, at least in Olcott's perspective. The Sri Lankan Buddhist reformer Dharmapala later founded the Mahabodhi Society at Bodh Gaya, India in 1891. The Mahabodhi Society also eventually founded a Burmese branch.

6. Henry Olcott was associated with the founding of the Theosophical Society and the International Buddhist League. Alan Bennett founded the International Buddhist Society. Gordon Douglas was ordained in 1899 as Bhikkhu Aśoka. The following year, he passed away in Bassein, southern Burma, where the Aśoka Society, named after him, was established in 1902.

7. In contrast to his failed venture in Burma, Olcott is of course well known for his efforts to missionize Buddhism throughout much of Asia and particularly in Sri Lanka, where he fostered and inspired, together with his companion Helen Blavatsky (1831–1891), the Buddhist revival carried out by his protegé Anagarika Dharmapala (1864–1933).

8. See Prothero. *The White Buddhist,* pp. 117–118, 127–130.

9. For further information on his missionary efforts, see the pamphlet he authored, as Ananda Metteya, entitled "Extension of the Empire of Righteousness to the Western Lands."

10. See Sarkisyanz, *Buddhist Backgrounds of the Burmese Revolution,* p. 128.

11. See Mendelson, *Sangha and State in Burma,* pp. 73–235.

12. See ibid.

13. Maung Maung, *From Sangha to Laity,* p. 2.

14. In 1898 C. S. Dissanayake collaborated to found the Young Men's Buddhist Association in Sri Lanka as an offshoot of Olcott's Buddhist Theosophical Society. Frost ("Wider Opportunities," p. 953) mentions in passing the view held among members of the Sri Lankan YMBA that the Burmese YMBA was a branch of its organization. In Burma, however, the Burmese YMBA is seen as entirely independent of and unrelated to its Sri Lankan namesake.

15. See Furnivall, *Colonial Policy and Practice,* p. 143, where he notes the general admiration of Japan throughout Asia that followed the Japanese victory over Russia in 1904–1905.

16. Concerning the lack of opportunities for the Burmese intelligentsia who returned from studying abroad, one is reminded of Gandhi's exasperation with his own professional trajectory, when, after returning to India from Britain, he described his role as "Arjuna in a small claims court" (Rudolph and Rudolph, *Gandhi*, pp. 25–29).

17. See Lincoln's discussion of maximalists and minimalists in *Holy Terror,* p. 32.

18. *Bouddha batha bama lu myo,* literally, "We Burmese are Buddhists." This slogan has been appropriated by, and attributed to, many leading figures, including U Nu and Aung San Suu Kyi. Even the British Bhikkhu Ananda Metteya employs the phrase in *Extension of the Empire of Righteousness to the Western Lands.*

19. See Bečka. "The Role of Buddhism," pp. 389–405; and Schober, "Religious Merit and Social Status among Burmese Lay Buddhist Organizations."

20. Ibid., 3.

21. Ibid., 4

22. Ibid., 4, 15.

23. Ibid., xvi.

24. Ibid. 4.

25. Sarkisyanz, *Buddhist Backgrounds of the Burmese Revolution,* p. 13.

26. Although I use the terms Burma, Burmese, Myanmar, and Burman interchangeably, it is important to draw some distinctions in this context. To be Burman and to be Buddhist was a way of distinguishing the majority of Burmans from other groups along ethnic, religious, and political lines.

27. Colonial Burmese society was socially fragmented. J. S. Furnivall advocated nationalism as a means to overcome these social ills and form a "plural society" in Burma (*Colonial Policy and Practice*). Although Furnivall was critical of colonial policy, which he saw as obstructing Burmese national goals, he was sufficiently convincing of some factions within the Indian Civil Service to obtain support from Clayton's Committee on the Imperial Idea, which was charged with muting popular unrest and developing a pacified, prosperous colony (Pham, "Ghost Hunting in Colonial Burma," pp. 245–249).

28. See Bečka, "The Role of Buddhism," p. 399. See also Sarkisyanz, *Buddhist Backgrounds of the Burmese Revolution,* p. 108.

29. Maung Maung, *From Sangha to Laity,* p. 4.

30. See Bečka, "The Role of Buddhism," p. 401.

31. Maung Maung, *From Sangha to Laity,* p. 4.

32. Singh, *Growth of Nationalism in Burma,* pp. 30–31.

33. Ong, "The Modern Burman," pp. 5–6.

34. Ibid., p. 2.

35. Ibid., p. 3.

36. Ibid., p. 7.

37. Von der Mehden (*Religion and Nationalism,* p. 32) reports that the activities of the YMBA languished from 1910 to 1912 because most of its leaders were studying abroad.

38. The "dawn of nationalism" is an expression Furnivall coined in his preface to U May Ong's speech on the Modern Burman; see Furnivall and Ong, "The Dawn of Nationalism."

39. Bruce Lincoln (*Holy Terror*) defines maximalists as those social groups who seek to subordinate matters of civil society and the authority of the state to religious principles. We will return to his distinction between maximalists and minimalists in later chapters.

40. After sinking under the nationalist movements of the 1920s, the YMBA was resurrected during Ne Win's era and currently functions at a reduced scale in Yangon as a social and religious organization.

41. Singh (*Growth of Nationalism in Burma,* p. 33) reports that popularization of this issue involved the YMBA's collaboration with the Burma Provincial Congress Committee, which formed in 1908 and was supported by Indians in Burma. He indicates that there had been considerable collaboration between Burmese and Indian nationalists until 1917.

42. Ibid., p. 32.

43. See Keyes, "Buddhist Economics and Buddhist Fundamentalism," p. 374. In 1911 the Ledi Sayadaw was awarded the title of Agga Mahapandita by the Government of India. He authored numerous commentaries and was a popular preacher throughout Burma. Guy Lubeigt, in his "Introduction of Western Culture in Burma," argues that later biographers attributed to the Ledi Sayadaw a nationalist stance. Lubeigt claims that this orientation was absent from the Ledi Sayadaw's public preaching. His observation may be correct as the "foot wearing" debate, in which the Ledi Sayadaw eventually did take a public stance, emerged only near the end of his life. See also Braun, "The Birth of Modern Buddhism."

44. This colonial reform also led to the establishment of Rangoon University as a residential institution with strict educational standards. According to Cady (*A History*

of Modern Burma, pp. 217–221), the opening of Rangoon University in December 1920 was followed immediately by a general university-wide strike during which the YMBA launched its National Schools Movement. The National Schools Movement was led by U Ba Lwin. His sons, U Kyaw Nyein, U Than Lwin, and U Yan Naing Lwin, upheld their family's high regard for education throughout their careers in Burma and in the United States. Each of them has been instrumental, along with many others, in facilitating my research in Burma.

45. This source of tension within the YMBA had been building up since the Craddock Reforms of 1919–1923 and the refusal to grant Burma increased authority in the determination of home rule.

Chapter 5: The Politics of the Modern State as Buddhist Practice

1. Mendelson, *Sangha and State in Burma*; and Ferguson, "The Arahat Ideal."

2. See Michael Aung-Thwin, *Pagan,* pp. 184–185.

3. Turner, "Buddhism, Colonialism, and the Boundaries of Religion."

4. For a comprehensive treatment of reforms during the Ne Win period, see Tin Maung Maung Than, "The Sangha and Sāsana in Socialist Burma"; and his "Sangha Reforms and Renewal of Sāsana in Myanmar."

5. See Mendelson, *Sangha and State in Burma.*

6. As a college student, U Nu translated books into Burmese (such as Dale Carnegie's *How to Win Friends and Influence People*). He also wrote plays, novels, political speeches, and essays on Buddhism. His novel, *Man, the Wolf of Man,* emphasized personal themes, while his best-known play, *The People Win Through,* focused on what he saw as immoral activities, such as communist insurrection and political rule by force. Of his other plays, *Converting the Elder Brother* is a drama about political and personal betrayal, and *Thurya* is an allegorical fable about political corruption under colonialism. In *Saturday's Son,* an autobiographical novel, he recounted the turbulent events of his life until 1962. His religious writings primarily followed traditionalist forms. In *Buddhism: Theory and Practice* he detailed the moral and mental stages of meditation.

7. For a discussion of early instances of meditation during late Konbaun period in Upper Burma, see Mendelson, *Sangha and State in Burma,* pp. 66–119.

8. I am grateful to Steven Collins for pointing out that Buddhaghosa's work is an extended commentary on one verse from the *Sanyutta Nikāya.*

9. See Jordt, *Burma's Mass Lay Meditation Movement.*

10. See also Sai Khma Maung, *Changing Buddhist Practice in Burma*; Houtman, "The Tradition of Practice among Burmese Buddhists"; and Houtman, *Mental Culture in Burmese Crisis Politics.*

11. See D. E. Smith, *Religion and Politics in Burma,* pp. 157–165.

12. Ibid., pp. 253–254, 256.

13. See Bechert, *Buddhismus, Staat und Gesellschaft*; and D. E. Smith, *Religion and Politics in Burma.*

14. In his introduction to *Fundamentalisms Observed*, Martin Marty defines modernity as characterized by secular rationality, religious tolerance, relativism, and individualism. He contrasts this concept with the global phenomenon of fundamentalism, which he construes as a traditionalist, conservative reaction to modernity centered on orthodoxy and orthopraxy, but using the instruments of modernization, such as mass media and other communication technologies, to promote fundamentalist goals. Donald Swearer's contribution to that volume expands on the postmodern features of fundamentalist Theravada Buddhist movements in Sri Lanka and Thailand and affirms their "simplistic, moralistic Buddhist ideology aimed at restoring national pride" and their appeal to "a new class of civil servants, business people, and professionals" ("Fundamentalistic Movements in Theravāda Buddhism," p. 636). He sees Theravada fundamentalism as shaped by the postcolonial revival of meditation, the activism of the laity, a new apologetic, and the renewal of a religiously grounded community identity (ibid., p. 633). As such, it shares with Islam and Christianity elements of religious fundamentalism, including a commitment to authoritative scripture, concern for orthodox belief, and a history of involvement with the state.

The discussion by Charles Keyes, in his article on "Buddhist Economics and Buddhist Fundamentalism," presents Theravada Buddhist fundamentalism as developing from the reformist Buddhist encounter with modernity in the nineteenth century. Keyes concludes that fundamentalism in Theravada Buddhism entails a retreat to an essentialist view of the fundamental principles of Buddhism.

15. See Bechert, "Sangha, State, Society, Nation"; Bechert, "Neue Buddhistische Orthodoxie"; Schober, "Religious Reform in Burma"; and Tin Maung Maung Than, "The Sangha and Sāsana in Socialist Burma."

16. Steinberg, *Burma, a Socialist Nation in Southeast Asia*; and Steinberg, *Burma's Road Toward Development.*

17. I am grateful to Steven Collins for noting the literal translation of Sangha Mahanayaka, namely, the Great Leadership of the Monastic Order.

18. See Tin Maung Maung Than, "The Sangha and *Sāsana* in Socialist Burma"; and his "Sangha Reforms and Renewal of *Sāsana* in Myanmar."

19. The State Law and Order Restoration Council Law No. 20/90, October 31, 1990, officially recognizes the following nine *nikāya*: Sudhamma or Thudhamma, who make up the majority of monks, Shwegyin, who constitute the second largest monastic lineage; with the other officially recognized lineages being Weiluwun Nikāya, Dhammanudhamma Mahadwaya Nikāya, Dhammavinayanuloma Muladwaya Nikāya, Dhammayuttika Nikāya Mahayin, Catubhummika Mahasatipatthana Hngettwin, Ganavimut Gado, and the Anauk Kyaun Dwaya. While their legal standing has been

reaffirmed several times, most of these ordination lineages trace their beginnings to Mindon's Fifth Buddhist Council (see Mendelson, *Sangha and State in Burma*).

20. See Bechert, "Neue Buddhistische Orthodoxie," pp. 24–56; and Mathews, "The Iron Heel."

21. The official perception was that available translations by the Pāli Text Society did not reflect a Burmese understanding of Buddhism, but an orientalist and colonial one.

22. The best-known case of a heretical doctrine concerned the followers of *lu thei lu phyi*, who claimed that people could be reborn only as human beings and not in any other form or Buddhist realm. This doctrine implicitly advocated a shortcut to enlightenment, and this had tremendous popular appeal during the 1980s. Following prolonged doctrinal debates during the hearings, the monastic courts determined the teachings to be heretical (*adhamma*) and forced monastic adherents to recant or be disrobed.

23. See especially Robert Taylor, *The State in Burma*, p. 360; and Tin Maung Maung Than, "The Sangha and Sāsana in Socialist Burma."

24. See Keyes, "Millennialism, Theravada Buddhism, and Thai Society"; and Sarkisyanz, *Buddhist Backgrounds of the Burmese Revolution.*

25. See Mendelson, "A Messianic Association in Upper Burma"; Sarkisyanz, *Buddhist Backgrounds of the Burmese Revolution;* and Schober, "The Path to Buddhahood."

26. Throughout these chapters, I argue that expressions of religion and politics are inseparable in Burmese forms of Buddhism. The category of "political monks" emerged from the scholarship of colonial historians, who accepted Weber's notion of Theravada monks as ascetic world renouncers. This discussion is taken up in detail in chapter 8.

27. I follow Benedict Anderson's position in *Imagined Communities* in my treatment of nationalism as a cultural form. See also Schober, "Buddhist Just Rule and Burmese National Culture."

28. See Bechert, "Sangha, State, Society, Nation"; Schober, "Religious Reform in Burma"; and Maung Maung Than Tin, "The Sangha and Sāsana in Socialist Burma."

29. See Schober, "Buddhist Visions of Moral Authority and Civil Society."

30. Aung San Suu Kyi, *Freedom from Fear and Other Writings;* Aung San Suu Kyi, *Letters from Burma;* Aung San Suu Kyi, "Letter from Burma, 1997(4)"; Houtman, *Mental Culture in Burmese Crisis Politics;* Pradhan, *Burma, Dhamma, and Democracy*; and Shwe Lu Maung, *Burma, Nationalism and Ideology.*

31. In *Relics of the Buddha,* John Strong offers an excellent theory of the biographical processes associated with the veneration of relics. See also Schober, "Venerating the Buddha's Remains in Burma."

32. The violent human rights abuses against lay people and monks committed by successive military regimes in the aftermath of 1988 are documented in several places. One report composed of detailed interviews and photos of detained monks is entitled

"Burma: The Land Where Buddhist Monks Are Disrobed and Detained in Dungeons." See also the All Burma Young Monks' Union report, "The Buddha Sāsana and Burma Military Regime." Similar reports were distributed by the Buddhist Relief Mission and the Buddhist Relief Center–Japan, among others.

33. The Mahanayaka Council supervises the affairs of all nine officially recognized ordination lineages, the registration of individual monks, monastic education, and the leadership training programs for abbots. Its central body is housed at Kaba Aye, adjacent to the ministerial offices. Monastic representatives to the central Mahanayaka Council rotate every few months, which renders their presence largely ceremonial and keeps the council's agenda firmly under the control of the ministry. In the opening address to an advanced course on Buddhist culture in North Okkalapa Township, where some of the most violent antigovernment riots occurred in 1988, Minister of Religious Affairs Lt.-Gen. Myo Nyunt was reported to have stated: "Each of the trainees is to help preserve national culture through religious education." The report stated also that Myo Nyunt "stressed the need to safeguard the nation against the threat of extinction of race and culture" (*New Light of Myanmar,* April 25, 1994).

34. See Schober, "Buddhist Just Rule and Burmese National Culture."

35. This form of Theravada Buddhist practice has characterized the history of traditional polities from the time of Aśoka and inspired the construction of grand Buddhist monuments. Stanley Tambiah (*Culture, Thought, and Social Action*) calls this religio-political constellation a galactic polity. The just ruler acts within the ritual and social structures of an economy of merit. Homage and generosity toward the Buddha's spiritual and material remains are seen as indications of devout religious practice, social status, and political legitimacy. Regarding relics in Buddhist polities, in this case the Tooth Relic in precolonial Kandy, Sri Lanka, John Strong writes that "possession of the Buddha's tooth was seen as an indispensable attribute of kingship. Its cult was the privilege and duty of the legitimate ruler and was thought to ensure social harmony, regular rainfall, bountiful crops, and righteous rule. Its possession meant power" ("Relics," vol. 12, p. 280).

36. In his reflections on imagined communities and nationalism, Anderson, in *Imagined Communities,* observes the significant role that print capitalism plays in the development of national histories and the ideologies of modern nation-states.

37. For an explication of the conceptual link between status and merit-making in Burmese culture, see Schober, "Religious Merit and Social Status."

38. See Schober, "Buddhist Just Rule and Burmese National Culture."

39. For a discussion of cosmological Buddhism, see Reynolds and Reynolds, *Three Worlds According to King Ruang*; and Keyes, Kendall, and Hardacre, "Contested Visions of Community in East and Southeast Asia."

40. My use of ritual theater and the dramaturgy of power follows Clifford Geertz, who writes of the theater state in nineteenth-century Bali and the doctrine of the exemplary center: "This is the theory that the court-and-capital is at once a microcosm of the

supernatural order—'an image of . . . the universe on a smaller scale'—and the material embodiment of political order" (*Negara*, p. 13). He continues later: "The competition to be the center of centers, the axis of the world, was just that, a competition; and it was the ability to stage productions of an eleven-roof scale, to mobilize the men, the resources, and, not least, the expertise, that made one an eleven-roof lord" (ibid., p. 120). He concludes by stating: "The confinement of interpretive analysis . . . to the supposedly more 'symbolic' aspect of culture is a mere prejudice, born out of the notion . . . that 'symbolic' opposes to 'real.' . . . To construe the expressions of the theatre state, to apprehend them as theory, this prejudice, along with the allied one that the dramaturgy of power is external to its workings, must be put aside. The real is as imagined as the imaginary" (ibid., p. 136). I would add a cautionary note about using this characterization of premodern state ritual as describing SLORC's hegemonic intent that the modern theatre of the state is a self-consciously constructed legitimation of its highly contested hegemony.

41. The Chinese Tooth Relic, believed to be a genuine relic of the Buddha, was clouded in oblivion for nearly 800 years, until it was rediscovered in China around 1900 CE; it is now housed in a temple outside Peking. This relic toured Burma during U Nu's period to usher in his monastic convocation and reform. After leaving Burma, it traveled to Sri Lanka, where a second tooth relic of the Buddha is enshrined at Kandy.

42. After SLORC opened its economy to joint foreign capital ventures in the early 1990s, a trend that continued under the SPDC, a large number of foreign investors, including Burmese expatriates, were invited to capitalize on a market characterized by high demands, few supplies, cheap labor, and untapped natural resources. Due to the high taxation SLORC imposed on all transactions involving foreign currency, however, few investors have been willing to make long-term financial commitments. In the absence of political stability and modern infrastructure, most businesspeople remain leery of unpredictable changes in government policies and seek out opportunities to garner favors from the political elite.

43. A popular counterhegemonic discourse deserves mention in this context. Although the Pagan Museum receives a considerable number of Burmese visitors, hardly anyone goes to worship at Ne Win's pagoda or at the replicas of the Tooth relic in Mandalay or Rangoon that, incidentally, were built on the model of the famous Ananda Pagoda in Pagan. Further, Cyclone Nargis caused considerable damage to Shwedagon Pagoda in 2008. Rumors abound that the diamonds, sapphires, and rubies that studded the spire were scattered across the pagoda's platform. This is popularly understood to be a particularly bad omen, one which speaks to the moral authority of the current regime that restored this national treasure.

44. In contrast to the 1980s and 1990s, when the Mahasi Meditation Center in Rangoon housed many western meditators, only nineteen foreigners were residing there when I visited in July 2006. Three were American citizens.

45. On my visit there I went to purchase some of their publications, only to find

that the key to unlock the display case of books had been locked in a wooden cabinet, and the keys to the cabinet had been lost. The clerks insisted in taking out the cabinet lock and retrieving the key that would let them open the display case. Perhaps this was an indication of the low demand for publications that visitors may purchase there.

46. For an analysis of Taw Sein Ko's complex role during the colonial era, see Edwards "Relocating the Interlocutor."

47. Like many landmarks and towns, Pagan has been renamed as Bagan. The difference is reflected mostly in the English transcription of names and less often in the actual Burmese pronunciation or writing of the name.

48. Beaded *kalaga* embroidery is one of the traditional arts of Burma.

49. The 88 Generation Prayer Campaign was a movement that emerged in 2006. It was led by individuals who had been student activists at the forefront of the 1988 uprising, including Min Ko Naing, Ko Ko Gyi, and others, most of whom were rearrested in connection with the events of September 2007. The movement advocated prayer campaigns among Buddhists, Hindus, Muslims, and Christians, all clothed in white and seeking to bring about a national reconciliation two decades after the watershed events of the 1988 uprising. It also instigated a letter-writing campaign in which people were encouraged to try to persuade Than Shwe, the head of the junta, to end recriminations against those who opposed the regime.

50. The following report from *Narinjara News* (September 2, 2003) articulates how Buddhist ritual can be understood as reifying national territory.

> Buddhist rites to prevent foreign invasion!
>
> Maungdaw: Burma's ruling junta, State Peace and Development Council, began to conduct a Buddhist religious ceremony at the border town of Maungdaw on the Naaf River in the western part of the country on 27th August 03. Sources said that the ceremony began at 0441 hours local time and ended at 5:45 pm (1745 hrs).
>
> U Pandithara, the abbot of Alodawbreh Monastery, and fifteen other monks initiated the ceremony. For the first thirty-five minutes they chanted the Upakathindhi Sutta while nine other groups of lay people continued to chant the same sutta. The ceremony was conducted in a stage built so as to face Bangladesh in the garden in front of the Mroma Market. The cost of the building of the stage and the entire ceremony was collected from the townspeople by force.
>
> For the ceremony each of the quarters of the township had to bear the cost of nine sets of ritualistic offerings of mostly fruits. According to a Buddhist monk attending the function, the ceremony will be continued to be held at nine hours a day, nine times a month and nine months in a year. The monk said that the number nine so used shows that the entire

ceremony is a practice of magic aimed at lengthening the rule of the junta. In the township the people have been forced to take civil defence training, what the junta termed as preparation for defending the country from foreign invasion that has greatly hampered the agricultural and other works for their own sustenance. The ceremony has been conducted throughout Burma since that day, the first day of the Burmese month of Tawthaling. The ceremony was attended by six hundred people including Brigadier General Maung Oo, the chairman of the Rakhine State Peace and Development Council. The junta believes that the sutta helped the ancient Burmese kings to prevent war with China on many occasions.

Chapter 6: Buddhist Resistance against the State

1. Chatterjee, *The Nation and Its Fragments,* p. 120. See also Edwards, "Grounds for Protest, pp. 208–209.

2. See Turner, "Buddhism, Colonialism, and the Boundaries of Religion."

3. In his book *Holy Terror* (p. 70), Bruce Lincoln distinguishes between minimalists, who are content to keep religion separated from the goals of the state, and maximalists, who seek to have religious concerns reflected in the foundation of the state.

4. See Maung Maung, *From Sangha to Laity,* p. 19. See also Chie Ikeya's account of the public presence of women wearing homespun cotton as a symbol of their support for the nationalist movement and of their solidarity with the GCSS ("Gender, History, and Modernity," pp. 102–136).

5. Sir Reginald Craddock was a British governor of Burma from 1918–1923 and much disliked for his plans to diminish Burmese national aspirations. Known as the Craddock Scheme, his reforms envisioned limited opportunity for the Burmese to shape their political future because Burma was a province within British India. Diarchy, or the dual-government reform implemented between 1923 and 1935, recognized Burma as a province of British India and increased the number of elected members of the Legislative Council in Burma.

6. Singh (*Growth of Nationalism in Burma,* p. 48) is likely correct in claiming that the indigenization of the nationalist struggle in Burma came initially from India and was popularized though charismatic figures like U Ottama and U Wisara. Many of the early nationalists emulated the methods of the Indian Congress Party and adopted Gandhian strategies. Gandhi visited Rangoon in March 1929 and spoke publicly to inspire the nationalist struggle.

7. See Maung Maung, *From Sangha to Laity,* p. 21.

8. Maung Maung (ibid., p. 37) does not hide his disappointment with the loss of the secularist cause to the sangha.

9. Relations between Soe Thein and Saya San must have been complex, for Saya

San was part of a faction of monks who opposed Soe Thein's leadership of the GCBA in 1926, as Maung Maung (ibid., p. 59) points out.

10. Ibid., p. 25.

11. See Maitrii Aung Thwin, "Genealogy of a Rebellion Narrative"; and Maung Maung, *From Sangha to Laity*, p. 42.

12. Stanley Tambiah has noted on several occasions the ways in which the Buddhist sangha traditionally facilitated an intellectual career at political centers for gifted young monks from rural areas. In the case of U Ottama, one may extend Tambiah's observation to argue that the sangha facilitated the career of a politician of modest means to travel, in the robes of a monk, across various ethnic, colonial, and Buddhist boundaries.

13. Mendelson, *Sangha and State in Burma*, p. 201.

14. Ibid., p. 202; see also Maitrii Aung Thwin's argument ("Genealogy of a Rebellion Narrative," pp. 393–419) that U Ottama likely aided the agitation of Bengali insurgents to extend into Burma, and that this, and probably not millennial aspirations among the Burmese, lie at the core of the events colonial administrators and historians have come to label as the end to Saya San Rebellion (1930–1931).

15. The Japanese victory over Russia in 1905 clearly made an impression upon Burmese nationalists. However, their focus remained primarily on the activities of Indian National Congress.

16. Mendelson (*Sangha and State in Burma*, pp. 199–206) mentions that U Ottama may not have been mentally stable toward the end of his life, which, perhaps, contributed to the location and manner of his passing.

17. See ibid., pp. 199–205.

18. See Maung Maung, *From Sangha to Laity*, p. 24.

19. Diarchy envisioned the separation of Burma from India under colonial rule. The plan was to award India greater rights of self-determination, while withholding them from Burma. The nationalist struggle during the 1920s and 1930s took issue with the administrative reforms, mentioned above, that Sir Reginald Craddock advocated.

20. See Mendelson, *Sangha and State in Burma*, p. 99; and Maitrii Aung Thwin, "Genealogy of a Rebellion Narrative."

21. See Bečka, *Historical Dictionary of Burma*, p. 179.

22. See Mendelson, *Sangha and State in Burma*, pp. 211ff; Cady. *A History of Modern Burma*, p. 395; and Ikeya, "Gender, History, and Modernity," pp. 158, 159, who writes that in 1938 alone, 200 deaths and 926 injuries were reported because of the riots.

23. Mendelson, *Sangha and State in Burma*, p. 211.

24. Ikeya ("Gender, History, and Modernity," pp. 166–167) discusses the antimodern activism of the Yahan Pyo monks who, in the 1920s and 1930s, accosted in public women dressed in western clothes these monks found objectionable. This monastic organization is known for its nationalist orientation and for its support of the Ne Win coup in 1962.

25. In "Colonial Knowledge and Buddhist Education in Burma," I explore the ways in which monks in Burma have been both victims and perpetrators of violence and militancy. Here I simply want to mention the involvement of monks in anti-Muslim riots during 2003.

26. See Mathews, "Myanmar's Agony."

27. The All Burma Young Monks Union, which operates from the Thai border, is involved in a variety of civil projects. Another organization in the region is the Overseas Mon Young Monks Union (OMYMU), which publishes a magazine with the title *Buddhist Way to Democracy.* The first issue appeared in April 1992 in Bangkok. In this inaugural pamphlet, the OMYMU defined their work as revitalizing their monastic lineage, missionizing internationally, working for the Buddhist way to democracy, and achieving the SLORC handover of power to the NLD.

28. Mathews, "The Iron Heel."

29. Mendelson, "A Messianic Association in Upper Burma"; Sarkisyanz, *Buddhist Backgrounds of the Burmese Revolution*; and Schober, "The Path to Buddhahood."

30. A bizarre set of events led to her most recent detention. A few months before her previous house arrest was to expire, an American intruder swam across Inya Lake to visit her and attempt to convert her to Mormonism. While his motives appear irrational, one can only speculate about the fact that he accomplished this feat without being detected by the military guarding access to her house. The man pleaded exhaustion, and Suu Kyi agreed to let him stay and recuperate. It was upon his return that he was caught. The ensuing trial triggered international outrage. It ended in the intruder's eventual release into American custody and with the extension of Aung San Suu Kyi's house arrest.

31. Aung San Suu Kyi, *Letters from Burma.*

32. Jordt's *Burma's Mass Lay Meditation Movement* contributes much to our understanding of the messianic qualities of mass meditation movements among lay people in Burma.

33. See Houtman, *Mental Culture in Burmese Crisis Politics.*

34. Aung San Suu Kyi, "The Benefits of Meditation and Sacrifice."

35. *Letters from Burma* was a year-long series of weekly commentaries published in the Japanese newspaper *Mainichi Daily News.* The fifty-some essays were then collected and published by Penguin in 1997, and the book was awarded recognition by a professional association of the Japanese press.

36. See Aung San Suu Kyi, *Letters from Burma*, pp. 115–116.

37. The Eightfold Noble Path, also known as the Middle Path, provides a summation of the Buddha's teachings, which emphasize that in the conduct of one's daily life one should observe right understanding, right thought, right speech, right action, right livelihood, right effort, right mindfulness, and right concentration.

38. Aung San Suu Kyi, "Faith Eases the Mind in Times of Political Turmoil."

39. Ibid.

40. Swearer (*The Buddhist World of Southeast Asia*) and Queen and King (*Engaged Buddhism*) have characterized Aung San Suu Kyi's politics of resistance as grounded in the liberation theologies of modern Buddhist Asia.

41. Aung San Suu Kyi, "In Quest of Democracy," p. 168.

42. Democratic activists in Theravada countries appear to be partial to this story, for it is also found in contemporary Thai discourse advocating socially engaged Buddhism. See, for example, Peter Jackson's essay on contemporary Thai political discussions of King Ruang's Three Worlds ("Re-interpreting the Traiphuum Phra Ruang"). See also Sulak Sivaraksa's *A Buddhist Vision for Renewing Society* for discussions that similarly justify democracy as a desired political ideology that is grounded in Buddhist ethical precepts, and Collins and Huxley, "The Post-Canonical Adventures of Mahāsammata."

43. Aung San Suu Kyi, "Faith Eases the Mind in Times of Political Turmoil," p. 122.

44. Aung San Suu Kyi, "Letters from Burma," p. 17.

45. Aung San Suu Kyi, "Empowerment for a Culture of Peace and Development," Address to the World Commission on Culture and Development, Manila, 1995.

46. Western converts to Buddhism in America are already acquainted with the variant of Buddhist ethical universalism advocated by the Dalai Lama, who also received the Noble Peace Prize for focusing global attention on the plight of the Tibetan Buddhist diaspora.

47. Aung San Suu Kyi discussed human rights, economic development, and ethics in a speech delivered on her behalf in Manila in November 1994. Similarly, the well-known Burmese monk, U Rewata Dhamma, spoke on "Dhamma, Ethics, and Human Rights" at a convention in Seoul, Korea. While such public statements delivered outside of Myanmar can be interpreted within the broader context of socially engaged Buddhism advocated by such prominent religious and social thinkers as Sulak Sivaraksa, Bhikkhu Buddhadassa, or Thich Nhat Hanh, such discourse within Myanmar is limited and very private. Yet it is also apparent that many chose to voice their political opposition to SLORC through religious preferences, such as donations to selected monks, monasteries, and meditation centers.

48. For an analytical overview of the movement, see Bertil Lintner's essay "Myanmar's 88 Generation Comes of Age."

49. See Maung Oo, "88 Generation Students to step up peaceful protests."

50. See "The 88 Generation Students' policy announcement regarding the emergence of the State Constitution."

51. See "The 88 Generation Students" on oppression against economic and social equalities of political activists."

52. See Swearer, "Fundamentalistic Movements in Theravada Buddhism."

53. For a discussion of Buddhism, the state, and violence, see Schober "Buddhism, Violence, and the State."

Chapter 7: The Limits of Buddhist Moral Authority in the Secular State

1. Revolutionary change did not come about, and the naming of the events of September 2007 reveals, perhaps, romantic aspirations of some organizers and their western sympathizers.

2. As noted in the Introduction, I follow David Scott's notion of conjuncture in *Refashioning Futures*, where he points to pivotal moments in history, when social, economic, cultural, and political forces combine to indicate the parameters for possible future developments.

3. On August 21, Burmese authorities arrested several activists of the 88 Generation students group, including Min Ko Naing, Ko Ko Gyi, Htay Win Aung, Min Zeya, Mya Aye, Kyaw Min Yu, Zeya, Kyaw Kyaw Htwe, Arnt Bwe Kyaw, Panneik Tun, Zaw Zaw Min, Thet Zaw, and Nyan Lin Tun, according to the state-run newspaper, *The New Light of Myanmar.*

4. The following list of protest sites shows the gradual escalation of marches from local protests motivated by economic concerns to large-scale demonstrations led by monks. The sites listed in the *Irrawaddy News*, September 25, 2007, include: "Different parts of Rangoon—August 21; Rangoon, Mandalay—August 22; Rangoon, Yenanchaung—August 23; Rangoon, Bassein (Irrawaddy Division)—August 24; Rangoon, Mogok (Mandalay Division)—August 25; Pegu—August 27 (over 100 Buddhist monks); Rangoon, Sittwe (Arakan State), Meikhtila (Mandalay Division)—August 28; Tavoy (Tenasserim Division)—August 29; Aung Lan—August 30; Kyaukpadaung, Mandalay—August 30; Taungkok (Arakan State)—August 31; Myintkyina, Latputta, Kyaukse, Pakhokku—September 3; Taungkok, Taungyi (Shan State), Hakha (Chin State)—September 4; Bokalay—September 5; Pakhokku—September 5 and 6 (Buddhist Monks Held SPDC officials hostage); Gwa (Arakan State)—September 7; Daw Pone—September 8; Taungkok—September 12; Kyaukpadaung (Mandalay Div.), Rangoon, Monywa, Mogok, Chauk, Pwint Phyu (Magwe Division) by monks—September 17, 18, 19, 20, 21, 22."

5. Aung Zaw, "Burmese Monks in Revolt," *The Irrawaddy,* September 11, 2007.

6. *Pattam nikkujjana kamma,* the refusal to accept a donation from a donor, is discussed in the Cullavagga V, 20, of the Vinaya.

7. "Burma: A Land Where Buddhist Monks Are Disrobed and Detained in Dungeons."

8. The following statement details the events triggering the pronouncement of the monastic boycott: "Announcement of the All Burma Monks Alliance: 12th Waning Day of Wagaung, 1369 B.E., Sunday, Letter No. (1/2007), Monday, September 10, 2007.

> The local authorities under SPDC military regime brutally cracked down, arrested and tortured the monks and people demonstrators who were

protesting over the current fuel price hike in Burma. They did such a brutal crackdown in Pakhokku where the peaceful monk demonstrators protested over the fuel price hike by reciting Metta Sutra, by lassoing them and tied them at the lamp post, and slapped them, kicked them and beat them up in public by the SPDC thugs of USDA and Swan Ah Shin. One of the monks died of these brutal treatments. Thus it becomes the cause of Theravada Buddhism and the whole monks residing in Burma.

We, 'All Burma Young Monks Union', 'Federation of All Burma Monks Union', 'Young Monks Union (Rangoon)', 'Monk Duta' and all Monks Unions in different States and Divisions joined hands together and establishing this Monks Alliance Group representing all monks living in Burma, today make and announce the following demands to SPDC.

1. The SPDC must apologize to the monks until they satisfy and can forgive and pardon them.
2. Reduce all commodity prices, fuel prices, rice and cooking oil prices immediately.
3. Release all political prisoners including Daw Aung San Suu Kyi, and all detainees arrested in ongoing demonstrations over fuel price hike.
4. Enter [into a] dialogue with democratic forces for national reconciliation immediately to resolve the crises and difficulties facing and suffering.

Unless SPDC give[s] in and compl[ies] with our demand on or before the deadline of 17th September 2007 (the 6th waxing day of Tawthalin), we hereby announce that this Monks Alliance Group will boycott SPDC until our demands are met.—All Burma Monks Alliance Group.

9. For a discussion of Victor Turner's concept of *communitas* and its centrality in the structure of rituals, see his *Ritual Process*, pp. 94–113 and 125–130.

10. For discussions of the significance of sacred sites in public protests, see Edwards, "Grounds for Protest"; see also Philp and Mercer, "Politicised Pagodas and Veiled Resistance."

11. Wahyuana, "A Burmese Monk's Reflections."

12. See his essay, "Thai Buddhism in the 21st Century" and personal communication, March 2009.

13. Paulo Sérgio Pinheiro, *Report of the Special Rapporteur*; and Human Rights Watch, *Crackdown*. Kyaw Yin Hlaing's "The State of the Pro-Democracy Movement in Authoritarian Burma" describes the failed strategies of the democratic resistance prior to

September 2007. A useful comparison to Kyaw Yin Hlaing's essays describes the dangers of living in hiding from government reprisals and is found in Packer, "Drowning."

14. Tambiah, *Buddhism Betrayed?* p. 81.

15. A regional USDA representative asserted in an interview in 2006 that the impact of western sanctions was felt strongly, not only because of a loss in trade with the west, but also because it entailed a loss of funding from the United Nations for a range of public purposes, including public health projects.

16. A useful economic survey is found in Turnell, "Burma's Economy 2008."

17. The practices of socially engaged Buddhism within globalizing economies, such as China's emerging consumer society, require further investigation. It is worth noting that in Myanmar, as in Tibet during the unrest of 2008, increased economic pressures brought Buddhist monks into violent confrontation with the military agents of the state.

18. This was the title of an article written by Choe Sang-Hun in the *International Herald Tribune* on October 23, 2007.

19. The Ten Duties of Kings include generosity (*dāna*), morality (*sīla*), dedication (*paricagga*), integrity (*ajjava*), kindness (*maddava*), austerity (*tapas*), the absence of anger (*akkodha*), nonviolence (*avihimsa*), patience (*khanti*), and respect for the will of the people (*avirodha*). The Venerable Rewata Dhamma, one of the early proponents of socially engaged Buddhism and democracy in Burma, discussed these qualities as the foundation for human rights and justice in Burma in an address he delivered in November 1989.

20. Min Zin, "Burmese Buddhism's Impact on Social Change."

21. Bechert in "Neue Buddhistische Orthodoxie" and Mathews in "The Iron Heel" both propose that the Burmese sangha is tradition-bound and unfamiliar with issues of modernity. But I argue that the Burmese monastic confrontation with modernity is multifaceted and includes its traditional concern for social ethics as well as its involvement with the international mission of Buddhist activism and the economic and political struggle for modernization. The interpretations of social ethics by monastic groups and their lay supporters encompass a pluralist, multifaceted spectrum of religious voices and practice in Burma. The resolution of the on-going struggle for modernity will be a critical element in the popular legitimation of the future Burmese state. Against the context of this multivocal quest for modernity among members of the state, the sangha, and the laity, the welfare of the Burmese nation will depend on the development of a civil society and civil institutions resilient enough to withstand both coercive power and charismatic appeal.

22. Jackson, *Buddhism, Legitimation, and Conflict*; Keyes, "Buddhism and National Integration in Thailand"; Keyes, "Buddhist Politics and Their Revolutionary Origins in Thailand"; Suksamran, *Political Buddhism in Southeast Asia;* Sulak Sivaraksa, *A Buddhist Vision for Renewing Society*; Bond, *The Buddhist Revival in Sri Lanka*; Tambiah,

Buddhism Betrayed?; Tambiah, "The Persistence and Transformation of Tradition in Southeast Asia"; Anderson, *Imagined Communities*; James Scott, *Weapons of the Weak*; James Scott, *Domination and the Arts of Resistance*.

23. A full description of Sāsana Moli can be found at http://sasanamoli.blogspot.com/. Similar advocacy of Buddhist causes is also accessible at http://www.buddhistchannel.tv/.

24. Aung Zaw, "Burmese Monks in Revolt."

25. Currently the Burmese sangha also does not advocate a nationalist agenda that excludes ethnic minorities.

26. Wahyuana, "A Burmese Monk's Reflections."

27. One need only recall here the reasons Sinhalese monks cite to justify their involvement in nationalist politics.

28. Wai Moe, "Myanma Media Claims Monks Possessed Weapons, Pornography," *The Irrawaddy,* October 8, 2007.

29. Min Lwin, "Burmese Armed Forces day to mark decades of Military Rule," *The Irrawaddy,* March 26, 2008. Accessed on March 26, 2008 at http://www.irrawaddy.org/article.php?art_id=11126.

30. For a discussion of violence and Buddhist practice, see Schober, "Buddhism, Violence, and the State."

31. Similarly, Christianity espouses normative values of altruism, but we do not expect actual Christian practice to contravene all issues of self-interest in economic and political transactions.

32. See Ingrid Jordt's interview by Seth Mydans, "What Makes a Monk Mad," *The New York Times,* September 30, 2007.

33. Mendelson, *Sangha and State in Burma,* pp. 174–179.

34. See Harvey, *History of Burma*, p. 26.

35. Maitrii Aung Thwin has argued that Buddhist culture in general was criminalized during colonial rule in Burma in "Genealogy of a Rebellion Narrative."

36. Founded in 1921, the General Council of Sangha Sammeggi fostered a largely traditionalist nationalism, which was advocated by the monks who came to be known as Burma's political monks.

37. During November 2008, several other prominent protest leaders, including actors and poets, received harsh prison terms for their roles in the events of September 2007.

38. Wahyuana, "A Burmese Monk's Reflections on the Struggle for Democracy."

Chapter 8: Potential Futures

1. Justin McDaniel's analysis of trends in modern Thai Buddhism similarly distinguishes between Buddhist movements that have either contested or supported the Thai state; see his "Buddhism in Thailand."

2. Scholars concerned with the emergence of secularism in the west have similarly noted that in western traditions as well, the idea of the absence of religious ethics from public life is derived from primarily Christian ethics.

3. Critical reflections on orientalism in Buddhist studies have been most profitably articulated by Donald Lopez in *Curators of the Buddha*; by Charles Hallisey in "Roads Taken and Not Taken," concerning colonial scholarship on Theravada traditions; by Ananda Abeyeskera in *Colors of the Robe*, on authenticity in Buddhist practice; and by David McMahan in *The Making of Buddhist Modernism*, on the emergence of Buddhist modernism. In regards to the study of Burmese Buddhism, the recognition of ethnographic authenticity is expressed in the works of Mendelson, F. K. Lehman, and many others who have written about these concerns more recently.

4. In "Weber and Anthropology," Keyes offers an insightful discussion of Weber's contributions.

5. See Han's essay, "Introduction: Political Society and Civil Anthropology," for a useful overview of Weberian approaches to the study of civil society. Perez-Diaz, "The Possibility of Civil Society," offers a persuasive critique of approaches that exhibit a Christian or western bias.

6. Steinberg, "A Void in Myanmar."

7. Ironically, the regime labeled Aung San Suu Kyi's renewed house arrest as "preemptive," in order to prevent her from mobilizing Burmese youths and avoid attacks on her person like the one during the Depyin Massacre her followers endured in 2003. For further discussion, see my essay "Buddhism, Violence, and the State."

8. Although this organization is represented to be a voluntary business organization, it resembles a grassroots party organization, for its leadership is made up almost entirely of retired military officers.

9. USDA activities include social causes, such as fundraising in support of local libraries, blood drives, and improvements to schools.

10. Tourists are expected to pay in U.S. dollars at government offices for items such as road tolls when crossing into another state or division or for entrance fees when visiting monuments and museums.

11. See Myat Thein, *Economic Development of Myanmar,* on state control over economic investments. For a discussion of USDA's economic involvements, see Steinberg, *Burma: The State of Myanmar*. I thank Joerg Schendel for sharing these references with me.

12. Some observers may suggest that a more substantive answer to that question could be gleaned from the state's response to the devastation caused by Cyclone Nargis in 2008.

13. See the *Myanmar Times,* June 26–July 2, 2006, p. 4. This complex set of national objectives has been widely publicized by the government.

14. The news site, *Mizzima*, reported on June 25, 2009: "Gambira, leader of the

All Burma Buddhist Monks Association for five years, was charged under the Electronics Act. The reverend monk, who was charged on 16 counts, will now have to serve 63 years in prison. The Electronics Act 33 (a) stipulates that using the internet without the permission of the authorities is an offence and is punishable. The law has become a tool for the authorities to sentence the reverend monk, who took a lead role in the September 2007 monk-led protests."

GLOSSARY

(B) designates Burmese terms; (P) designates Pāli terms..

acaryāvadin (P) transmitted by "unorthodox" teachers
adhamma (P) heretical teachings
adhammavadi (P) heresy
alajji (P) shameless
amyo (B) race
ana (B) power, authority, strength
arahant (P) perfected individual, saint
aun myei (B) place of victory
batha (B) erudition, knowledge of a subject like Burmese literature and religion
cakkavatti (P) wheel-turning monarch, world conqueror, Buddhist universal monarch
dāna (P) donations, generosity, a Buddhist virtue
dat loun: (B) alchemist's stone
dhamma (P) the Buddhist Law
dhammakathika (P) monastic teachers of Buddhism appointed to Burmese government school
dhammakāya (P) the Buddha's spiritual body, teachings
dhammarāja (P) righteous Buddhist ruler
gain: (B) monastic grouping, often based on ordination lineages
hluttaw (B) council of ministers during royal times; the legislative body of the modern state
hpoun (B) one's store of merit, the quality of one's merit
hti (B) spire atop a stupa or pagoda; symbolizes enlightenment; is often adorned with gems
kandaw (B) paying respect to the Buddha, monks, or one's superiors
kuthou shin (B) owner of merit
kyaun: (B) monastery or monastic school
lokiya (P) worldly realm of existence
lokuttera (P) transcendent realm of existence
metta (P) loving kindness, a Buddhist virtue
nat (B) local spirit lord
nibbāna (P) moral perfection, enlightenment
nikāya (P) ordination lineages of monastic groups

oza (B) influence, authority, command
pārājika (P) transgression meriting expulsion from the sangha
pativedha sāsana (P) ideal Buddhist society
pattam nikkujjana kamma (P) the formal act of the sangha to refuse donations
pwè kyaun: (B) heterodox monastery
pyinnya (B) formal education
rūpakāya (P) the Buddha's physical remains
samsāra (P) the realm of rebirth, by extension, the Buddhist world
sangāyana (P) the Buddhist Council
sangha (P) the Buddhist monastic community, the fully Romanized designation of sangha is used here due to its relative currency in contemporary English
sāsana (P) the Buddha's dispensation
satyagraha nonviolent resistance, "seizing the truth" (a Sanskrit term)
setkya min: (B) a wheel-turning monarch, a universal monarch
sīla (P) precepts, morality
sīmā (P) consecrated ordination hall
stūpa (P) a reliquary mount or a monument containing the remains of an enlightened person, often also a pilgrimage destination
tagou (B) one's personal power
thabeik hmauk (B) to overturn the alms bowl, to refuse donations, to go on strike
thathana (B) the Buddha's dispensation
thathana pyu thi (B) missionizing Buddhism, making the world safe for the Buddhist dispensation
thathana win (B) religious chronicles, genealogy of Buddhist history
thathanabain (B) patriarch of the Burmese sangha
tipitaka (P) the Theravada canon, consisting of the rules for monastic discipline, *vinaya pitaka*; the *sutta pitaka* containing narratives about the Buddha and his preaching; and the *abhidhamma pitaka*, a collection of Theravada philosophy concerning the causality that governs the path to enlightenment
vinaya (P) rules of monastic conduct, monastic discipline
vipassanā (P) insight meditation
wunthanu athin (B) grassroots organizations promoting nationalism during colonialism

BIBLIOGRAPHY

"The 88 Generation Students on oppression against economic and social equalities of political activists." BurmaNet News, April 5, 2007. http://www.burmanet.org/news/2007/04/05/the-88-generation-students-on-oppression-against-economic-and-social-equalities-of-political-activists/ (accessed July 13, 2007).

"The 88 Generation Students' policy announcement regarding the emergence of the State Constitution." BurmaNet News, June 28, 2007. http://www.burmanet.org/news/2007/06/28/the-88-generation-students-the-88-generation-students-policy-announcement-regarding-emergence-of-the-state-constitution/ (accessed July 13, 2007).

Abeysekara, Ananda. *Colors of the Robe: Religion, Identity and Difference.* Columbia: University of South Carolina Press, 2002.

All Burma Young Monks Union. "The Buddha Sāsana and Burma Military Regime." Revolutionary Area, Burma, 1991.

Altbach, Philip G., and Gavin. P. Kelly. *Education and the Colonial Experience.* New York: Advent Books, Inc., 1991.

Ananda Metteyya. "Extension of the Empire of Righteousness to the Western Lands." Address at the Sixth Annual Convention of the International Buddhist Society. December 27, 1908. Mandalay: Chanea Press, 1909.

Anderson, Benedict. *Imagined Communities: Reflections on the Origins and Spread of Nationalism.* New York: Verso, 1991.

Aung San Suu Kyi. "The Benefits of Meditation and Sacrifice." *Bangkok Post.* September 1996.

———. "Empowerment for a Culture of Peace and Development." Address to World Commission on Culture and Development. November 1994. BurmaNet News. http://burmanetnews.org (accessed April 5, 2000).

———. "Faith Eases the Mind in Times of Political Turmoil." *Letters from Burma* 40. *Mainichi Daily News,* Monday, September 9, 1996.

———. "In Quest of Democracy." In *Freedom from Fear and Other Writings*, ed. Michael Aris, pp. 167–179. New York: Viking Press, 1991.

———. "Intellectual Life in Burma and India under Colonialism." In *Freedom from Fear and Other Writings,* ed. Michael Aris, pp. 82–139. New York: Viking Press, 1991.

———. "Letter from Burma, 1997(4)." *Mainichi Daily News*, Monday, April 14, 1997.

———. *Letters from Burma.* New York: Penguin Books, 1997.

Aung Thwin, Maitrii. "Genealogy of a Rebellion Narrative: Law, Ethnology, and Culture in Colonial Burma." *Journal of Southeast Asian Studies* 34, no. 3 (2003): 393–419.

Aung-Thwin, Michael. "Of Monarchs, Monks and Men: Religion and the State in Myanmar." Asia Research Institute, National University of Singapore: Working Paper series 127, 2009.

———. *Pagan: The Origins of Modern Burma.* Honolulu: University of Hawai'i Press, 1985.

Aung Zaw. "Burmese Monks in Revolt." *The Irrawaddy.* September 11, 2007.

Bagshawe, L. E. "A Literature of School Books." M. Phil. Thesis, School of Oriental and African Studies, University of London, 1976.

Bechert, Heinz. *Buddhismus, Staat und Gesellschaft in den Ländern des Theravada-Buddhismus.* Vol. 1. Frankfurt am Main: Schriften des Instituts für Asienkunde, 1966.

———. "Neue Buddhistische Orthodoxie: Bemerkungen zur Gliederung und zur Reform des Sangha in Birma." *Numen* 35, no. 1 (1988): 24–56.

———. "Sangha, State, Society, Nation: Persistence of Traditions in 'post-traditional' Buddhist Societies." *Daedalus* 102, no. 1 (1973): 85–95.

———, Daw Khin Su, and Daw Tin Tin Myint, compilers. *Burmese Manuscripts.* 2 vols. Wiesbaden: Steiner, 1978–1985.

Bečka, Jan. *Historical Dictionary of Burma.* London: Scarecrow Press, 1995.

———. "The Role of Buddhism as a Factor of Burmese National Identity in the Period of British Rule in Burma (1886–1948)." *Archiv oriental* 59, no. 4 (1991): 389–405.

Bellah, Robert, and Phillip E. Hammond, eds. *Varieties of Civil Religion.* San Francisco: Harper & Row, 1980.

Bond, George. *The Buddhist Revival in Sri Lanka: Religious Tradition, Reinterpretation, and Response.* Columbia: University of South Carolina Press, 1988.

Braun, Erik. "The Birth of Modern Buddhism: Ledi Sayadaw, Abhidhamma, and the Development of the Modern Insight Meditation Movement in Burma." Ph.D. diss., Harvard University, 2008.

Burma, Department of Education. *Annual Reports of Public Instruction in Burma, 1867–.* Rangoon: Suptd., Government Printing Office, 1891–1892.

Burma Human Rights Year Book 2002–2003: Rights to Education and Health. Online Burma/Myanmar Library. November 10, 2003. Originally published by Human Rights Documentation Unit, NCGUB. http://www.burmalibrary.org/show.php?cat=333 (accessed August 9, 2007).

"Burma: The Land Where Buddhist Monks Are Disrobed and Detained in Dungeons." The Assistance Association for Political Prisoners (Burma), November 2004. http://mailto:aappb@cscoms.com and http://www.aappb.net.

Cady, John F. *A History of Modern Burma.* Ithaca, NY: Cornell University Press, 1958.

———. "Religion and Politics in Modern Burma." *The Far Eastern Quarterly* 12, no. 2 (1953): 149–162.

Chan Htoon. "Address to the Conference on Religion in the Age of Science." Address to the Conference on Religion in the Age of Science, Star Island, NH, 1958.

Charney, Michael W. *Powerful Learning: Buddhist Literati and the Throne in Burma's Last Dynasty, 1752–1885.* Ann Arbor: University of Michigan, Centers for South and Southeast Asian Studies, 2006.

Chatterjee, Partha. *The Nation and Its Fragments: Colonial and Postcolonial Histories.* Princeton: Princeton University Press, 1993.

Choompolpaisal, Phibul. "Constrictive Constructs: Unravelling the Influence of Weber's Sociology on Theravada Studies since the 1960s." *Contemporary Buddhism* 9, no.1 (2008): 7–51.

Cohn, Bernard S. *Colonialism and Its Forms of Knowledge: The British in India.* Princeton, NJ: Princeton University Press, 1996.

Collins, Steven. *Nirvana and Other Buddhist Felicities: Utopias of the Pāli Imaginaire.* Cambridge: Cambridge University Press, 1998.

———. "On the Very Idea of the Pali Canon." *Journal of the Pali Text Society* 15 (1990): 89–126.

———, and Andrew Huxley, "The Post-Canonical Adventures of Mahāsammata." *Journal of Indian Philosophy* 24, no. 6 (1996): 623–648.

Cuttriss, C. A. "Early Newspapers in Burma." *Journal of Burma Research Society, Fiftieth Anniversary Publications.* Vol. 2, pp. 43–47. Rangoon: Sarpay Beikman Press, 1960. Originally published in *Journal of the Burma Research Society* 27, no. 3 (1937): 277–282.

Edwards, Penny. "Grounds for Protest: Placing Shwedagon Pagoda in Colonial and Postcolonial History." *Postcolonial Studies* 9, no. 2 (2006): 197–211.

———. "Relocating the Interlocutor: Taw Sein Ko (1864–1930) and the Itinerancy of Knowledge in British Burma." *South East Asia Research* 12, no. 3 (2004): 277–335.

Ferguson, John P. "The Arahat Ideal in Modern Burmese Buddhism." Paper presented at the Meetings of the Association for Asian Studies, New York, March 1977.

———. "The Symbolic Dimensions of the Burmese Sangha." Ph.D. diss., Cornell University, 1975.

Fraser-Lu, Sylvia. *Splendour in Wood: The Buddhist Monasteries of Burma.* Trumbull, CT: Weatherhill, 2001.

Frost, Mark. "Wider Opportunities: Religious Revival, Nationalist Awakening and the Global Dimension in Colombo, 1870–1920." *Modern Asian Studies* 36, no. 4 (2002): 937–967.

Furnivall, J. S. *Colonial Policy and Practice.* Cambridge: Cambridge University Press, 1948.

———. *Educational Progress in Southeast Asia.* New York: Institute of Pacific Relations, 1943.

———, and May Ong. "The Dawn of Nationalism." *Journal of the Burma Research Society* 33, no. 1 (1950): 1–7.

Geertz, Clifford. *Negara: The Theater State in 19th Century Bali.* Princeton: Princeton University Press, 1980.

Gellner, David. *The Anthropology of Buddhism and Hinduism.* Oxford: Oxford University Press, 2001.

Gravers, Mikael. *Nationalism as Political Paranoia: An Essay on the Historical Practice of Power.* Richmond: Curzon, 1999.

Hall, D. G. E. *Burma.* London: Hutchinson's University Library, 1956.

Hallisey, Charles. "Roads Taken and Not Taken." In *Curators of the Buddha: The Study of Buddhism under Colonialism,* ed. Donald S. Lopez, Jr., pp. 31–62. Chicago: University of Chicago Press, 1995.

Hann, Chris. "Introduction: Political Society and Civil Anthropology." In *Civil Society: Challenging Western Models,* ed. Chris Hann and Elizabeth Dunn, pp. 1–27. London: Routledge, 1996.

Harvey, Godfrey E. *History of Burma: From the Earliest Times to 10 March 1824.* London: Frank Cass and Co., 1925.

Herbert, Patricia. "Burmese Cosmological Manuscripts." In *Burma: Art and Archaeology,* ed. Alexandra Green and Richard Blurton, pp. 277–298. London: The British Museum Press, 2000.

———. *The Hsaya San Rebellion (1930–1932).* London: The British Library London, 1982.

Houtman, Gustaaf. *Mental Culture in Burmese Crisis Politics.* Tokyo: Institute for the Study of Languages and Cultures of Asia and Africa, Tokyo University of Foreign Studies, 1999.

———. "The Tradition of Practice among Burmese Buddhists." PhD diss., University of London, 1990.

Human Rights Documentation Unit. *Bullets in the Alms Bowl: An Analysis of the Brutal SPDC Suppression of the September 2007 Saffron Revolution.* National Coalition Government of the Union of Burma. March 2008.

Human Rights Watch. *Crackdown: Repression of the 2007 Popular Protests in Burma.* Vol. 19, no. 18 (C), December 2007.

Ikeya, Chie. "Gender, History, and Modernity: Representing Women in Twentieth Century Colonial Burma." PhD diss., Cornell University, 2006.

Jackson, Peter. *Buddhism, Legitimation, and Conflict: The Political Functions of Urban Thai Buddhism.* Singapore: Institute of Southeast Asian Studies, 1989.

———. "Re-Interpreting the Traiphuum Phra Ruang: Political Functions of Buddhist Symbolisim in Contemporary Thailand." In *Buddhist Trends in Southeast Asia,* ed. Trevor Ling, pp. 64–100. Singapore: Institute for Southeast Asian Studies, 1993.

James, Helen. *Governance and Civil Society in Myanmar: Education, Health and Environment.* London: Routledge, 2005

Jordt, Ingrid. *Burma's Mass Lay Meditation Movement: Buddhism and the Cultural Construction of Power.* Athens: Ohio University Press, 2007.

Judson, Adoniram. *Judson's Burmese-English Dictionary.* Rangoon: Baptist Board of Publications, 1953.

Keyes, Charles. "Buddhism and National Integration in Thailand." *Journal of Asian Studies* 30, no. 3 (1971): 551–567.

———. "Buddhist Economics and Buddhist Fundamentalism in Burma and Thailand." In *Fundamentalisms and the State: Remaking Polities, Economies, and Militance,* ed. Martin Marty and Scott Appleby, pp. 367–409. Chicago: University of Chicago Press, 1993.

———. "Buddhist Politics and Their Revolutionary Origins in Thailand." *International Political Science Review* 10, no. 2 (1989): 121–142.

———. "Millennialism, Theravada Buddhism, and Thai Society." *Journal of Asian Studies* 36 (1977): 283–302.

———. "Weber and Anthropology." *Annual Review of Anthropology* 31 (2002): 233–255.

———, Laurel Kendall, and Helen Hardacre. "Contested Visions of Community in East and Southeast Asia." In *Asian Visions of Authority: Religion and the Modern States of East and Southeast Asia,* ed. Charles Keyes, Laurel Kendall, and Helen Hardacre, pp. 1–18, Honolulu: University of Hawai'i Press, 1994.

Khammai Dhammasami. "Idealism and Pragmatism: A Dilemma in the Current Monastic Education Systems of Burma and Thailand." In *Buddhism, Power and Political Order,* ed. Ian Harris, pp. 10–25. New York: Routledge, 2007.

King, Richard. "Colonialism and Buddhism." In *Encyclopedia of Buddhism,* ed. Robert E. Buswell, Jr., pp.162–165. New York: Macmillan Reference, 2003.

Kitiarsa, Pattana. "Beyond the Weberian Trials: An Essay on the Anthropology of Southeast Asian Buddhism." *Religion Compass* 3, no. 2 (2009): 200–224.

Kyaw Yin Hlaing. "The State of the Pro-Democracy Movement in Authoritarian Burma." East-West Center Washington Working Papers No. 11, December 2007.

Lehman, Kris F. "Doctrine, Practice and Belief in Theravada Buddhism." *Journal of Asian Studies* 31, no. 2 (1972): 373–380.

———. "On the Vocabulary and Semantics of 'Field' in Theravada Buddhist Society." In *Essays on Burma,* ed. J. P. Ferguson, pp. 101–111. Leiden: E. J. Brill, 1980.

Leider, Jacques P. "Text, Lineage and Tradition in Burma: The Struggle for Norms and Religious Legitimacy under King Bodawphaya (1782–1819)." *Journal of Burma Studies* 9 (2004): 82–129.

Lieberman, Victor. *Strange Parallels: Southeast Asia in Global Context, c. 800–1830.* Vol. 1, *Integration on the Mainland.* New York: Cambridge University Press, 2003.

Lincoln, Bruce. *Holy Terror: Thinking about Religion after September 11.* Chicago: University of Chicago Press, 2003.

Ling, Trevor, ed. *Buddhist Trends in Southeast Asia.* Singapore: Institute of Southeast Asian Studies, 1993.

Lintner, Bertil. "Myanmar's 88 Generation Comes of Age." *Asia Times online,* January 27, 2007. http://www.atimes.com/atimes/southeast_asia/IA25Ae04.html (accessed July 13, 2007).

Lopez, Donald S. *Buddhism and Science.* Chicago: University of Chicago Press, 2008.

——, ed. *Curators of the Buddha: The Study of Buddhism under Colonialism.* Chicago: University of Chicago Press, 1995.

Lubeigt, Guy. "Introduction of Western Culture in Burma in the 19th Century: From Civilian Acceptance to Religious Resistance." Manuscript from the Fourth Euro-Japanese Symposium on Mainland Southeast Asian History, 1999.

Marty, Martin, and Scott Appleby, eds. *Fundamentalisms Observed.* Chicago: University of Chicago Press, 1992.

Mathews, Bruce. "The Iron Heel: Buddhism under a Military Regime in Burma." Paper presented at the Burma Studies Colloquium, DeKalb, IL, 1992.

——. "Myanmar's Agony: The Struggle for Democracy." *The Round Table,* no. 325 (1993): 37–49.

Maung Maung. *Burmese Nationalist Movements (1940–1948).* Edinburgh: Kiscadale, 1989.

——. *From Sangha to Laity: Nationalist Movements of Burma (1920–1940).* Columbia, MO: South Asia Books, 1980.

Maung Oo. "88 Generation students to step up peaceful protests." Democratic Voice of Burma, May 21, 2007. http://english.dvb.no/news.php?id=121 (accessed July 13, 2007).

May Ong. "The Modern Burman." A lecture reported by the Rangoon Gazette, August 10, 1908. Reprinted in the *Journal of the Burma Research Society* 33, no.1 (1950): 1–7.

McDaniel, Justin. "Buddhism in Thailand: Negotiating the Modern Age." In *Buddhism in World Cultures: Contemporary Perspectives,* ed. Stephen Berkwitz, pp. 101–128. Santa Barbara, CA: ABC-CLIO, 2006.

McMahan, David L. *The Making of Buddhist Modernism.* Oxford: Oxford University Press, 2008.

——. "Modernity and the Early Discourse of Scientific Buddhism." *Journal of the American Academy of Religion* 72, no. 4 (2004): 897–933.

Mendelson, Michael E. "A Messianic Association in Upper Burma." *Bulletin of the School of Oriental and African Studies* 24 (1961): 560–580.

——. *Sangha and State in Burma, A Study of Monastic Sectarianism and Leadership.* Ithaca, NY: Cornell University Press, 1975.

Mi Mi Khaing. *Burmese Family.* Bloomington: Indiana University Press, 1962.

Min Lwin. "Burmese Armed Forces Day to Mark Decades of Military Rule," *The Irrawaddy,* March 26, 2008. http://www.irrawaddy.org/article.php?art_id=11126 (accessed March 26, 2008).

Min Zin. "Burmese Buddhism's Impact on Social Change: The Fatalism of Samsara and Monastic Resistance." *The Irrawaddy* 11, no. 2 (June 3, 2003).

Moscotti, A. *British Policy and the Nationalist Movement in Burma, 1917–1937.* Honolulu: University of Hawai'i Press, 1974.

Myat Thein. *Economic Development of Myanmar.* Singapore: Institute of Southeast Asian Studies, 2004.

Mydans, Seth. "What Makes a Monk Mad," *The New York Times,* September 30, 2007.

Myo Myint. "The Politics of Survival in Burma." Ph.D. diss. Cornell University, 1987.

Narinjara News. "Buddhist Rites to Prevent Foreign Invasion!" September 2, 2003.

Network for Democracy and Development. "The White Shirts: How the USDA will become the New Face of Burma's Dictatorship." Mae Sot Tak Thailand, NDD Headquarters, May 2006.

Ono Toru. "The Development of Education in Burma." *East Asian Cultural Studies* 20, no. 1–4 (March 1981): 107–133.

Overseas Mon Young Monks Union. *Buddhist Way to Democracy* 1, no. 1 (April 1992), Bangkok.

Packer, George. "Drowning: Can the Burmese People Rescue Themselves?" *The New Yorker,* August 25, 2008.

Perez-Diaz, Victor. "The Possibility of Civil Society: Traditions, Character and Challenges." In *Civil Society: Theory, History, Comparison,* ed. John Hall, pp. 80–109. Cambridge: Polity Press, 1995.

Pham, Julie. "Ghost Hunting in Colonial Burma: Nostalgia, Paternalism and the Thoughts of J. S. Furnivall." *South East Asia Research* 12, no. 2 (July 2004): 237–268.

Philp, Janette, and David Mercer. "Politicised Pagodas and Veiled Resistance." *Urban Studies* 39, no. 9 (2002): 1587–1610.

Pinheiro, Paulo Sérgio. *Report of the Special Rapporteur on the Situation of Human Rights in Myanmar,* December 7, 2007.

Pradhan, M. V. *Burma, Dhamma, and Democracy: Being a Historical and Cultural Survey of Burma and an Account of the Pro-democracy Struggle.* Bombay: Mayflower Publishing House, 1991.

Pranke, Patrick Arthur. "Treatise on the Lineage of Elders (*Vamsadipani*): Monastic Reform and the Writing of Buddhist History in Eighteenth-century Burma." Ph.D. diss., University of Michigan, 2004.

Prothero, Stephen. *The White Buddhist.* Bloomington: University of Indiana Press, 1996.

Queen, Christopher, and Sallie King. *Engaged Buddhism: Buddhist Liberation Movements in Asia.* Albany: SUNY Press, 1996.

Rewata Dhamma. "Dhamma, Ethics, and Human Rights." Speech given at a convention in Seoul, Korea, September 1994.

Reynolds, F. E. "Civic Religion and National Community in Thailand." *Journal of Asian Studies* 36, no. 2 (1977): 267–282.

——, and M. B. Reynolds. *Three Worlds according to King Ruang: A Thai Buddhist Cosmology.* Berkeley, CA: Asian Humanities Press, 1982.

Rives, Nang Mo Lao. "The Teaching of English in Burma (Myanmar) from 1824–1988." PhD diss., University of Kansas, 1999.

Rudolph, Susanna Hoeber, and Lloyd I. Rudolph. *Gandhi: The Traditional Roots of Charisma.* Chicago: University of Chicago Press, 1983.

Sai Khma Maung. "Changing Buddhist Practice in Burma." Honors thesis. The Australian National University, November 2004.

Sarkisyanz, E. *Buddhist Backgrounds of the Burmese Revolution.* The Hague: Martinus Nijhoff, 1965.

Schober, Juliane. "Buddhism and Modernity in Myanmar." In *Buddhism in World Cultures: Contemporary Perspectives,* ed. Steven Berkwitz, pp. 73–100. Santa Barbara, CA: ABC-CLIO, 2006.

——. "Buddhism, Violence, and the State in Burma (Myanmar) and Sri Lanka." In *Religion and Conflict in South and Southeast Asia: Disrupting Violence,* ed. Linell E. Cady and Sheldon W. Simon, pp. 51–69. New York: Routledge, 2007.

——. "Buddhist Just Rule and Burmese National Culture: State Patronage of the Chinese Tooth Relic in Myanma." *History of Religions* 36, no. 3 (February 1997): 218–243.

——. "Buddhist Visions of Moral Authority and Civil Society: The Search for the Post-Colonial State in Burma." In *Burma at the Turn of the Twenty-First Century,* ed. Monique Skidmore, pp. 113–132. Honolulu: University of Hawai'i Press, 2005.

——. "Colonial Knowledge and Buddhist Education in Burma." In *Buddhism, Power and Political Order,* ed. Ian Harris, pp. 52–70. New York: Routledge, 2007.

——. "In the Presence of the Buddha: Ritual Veneration of the Burmese Mahamuni Image." In *Sacred Biography in the Buddhist Traditions of South and Southeast Asia,* ed. Juliane Schober, pp. 259–288. Honolulu: University of Hawai'i Press, 1997.

——. "Mapping the Sacred in Theravada Buddhist Southeast Asia." In *Modern Landscapes: Sacred Geography and Social-Religious Transformations in South and Southeast Asia,* ed. Ronald Lukens-Bull, pp. 1–29. Tempe: Program for Southeast Asian Studies, Arizona State University, 2004.

——. "The Path to Buddhahood: Spiritual Mission and Social Organization of Mysticism in Contemporary Burma." *Crossroads* 4, no. 1 (1989): 13–30.

——. "Paths to Enlightenment: Theravada Buddhism in Upper Burma." Ph.D. diss., University of Illinois at Urbana-Champaign, 1989.

——. "Religious Merit and Social Status among Burmese Lay Buddhist Organizations." In *Blessings and Merit in Mainland Southeast Asia,* ed. N. Tannenbaum and C. Kammerer, pp. 197–211. New Haven, CT: Yale University, Southeast Asia Monograph Series, 1996.

——. "Religious Reform in Burma, 1980-1982: Traditional Religion and the Pragmatics of Modern Statecraft." Paper presented at the Summer Institute for Southeast Asian Studies, Ann Arbor, MI, 1984.

———. "The Theravada Buddhist Engagement with Modernity in Southeast Asia: Whither the Social Paradigm of the Galactic Polity?" *Journal of Southeast Asian Studies* 26, no. 2 (1995): 307–325.

———."U Nu (1907–95)." In *Encyclopedia of Buddhism*, ed. Damien Keown and Charles Prebish, pp. 771–772. New York: Routledge, 2007.

———. "Venerating the Buddha's Remains in Burma: From Solitary Practice to the Cultural Hegemony of Communities." *The Journal of Burma Studies* 6 (2001): 111–139.

Scott, David. *Refashioning Futures: Criticism after Postcoloniality.* Princeton: Princeton University Press, 1999.

Scott, James. *Domination and the Arts of Resistance: Hidden Transcripts.* New Haven, CT: Yale University Press, 1990.

———. *Weapons of the Weak.* New Haven, CT: Yale University Press, 1985.

Seito, Teruko. "Rural Monetization and Land-Mortgage Thet-Kayits in Kon-baung Burma." In *Last Stand of Asian Autonomies,* ed. Anthony Reid, pp. 153–186. New York: St. Martin's Press, 1997.

Seneviratne, H. L. *The Work of Kings: The New Buddhism in Sri Lanka.* Chicago: University of Chicago Press, 2000.

Shwe Lu Maung. *Burma, Nationalism and Ideology: An Analysis of Society, Culture, and Politics.* Dhaka: University Press, 1989.

Shwe Zan Aung. "Some Key Buddhist Concepts." *Journal of Burma Research Society* 8, no. 2 (1918): 99–106.

Singer, Noel F. *Old Rangoon.* Garmore, Scotland: Kiscadale Publications, 1995.

Singh, Surendra Prasad. *Growth of Nationalism in Burma, 1900–1942.* Calcutta: Firma KLM Private Limited, 1980.

Smith, D. E. *Religion and Politics in Burma.* Princeton: Princeton University Press, 1965.

Spiro, Melford E. *Buddhism and Society: A Great Tradition and Its Burmese Vicissitudes.* 2nd ed. Berkeley: University of California Press, 1982.

Stargardt, Janice. "The Oldest Known Pali Texts, 5th–6th Century: Results of the Cambridge Symposium on the Pyu Golden Pali Text from Sri Ksetra, 18–19 April 1995." *Journal of the Pali Text Society* 21 (1995): 199–213.

Steinberg, David. *Burma, a Socialist Nation in Southeast Asia.* Boulder, CO: Westview, 1982.

———. *Burma: The State of Myanmar.* Washington, DC: Georgetown University Press, 2001.

———. *Burma's Road toward Development.* Boulder, CO: Westview, 1981.

———. "A Void in Myanmar: Civil Society in Burma." In *Strengthening Civil Society in*

Burma: Possibilities and Dilemmas for International NGOs, ed. Burma Center Netherlands, Translational Institute, pp. 1–15. Chiang Mai, Thailand: Silkworm Books, 1999.

Strong, John. *The Legend of King Aśoka: A Study and Translation of the Aśokavadana.* Princeton: Princeton University Press, 1983.

———. "Relics." In *The Encyclopedia of Religion,* vol. 12, ed. Mircea Eliade, pp. 275–282. New York: MacMillan, 1987.

———. *Relics of the Buddha.* Princeton: Princeton University Press, 2004.

Suksamran, Somboon. *Political Buddhism in Southeast Asia.* New York: St. Martin's Press, 1976.

Sulak Sivaraksa. *A Buddhist Vision for Renewing Society: Collected Articles by a Concerned Thai Intellectual.* Bangkok: Thai Watana Panchi, 1981.

Swearer, Donald. *The Buddhist World of Southeast Asia.* Albany: SUNY Press, 1995.

———. "Fundamentalistic Movements in Theravāda Buddhism." In *Fundamentalisms Observed,* ed. Martin Marty and Scott Appleby, pp. 628–690. Chicago: University of Chicago Press, 1992.

———. "Thai Buddhism in the 21st Century: Contesting Views." In *Destroying Mara Forever: Buddhist Ethics Essays in Honor of Damien Keown,* ed. Charles Prebish and John Powers. Boulder, CO: Snow Lion Books, 2010.

Symes, Michael. *Journal of His Second Embassy to the Court of Ava in 1802.* London: Allen and Unwin, 1955

Tambiah, Stanley J. *Buddhism Betrayed? Religion, Politics and Violence in Sri Lanka.* Chicago: University of Chicago Press, 1991.

———. *Culture, Thought, and Social Action: An Anthropological Perspective.* Cambridge, MA: Harvard University Press, 1985.

———. "The Persistence and Transformation of Tradition in Southeast Asia with Special Reference to Thailand." *Daedalus* 102, no. 1 (1973): 55–84.

———. *World Conqueror, World Renouncer.* Cambridge: Cambridge University Press, 1975.

Taw Sein Ko. *Burmese Sketches.* Rangoon: British Burma Press, 1913.

Taylor, James. *Buddhism and Postmodern Imaginings in Thailand.* London: Ashgate, 2008.

Taylor, Robert. The State in Burma. Honolulu: University of Hawaiʻi Press, 1987.

———. *The State in Myanmar.* Revised. Honolulu: University of Hawaiʻi Press, 2006.

Than Htun, ed. *Royal Orders of Burma, A.D. 1598–1885.* 9 vols. Kyoto: Center for Southeast Asian Studies, Kyoto University, 1989.

Thant Myint-U. *The Making of Modern Burma.* Cambridge: Cambridge University Press, 2001.

Tin Maung Maung Than. "The Sangha and Sāsana in Socialist Burma." *Sojourn* 3, no. 1 (February 1988): 26–61.

———. "Sangha Reforms and Renewal of Sāsana in Myanmar: Historical Trends and Contemporary Practice." In *Buddhist Trends in Southeast Asia,* ed. Trevor Ling, pp. 6–66. Singapore: Institute of Southeast Asian Studies, 1993.

Turnell, Sean. "Burma's Economy 2008: Current Situation and Prospects for Reform." Burma Economic Watch/Economics Department, Macquarie University, Sydney, Australia, Burmalibrary.org (uploaded November 28, 2008).

Turner, Alicia. "Buddhism, Colonialism, and the Boundaries of Religion: Theravada Buddhism in Burma, 1885–1920." Ph.D. diss., University of Chicago, 2009.

Turner, Victor W. *The Ritual Process: Structure and Anti-Structure.* Chicago: Aldine Publishing, 1969.

Von Der Mehden, Fred. *Religion and Nationalism in Southeast Asia: Burma, Indonesia, and the Philippines.* Madison: University of Wisconsin Press, 1963.

Wahyuana. "A Burmese Monk's Reflections on the Struggle for Democracy," 2007–07–18. http://www.theasiamediaforum.org/node/698 (accessed March 24, 2008).

Wai Moe. "Myanma Media Claims Monks Possessed Weapons, Pornography." *The Irrawaddy,* October 8, 2007.

Weber, Max. *The Religion of India: The Sociology of Hinduism and Buddhism.* Glencoe, IL: Free Press, 1958.

Young Men's Buddhist Association. *The Illustrated History of Buddhism.* Daly City: Theravada Buddhist Society of America, 1994. Reprint of Rangoon edition, 1951.

INDEX

Abeysekara, Ananda, 159n2, 160n12
Alaungpaya, 16, 26
All Burma Monks Alliance (ABMA), 124, 125, 143, 183n8
All Burma Young Monks Union (ABYMU), 107, 125
All Monks Union, 9, 124. *See also* General Council of Sangha Sammeggi
Alliance of All Burma Monks, 119
Ananda Metteyya, 63
Anawrahta, 18, 113
Anti-Fascist People's Freedom League (AFPFL), 79
Atulayasa, 26, 163n27
Aung San, 7, 79, 108, 130, 145, 156, 165n25
Aung San Suu Kyi, 7, 61, 108, 110–127, 130, 157, 165n26, 171n18, 181n30, 182nn40, 47, 187n7
Aung Thwin, Maitrii, 103, 165n16, 180n14, 186n35
Aung-Thwin, Michael, 18, 76, 159n3, 160n7
authority, 168nn34, 38, 172n39, 173n45. *See also* moral authority

Bhikkhu Aśoka (a.k.a. Alan Bennett), 170n6
Bigandet, Bishop, 50, 166n9
Bodawpaya, 6, 16, 25–29
Bodh Gaya, 170n5
Buddha Batha KalyanaYuwa Athin (Association to Care for the Wholesomeness of Buddhism), 56. *See also* Young Men's Buddhist Association
Buddha Sāsana Council (BSC), 59, 80
Buddha Sāsana Sangāyana, 13, 30, 80, 83
Burmese Buddhist Way to Socialism, 59, 80

Chatterjee, Partha, 99, 133
Chit Hlaing, 101
civil society, 2, 11, 42, 61; and Buddhism, 45, 98, 148, 154; and democracy, 14, 110, 113, 120; development of, 7, 8, 90, 147, 185n21; and education, 35, 47, 70; and private domain, 10, 67, 143, 148; and social institutions, 61, 117–118, 147, 149; and social justice, 14, 110–113
Cohn, Bernard S., 46, 168n42
Collins, Steven, 23, 161n6, 162nn8, 23, 173n8, 174n17
colonial government, 13, 35, 40, 43, 47, 52–53, 67–75, 99–106, 140–141, 146; knowledge, 12, 51–61, 101, 168n42; power, 4, 30, 54, 65, 106; practice, 5, 34, 68; project, 12–13, 35, 50, 54, 60, 67, 147, 168n42; rule, 1, 4–5, 8, 14, 25, 30–34, 37–40, 44, 47, 56, 62, 72, 99–103, 119–120, 134, 136, 141–142, 146, 180n19;

scholarship, 71; society, 13, 42, 64, 66, 68, 77
colonialism, 1, 2, 7, 12, 15, 34, 42, 52, 55, 66, 68, 78, 115, 119, 140–147, 173n6; postcolonial, l, 8, 101, 117, 145, 159n1, 174n14; precolonial, 2–4, 14–16, 18, 20, 25, 27, 49, 55, 86, 140, 160n7, 176n35
conjuncture, ix, 1–13, 37, 40–45, 58, 59, 65–67, 98, 102, 106, 117–121, 130, 141, 146–151, 159n2, 161n14
Craddock, Sir Reginald, 179n5, 180n19
Craddock Reforms, 100, 173n45, 179n5
Culagandhi, 26, 28, 32
cultural narratives, 1, 23, 37, 72, 127, 160n11, 162n23

Dalai Lama, 114, 131, 182n46
dhammakathika, 58, 70, 102, 106, 140
Dhammakay movement, 117, 148
dhammarāja, 3–4, 12, 16–19, 24–25, 29–32, 36–37, 56, 78, 81–82, 132, 162n23
Dharmapala, Anagarika, 170nn5, 7
Dobama (We Burmans), 44, 72, 79
Dwara Nikāya, 32, 39, 140

economy of merit, 3, 5, 10, 12, 15, 19–20, 87–88, 120–123, 138, 140, 142, 176n35
education: Buddhist, 12–13, 48, 50, 52, 58–60, 102, 146; colonial, 42, 46–47, 50–56; modern, 46, 52, 54, 58, 61, 66, 70; monastic, 12, 23, 35, 50, 53–55, 57–58, 60, 69, 86, 162n22, 166n17, 167n32, 169n50, 176n33; western, 12, 35, 38, 42–43, 47–48, 52, 56, 58, 70
Eightfold Noble Path, 13, 45, 49, 77, 80, 110–111, 147, 181
88 Generation, 100, 115–116, 121; Prayer Campaign, 94, 157, 178n49, 183n3

Fort Dufferin, 36. *See also* Mandalay Palace
fundamentalism, 82, 108, 174n14
Furnivall, J. S., 171nn15, 27, 172n38

Gambira, Ashin, 125, 132, 136, 143, 153
genealogy: of contestation, 7, 13, 60, 119, 120; cultural, 18, 28, 93, 162n9
General Council of Burmese Associations (GCBA), 14, 73, 75, 101
General Council of Sangha Sammeggi (GCSS), 14, 73, 75, 100, 102, 119, 124, 155, 186n36. *See also* All Monks Union
Gravers, Mikael, 8

hegemony: Buddhist, 3–5, 7, 12, 15–19, 30–31, 62, 95, 123, 166n11; cultural, 25, 28; political, 86, 95, 131, 176n40. *See also* subjugation
Houtman, Gustaaf, 110

Ikeya, Chie, 106, 179n4, 180nn22, 24
innovation, 1, 5, 9, 38, 52, 56, 111

Jordt, Ingrid, 80, 109, 139

Kaba Aye Pagoda, 80, 83–84, 93, 95, 176n33

Keyes, Charles, 11, 34, 172n43, 174n14
Khammai Dhammasami, Ashin, 166n4
Kinwuṇ Mingyi, 36
Konbaun dynasty, 3, 4, 16, 18, 24–25, 28, 35–37, 39, 168n38

Ledi Sayadaw, 41, 64, 73, 172n43
Leider, Jacques P., 27
Lieberman, Victor, 3, 15, 16, 23, 162n22
Lion Throne, 4, 31, 36, 94

Mahabodhi Society, 63, 170n5
Mahāsammata, 112
Mahasi Meditation, 80, 93, 177n44; Sayadaw, 80
Mahawizaya Pagoda, 85, 92, 95
Mandalay Palace, 4, 151
Maung Maung, U, 65, 68, 100, 179n8
maximalists, 72, 81, 100, 102, 103, 106, 179n3
May Ong, U, 65, 70, 75
McDaniel, Justin, 159n3, 186n1
meditation, lay, 9, 32, 41, 80, 84, 88; movement, 109, 142, 161n14; *vipassanā,* 80, 109
Mendelson, Michael E., 52, 65, 106, 139, 159n3, 167nn18, 26, 32, 180n16
Metta sutta, 126–127
Mindon, 25, 27, 29–33, 36, 39, 80, 140, 146, 152, 168n39, 174n19
Mingun Pagoda, 29; Sayadaw, 83
minimalists, 66, 171n18, 172n39, 179n3
modernity, 1, 5–6, 8, 9, 11, 12, 14, 37, 56, 59, 61, 146, 149, 154, 174n14, 185n21; Buddhist, 5, 14, 34, 38, 43, 58, 62, 90, 98, 117, 134, 148; colonial, 2, 5, 12, 15, 37, 39, 40, 147, 166n4; and precolonial Burma, 29; secular, 39, 44, 70, 95
moral authority, 5, 40; and Buddhism, 120, 121, 127, 154; and civil society, 2, 117; and meditation, 99, 110; and military power, 86, 115, 121, 149, 177n43; and politics, 14, 82, 110–111, 120, 136, 141; and the sangha, 121, 127, 131, 135, 145; and the secular, 5, 82, 119; and the state, 120, 143, 145, 146
Mt. Poppa Sayadaw, U Parama, 85

Nargis (cyclone), 120, 133, 152, 177n43, 187n12
national development, 10, 14, 45, 152
National League for Democracy (NLD), 108, 112, 121, 181n27
National Schools Movement, 58, 101, 102, 172n44
nationalism, 1, 2, 9, 38, 88, 91, 99; Buddhist, 62–72, 75, 79, 86, 88, 97, 100, 107, 109, 115, 117, 124, 131, 152, 186n36; secular, 43, 74, 171n27, 172n38; transnational networks, 40, 43, 45, 56, 65, 67, 72, 105, 147, 176n36
Naypyidaw, 50, 78, 97, 151, 152
Ne Win, 85, 86, 92, 95, 97, 107, 142
nibbāna, 9, 44, 45, 53, 81, 89, 110, 113, 147
Nu, U, 2, 7–10, 13, 45, 47, 59–60, 67, 77–85, 93, 95, 97, 107, 142, 147, 165n25, 171n18, 173n6, 177n41
Nyanissara, Ashin U, 127, 133

Olcott, Henry, 63, 170nn5, 6, 7, 171n14
Ottama, U, 101, 103–105, 134, 140, 165n16, 179n6, 180nn12, 14, 16
Overseas Mon Young Monks Union, 181n27

Pakokku, 23, 64, 122, 124, 125
pativedha sāsana, 25, 27, 45. *See also* utopia
pattam nikkujjana kamma, 123–124, 135, 138
Pranke, Patrick A., 28, 163n31
protestantization, 10

reform, 6–7, 146, 148, 149, 170n5; Buddhist/monastic, 6, 7, 11, 15, 20, 24–33, 57, 76, 88, 109, 121, 131, 148, 164n43; democratic, 108, 114, 132; educational, 43, 46, 47, 50–54, 70, 87, 172n44; after 1988, 86–87; under Konbaun dynasty, 24–33, 76–77, 163n27; modern, 68–70, 99; under Ne Win, 7, 82–85, 142; political, 6, 13, 65, 113, 180n19; reformist lineages, 39, 140; religious, 7, 12, 105, 140; under U Nu, 7, 80–81, 177n41
relic, 20–22, 80, 87–89, 93, 142, 176n35, 177nn41, 43
Rewata Dhamma, 182n47, 185n19
Rhys Davids, Thomas W., 170n5
ritual: exchange, 19, 20, 24, 78, 120, 122, 143; of the court, 3, 16, 24; merit-making, 3, 19, 24, 32, 85, 87, 88, 89, 93, 109, 110, 112; networks, 12, 20, 78, 86, 87; of the state, 13, 80, 88, 89, 95, 176n40

Saffron Revolution, 1, 116, 119, 120, 122, 130, 132, 134, 136, 156
samsāra, 44, 89, 121, 132, 136, 145
Sangha Mahanayaka Council, 7, 77, 82–83, 85–86, 89, 93, 107–108, 134, 137, 174n17, 176n33
Sāsana Moli, 121, 134
Sāsana Nuggaha Athin (Mission Association), 41, 64
Saya San Rebellion, 40, 47, 102, 106, 134, 139, 165n16, 179n9, 180n14
Scott, David, 159n2, 183n2
secular power, 1, 5, 7, 10, 34, 39, 43, 55, 81, 95, 118, 120–122, 140, 149
secularism, 5, 8, 43–45, 61, 70, 82, 95, 147, 187n2
setkya min, 13, 40, 81
Shwedagon Pagoda, 4, 22, 30, 39, 73, 92, 96, 105, 115, 129, 177n43
Sixth Buddhist Synod, 60, 80. *See also* Buddha Sāsana Sangāyana
social justice, 111, 132, 153
social status, 3, 12, 20, 120, 135, 138, 142, 176n35
Socialist Union of Burma, 2, 86
socially engaged Buddhism, 9, 14, 109, 111, 120, 122, 127, 131–133, 153, 182nn42, 47, 185nn17, 19
State Law and Order Restoration Council (SLORC), 13, 78, 82, 86–88, 90, 97, 100, 107, 142, 159n1, 177n42, 181n27
State Peace and Development Council (SPDC), 78, 86, 88, 90, 116, 143, 177n42, 183nn4, 8, 184n8
Strong, John, 176n35
subjugation, 1, 4, 5, 143. *See also* hegemony

Sulak Sivaraksa, 114, 117, 154, 182n47
Swearer, Donald, 127, 174n14, 182n40

Tambiah, Stanley J., 3, 10, 18, 130, 176n35, 180n12
Taungoo dynasty, 15, 16, 48
Ten Duties of Kings, 112, 132, 185n19
thabeik hmauk, 123. See also *pattam nikkujjana kamma*
thakin, 42, 79, 165n25
Than Shwe, 93, 95, 116, 178n49
thathana, 18, 19, 38, 57, 68–69, 77, 86, 127, 162n12
Thathana Hita Athin (Foreign Mission Society), 39, 64
thathana pyu thi, 45, 64, 67, 88, 99, 161n14
thathana win, 28
thathanabain, 22–23, 27, 30, 31, 32, 37, 39, 49, 53–55, 63, 101, 140, 168nn38, 41
Thibaw, 36–37, 63, 168n38
Thich Nhat Hanh, 114, 131, 182n47
Thirty Comrades, 75, 79
Thudhamma, 26, 28, 32, 39, 49, 163n31, 174n19
Thudhamma Council, 27, 28, 30–32, 141, 163n28
Thudhamma-zayat, 163n31

Treaty of Yandabo, 29, 35
Turner, Alicia, 77, 99
21 Party, 72, 102

Union Solidarity and Development Association (USDA), 149, 150, 183n8, 185n15, 187n9
utopia, 2, 13, 25, 27, 44, 45, 82, 84, 109, 113, 160n11

***V**inaya,* 6, 22, 24–28, 30, 32, 37, 39, 49, 53–55, 64–65, 84, 120–121, 135–148; courts, 84, 87

Weber, Max, 10, 11, 20, 70, 120–121, 140, 143, 148, 175n26
Wisara, U, 105, 134, 137, 140, 143, 179n6
wunthanu, 64, 66, 77, 80, 99–103, 140

Yahan Pyo Apwe (Young Monks Association, YBA), 72, 85, 106, 119, 180n24
Young Men's Buddhist Association (YMBA), 13–14, 38, 41, 42, 45, 56–58, 65–75, 77, 99–103, 105, 170n4, 171n14, 172nn37, 40, 41, 44, 173n45

ABOUT THE AUTHOR

Juliane Schober is professor of religious studies at Arizona State University. Trained as an anthropologist and historian of religion, she has published extensively on the intersections of modernity, culture, and politics in the Buddhist traditions in Burma. Her edited volumes include *Sacred Biography in the Buddhist Traditions of South and Southeast Asia* (1997) and *Buddhist Manuscript Cultures: Knowledge, Ritual, and Art* (2008, with Stephen Berkwitz and Claudia Brown).

Production Notes for Schober

Modern Buddhist Conjunctures in Myanmar

Jacket design by Julie Matsuo-Chun

Text in Minion Pro; display in ITC Lubalin Graph

Book design + composition by Julie Matsuo-Chun

Printing and binding by IBT Global

Printed on 60# House Opaque, 426 ppi

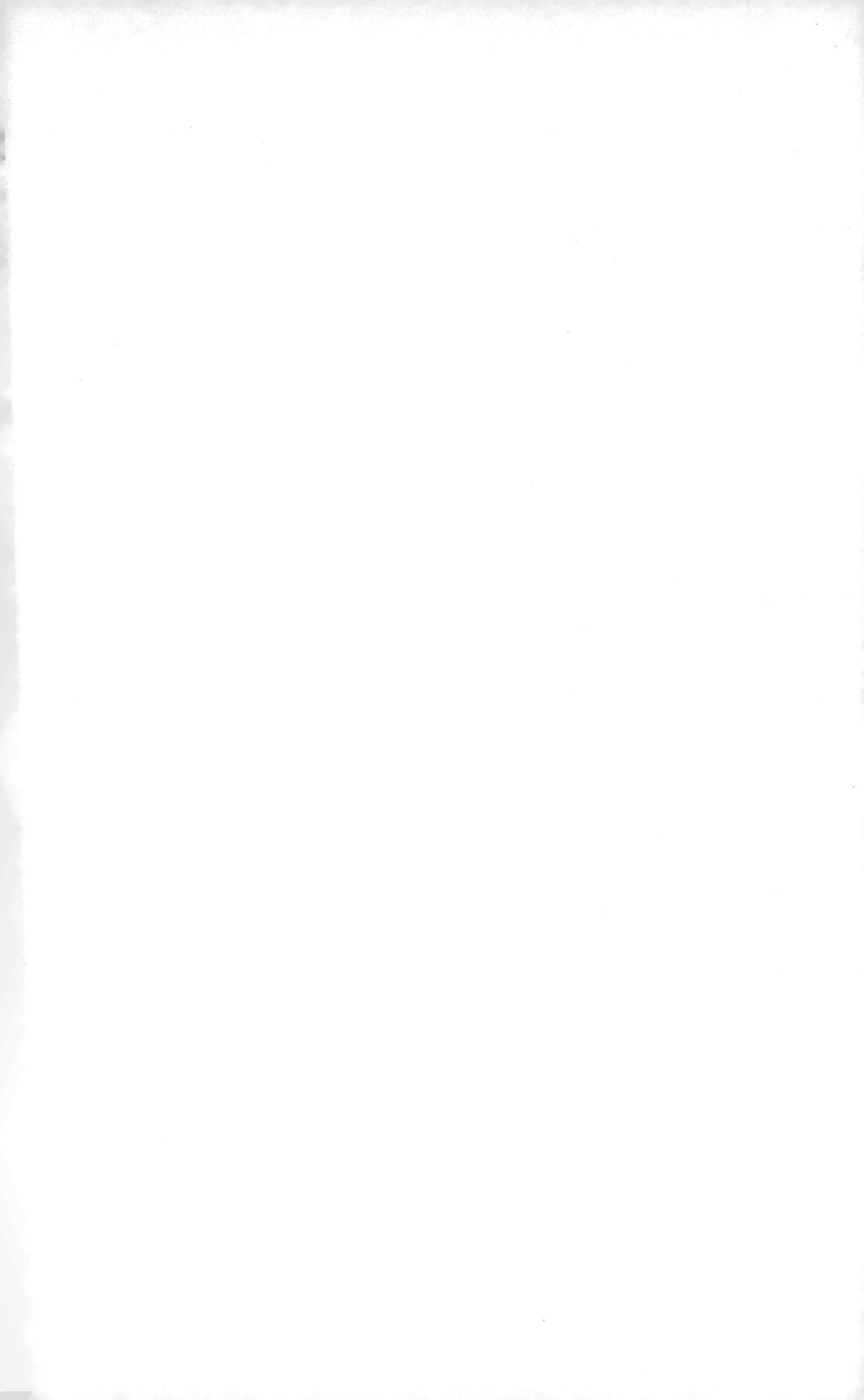